THE SUPER EASY KETO AIR FRYER COOKBOOK FOR BEGINNERS ON A BUDGET

500 Quick & Easy, Low-Carb Air Frying Recipes for Busy People on Ketogenic Diet

By

Dr. Fiona Griffith

TABLE OF CONTENTS

- Ketogenic nutrition at a glance 11
- RECIPES 13
  1. Spinach Cheddar Eggs 13
  2. Gaucho Keto Burger 13
  3. Frozen Mocha Almond Fat Bombs 14
  4. Berries with Coconut 14
  5. Mini Meatballs 14
  6. Cloud Buns (Keto Rolls) 15
  7. Crunchy Cinnamon Flaxseed 15
  8. Keto Jalapeño Cheddar Waffle 15
  9. Gooseberry Jam 16
  10. Chicken Breast Stuffed with Tomato, Mozzarella & Spinach 16
  11. Crispy Chicken Thighs 16
  12. Keto Cheeseburger with Egg & Bacon 17
  13. Asparagus Wrapped In Bacon 17
  14. Mini Eggplant Mushroom Pizza 17
  15. Keto Soft Air Fryer Cakes With Butter Syrup 18
  16. Egg Nest With Fresh Cream & Tomato 18
  17. Basil Quiche 18
  18. Salmon Fillet with Low-Carb Yogurt Dip 19
  19. Keto Asparagus Muffins 19
  20. Keto Bolognese Sauce 20
  21. Keto Pork Ribs 20
  22. Keto Mini Burger 21
  23. Slow Apple Low-Carb Dessert 21
  24. Low-Carb Carrot Cake 22
  25. Double Chocolate Cookies 22
  26. Cookies With Keto Marmalade 23
  27. Keto Air Fryer Cakes 23
  28. Keto Chocolate cake 23
  29. Buttercream Christmas Cookies 24
  30. Low-carb Zucchini Bread 25
  31. Lime Mousse 25
  32. Coconut Chocolate Fat Bombs 25
  33. Praline Fat Bombs 26
  34. Keto Breakfast Cake 26
  35. Keto Chocolate Mousse 26
  36. Chicken Cauliflower Casserole with Pesto 27
  37. Salad Wraps 27
  38. Salmon Cheese Air Fryer Cakes 28
  39. Grilled Trout 28
  40. Egg Avocado Wrapped In Bacon 28
  41. Salmon In Zucchini Bed 29
  42. Keto Breakfast Nut Yogurt 29
  43. Coconut Cinnamon Keto Fat Bombs 29
  44. Blueberry Keto Ice Cream 30
  45. Gooseberry Raspberry Keto Ice cream 30
  46. Shrimp Spiesse 30
  47. Stuffed Chicken Breast Fillet 31
  48. Low-carb Pizza Roll 31
  49. Zucchini Shrimp 31
  50. Smoked Pork Chops with Pickled Cabbage 32
  51. Keto Chicken Cauliflower Casserole 32
  52. Hot Chili Soup 33
  53. Paprika Cauliflower Soup 33
  54. Keto Salami Pizza 34
  55. Low-carb Pesto Chicken Roulade 34
  56. Low-carb Tomato Soup 35
  57. Cauliflower Pizza 35
  58. Keto Lasagna 36
  59. Avocado Tuna Salad 36
  60. Keto Muffin Rolls 36
  61. Meatloaf Pizza 37

62. Stewed Cabbage & Minced Meat 37
63. Keto Stromboli Snacks 38
64. Cucumber Gazpacho 38
65. Fish Sticks 38
66. Simple Spaghetti 39
67. Sausage Rolls 39
68. Pizza with Sour Cream & Bacon 40
69. Poppy Seed Bread 40
70. Rhubarb Pecan Pie 40
71. Spinach & Mushroom Quiche 41
72. Cheese Sauce 41
73. Cheese & Ham Omelet 42
74. Homemade Granola 42
75. Spinach & Cheese Flatbread 43
76. Crackers 43
77. Low-carb Bread 43
78. Keto Zucchini Boats with Tuna 44
79. Tomato-mozzarella Eggplant Fan 44
80. Pecan Ice Cream 44
81. Low-carb Vanilla Ice Cream 45
82. Cauliflower Hash Browns 45
83. Egg Wrap with Salmon & Spinach 45
84. Salmon with Lemon & Capers 46
85. Low-carb Pumpkin Squash 46
86. Low-carb Cheese Tacos 47
87. Bell Pepper Nachos with Minced Meat & Avocado 48
88. Big Mac Salad 48
89. Sugar-free Crème Brûlée 49
90. Low-carb Crepes 49
91. Hamburger Salad with Avocado 50
92. Lettuce Wraps with Asian Minced Chicken .. 50
93. Low-carb Chicken Meatballs 51
94. low-carb Hamburger Sticks 51
95. Low-carb Breakfast Porridge 52
96. Cream Puffs 52
97. Chocolate Coconut Pudding 53
98. Low-carb Cheese Crackers 53
99. Coconut Macaroons 54
100. Low-carb Cabbage Salad 54
101. Low-Carb Rösti 54
102. Chicken Cordon Bleu 55
103. Mushroom pizza 55
104. Stuffed Peppers with Chorizo & Egg 56
105. Egg & Bacon Breakfast Muffins 56
106. Air Fryer Scrambled Eggs 56
107. Cheddar & Bacon Stuffed Mushrooms 57
108. Savory Ham & Cheese Muffins 57
109. Broccoli in Almond-Lemon Butter 58
110. Grilled Salmon with Avocado Sauce 58
111. Baby Spinach Omelet 58
112. Blueberry Bowl with Fig, Pomegranate, Chia and Banana 59
113. Salmon in Cream Sauce with Peas & Lemon 59
114. Air Fryer Steamed Vegetables 59
115. Chicken Breast with Air Fryer Vegetables .. 60
116. Mushroom with Cream Sauce & Herbs 60
117. Yogurt with Cereal & Persimmons 61
118. Chicken Breast with Peppered Vegetables. 61
119. Fresh Cucumber Salad with Onions & Herbs 61
120. Beef Pot Roast 62
121. Orange Carrot Power Drink 62
122. Beef Steak with Arugula & Cherry Tomatoes 62
123. Fried Sea Bream with Mango Salsa 63
124. Red Cabbage Salad with Nuts & Seeds 63
125. Eggplant Tomato Omelet 64
126. Chickpea & Halloumi Salad 64
127. Chard, Avocado, Nut & Feta Salad 64
128. Tuna with Vegetables & Avocado 65
129. Colorful Vegetable Salad 65

3

130. Smoothie Bowl with Spinach, Mango & Muesli 66
131. Chickpea tomato & cucumber salad 66
132. Beef Steak with Broccoli........................... 67
133. Chicken Thighs with Vegetables 67
134. Green Smoothie with Avocado, Spinach & Banana 67
135. Sweet Pear, Pomegranate & Nuts Salad 68
136. Avocado & Mozzarella Salad Bowl 68
137. Chicken Breast with Arugula & Tomatoes.. 68
138. Zucchini Chips 69
139. Fried Egg & Bacon 69
140. Chocolate shake with almond milk 69
141. Kebab Skewers with Chicken & Tzatziki 70
142. Steamed Veggies 70
143. Spinach & Cream Cheese Frittata 70
144. Fresh Cucumber Salad with Onions & Herbs 71
145. Colorful Vegetable & Chicken Skewers 71
146. Mediterranean Vegetable Omelet............ 72
147. Grilled Pineapple 72
148. Celery Chive Puree 72
149. Tomato Avocado, Cucumber & Herb Salad 73
150. Broccoli Hummus with Pine Nuts 73
151. Braised Eggplant, Peppers, Olives & Capers 74
152. Fresh Garden Salad with Beef 74
153. Herbed Zucchini Patties with Yogurt Dip ... 74
154. Salmon, Egg & Parmesan Salad 75
155. Fried Eggs with Bacon, Avocado & Arugula 76
156. Chicken Breast with Green Beans............. 76
157. Grilled Salmon with Green Beans 76
158. Asian Chicken Salad 77
159. Zoodles with Shrimp & Cherry Tomatoes .. 77
160. Low-Carb Bread with Cream Cheese & Avocado 78
161. Salad with Avocado & Chicken 78

162. Cheese Stuffed Mushrooms 79
163. Pea Soup with Roasted Asparagus & Feta .. 79
164. Swiss Chard Salad with Feta & Dried Tomatoes 80
165. Broccoli & Quinoa Salad 80
166. Grilled Chicken Breast with Fresh Herbs 81
167. Arugula, Radish & Couscous Salad 81
168. Grilled Chicken Skewers with Onions & Peppers 82
169. Vegetables with Egg & Parsley 82
170. Fried Egg with Green Beans & Paprika 82
171. Asian Broccoli Salad 84
172. Jaair Fryerese Salad with Shrimp 84
173. Veal Skewers with Vegetables.................. 85
174. Salmon Steak with Green Asparagus 85
175. Ratatouille 86
176. Red Cabbage & Apple Salad 86
177. Eggplant Tomato Frittata 87
178. Low-Carb Bread with Arugula & Trout 87
179. Grilled Chicken Breast with Avocado, Salad & Cheese.. 87
180. Chicken Curry with Green Beans 88
181. Smoked Salmon Salad 88
182. Avocado Quinoa Buddha Bowl 89
183. Smoked Salmon with Lemon 89
184. Avocado with Grapefruit 89
185. Greek yogurt with Chia and Blueberries 90
186. Avocado Cream & Poached Egg Sandwich . 90
187. Margherita Omelet 90
188. Spinach and Ginger Smoothie 91
189. Rollmops.. 91
190. Caprese Salad with Parma Ham................ 92
191. Avocado Melon Coconut Smoothie 92
192. Low-Carb Almond Bar 92
193. Fried eggs and bacon 93
194. Green Kiwi & Ginger Smoothie................. 93

4

195. Tomato & Spring Onion Omelet 93	227. Blueberry Milkshake with Mint & Cocoa .. 105
196. Coconut Chia Pudding with Berries 94	228. Mediterranean Tomato Omelet 105
197. Eel with Scrambled Eggs & Low-Carb Bread 94	229. Zucchini Buffer with Salmon & Poached Egg 106
198. Parmesan, pepper and olive Omelet 95	230. Chia Power Yogurt with Fresh Fruit 106
199. Fried Egg with Broccoli & Paprika 95	231. Berry Fruit Drink 106
200. Mushroom & Onion Omelet 95	232. Scrambled Eggs with Tomatoes & Ham ... 107
201. Chia Coconut Pudding with Raspberries 96	233. Lavender Blueberry Chia Seed Pudding ... 107
202. Grilled Eggplant with Feta & Cherry Tomatoes 96	234. Raspberry Buttermilk Smoothie 108
203. Tomatoes, Peppers, & Ham Omelet 96	235. Chia Seeds with Mango & Blueberries 108
204. Melon Salad with Ham & Herbs 97	236. Broccoli Frittata 108
205. Arugula Salad with Colorful Tomatoes 97	237. Low-Carb Vanilla Muffins 109
206. Raspberry Banana Coconut Smoothie 97	238. Low-Carb Chocolate Chip Biscuits 109
207. Avocado Salmon Rolls 98	239. Low-Carb Air Fryer Cakes with Blueberries 109
208. Spinach, Strawberry & Avocado Salad 98	240. Strawberry-Orange-Mint Smoothie 110
209. Hot Salmon Snacks with Cream Cheese & Cucumber 98	241. Melon Shake 110
210. Blueberry Yogurt Cream 99	242. Tomato, Cheese & Basil Omelet 110
211. Strawberry Vanilla Shake 99	242. Chocolate Muffins with Strawberries 111
212. Pickled Salmon with Avocado 99	243. Strawberries On Spinach Leaves 111
213. Fruit Salad 99	244. Low-Carb Strawberry Dessert 111
214. Fresh Chanterelle Omelet 100	245. Cottage Cheese & Blueberry Cream with Fresh Mint 112
215. Hazelnut Muffins 100	246. Scrambled Eggs with Chives & Nutmeg ... 112
216. Vegetable Sticks with Dip 101	247. Zucchini Rolls with Cream Cheese & Salmon 112
217. Strawberry & Melon Coconut Shake 101	248. Buttermilk Wild Berry Shake 113
218. Melon Salad with Cucumber 101	249. Soy Yogurt with Strawberries, Mango, Mint & Nuts 113
219. Vanilla Cream with Blueberries & Redcurrants 102	250. Muffins with Blueberry Icing 113
220. Scrambled Eggs with Bacon & Chives 102	251. Blueberry-Yogurt Smoothie with Mint 114
221. Zucchini Omelet Cake 102	252. Fried Egg On Green Asparagus 114
222. Cottage Cheese & Radish Stuffed Peppers 103	253. Low-Carb Strawberry Cake 115
223. Ham & Zucchini Omelet 103	254. Low-Carb Chocolate Brownies 115
224. Vegetarian Omelet 104	255. Tuna & Egg Salad 115
225. Chia Seed Gel with Pomegranate & Nuts . 104	256. Sauerkraut with Pork Belly 116
226. Tomato & Egg Salad 105	257. Tomato Salad with Herbs & Basil 116

258. Low-Carb Vegetable Wraps 117
259. Fried Egg with Asparagus Bacon Rolls 117
260. Paprika with Vegetables & Meat 117
261. Chicken Breast Fillet with Shallots & Tomatoes In Red Wine Sauce 118
262. Colorful Air Fryer Vegetables with Herbs. 118
263. Brussels Sprouts & Bacon with Parmesan 119
264. Pork Fillet in Bacon Coat 119
265. Mozzarella Salad with Citrus Dressing 120
266. Grilled Sweet Potato with Avocado Cream & Egg 120
267. Vegetable Salad with Dried Tomatoes 121
268. Low-Carb Pumpkin Seed Bread 121
269. Low-Carb Klopse 121
270. Egg, Avocado & Chicken Salad with Basil. 122
271. Walnut Basil Pesto 123
272. Fried Fish Fillet with Vegetables 123
273. Beef Steak with Colorful Salad 123
274. Chicken Breast Fillet with Brussels Sprouts 124
275. Fish Patties 124
276. Zucchini Rolls with Ricotta & Parmesan Filling 125
277. Colorful Salad with Chicken Breast & Walnuts 125
278. Baked Cod with Spicy Crust 125
279. Arugula salad with chard, beetroot and orange fillets 126
280. Air Fryer Mushroom & Fennel 126
281. Zucchini Soup 127
282. Veal Schnitzel with Tomatoes & Cheese .. 127
283. Sweet Salad with Quail Eggs 127
284. Fruit Salad with Arugula, Avocado & Walnut 128
285. Zucchini, Tomato & Spinach Frittata 128
286. Tomato Salad with Cucumber & Apple 129
287. Grilled Cod with Tomato Salad & Herbs ... 129
288. Tuna with Spicy Herb Crust & Lemon 129
289. Roasted Pumpkin & Brussels Sprout Salad with Pecans 130
290. Paleo Hamburger with Avocado & Beans 130
291. Scrambled Eggs with Bacon & Chard 131
292. Cauliflower Rice with Eggs 131
293. Salmon Fillet with Vegetables 132
294. Grilled Chicken in Herb Marinade 132
295. Raw Salad with Orange Dressing 133
296. Grilled Lamb with Vegetables 133
297. Tuna Salad with Avocado, Tomato, & Mayonnaise 133
298. Avocado Chicken Paprika Omelet 134
299. Eggplant, Tomato & Basil Pizzas 134
300. Coleslaw with Mint & Lime Juice 135
301. Zucchini Salad with Cheese & Herbs 135
302. Roasted Broccoli with Garlic 135
303. Vegetable & Ham Frittata 136
304. Roast Pork with Herbs 136
305. Beetroot Spinach & Feta Salad 136
306. Meatloaf with Cheese Filling 137
307. Tomato Soup with Cream Cheese & Parsley 137
308. Salmon Fillet with Dill Dip 138
309. Green Salad with Beans, Cheddar & Lime Dressing 138
310. Roasted Butternut Squash with Cranberries & Walnut 139
311. Fish In Mediterranean Tomato Sauce 139
312. Meatball, Herb & Chili Frittata 140
313. Tomato Salad with Onions & Parmesan ... 140
314. Pumpkin Soup with Roasted Cashews 141
315. Zoodles with Feta & Tomatoes 141
316. Chinese Vegetables with Beef Strips 142
317. Fig, Kiwi & Pomegranate Salad 142
318. Mushroom & Boiled Ham Omelet 142
319. Tuna Salad with Eggs & Tomatoes 143

320. Cherry Tomato Frittata with Cucumber Salad ... 143
321. Grilled Salmon Steaks with Soy & Honey Marinade ... 144
322. Broccoli Salad with Peppers, Feta & Walnuts ... 144
323. Air Fryer Pepper Chicken ... 144
324. Zucchini with Tomato & Vegetable Sauce ... 145
325. Eggs Benedict ... 146
326. Scottish Eggs ... 146
327. Biscuits In Sausage Sauce ... 147
328. Portobello, Sausage & Cheese Breakfast Burger ... 147
329. Butter Glazed Muffins ... 148
330. Raspberry Scones ... 148
331. Waffles with Whipped Cream ... 149
332. Cream Cheese Air Fryer Cakes ... 149
333. Butter Coffee ... 150
334. Fried Eggs In Hambakjes ... 150
335. Bacon, Egg & Cheese Plates ... 150
336. Crustless Quiche Lorraine ... 151
337. Chia Yogurt Parfait ... 151
338. Naughty Avocado Fried Eggs ... 151
339. Broccoli & Cheese Quiche ... 152
340. Hot Dog Rolls ... 152
341. Garlic Pepperoni Chips ... 153
342. Caprese Salad Snacks ... 153
343. Bacon-Wrapped Mozzarella Sticks ... 153
344. French Onion Dip ... 154
345. Goat Cheese Stuffed Peppers ... 154
346. Spinach Artichoke Dip ... 154
347. Zucchini Mini Pizzas ... 155
348. Prosciutto & Cream Stuffed Mushrooms ... 155
349. Bleu Cheese Cauliflower ... 156
350. Crispy Kale Chips ... 156
351. Fried Avocado ... 157
352. Buffalo Dip ... 157
353. Black Forest Ham, Cheese & Chive Roll-Ups ... 158
354. Rosemary Roasted Almonds ... 158
355. Bacon Guacamole ... 158
356. Bacon Deviled Eggs ... 159
357. Asparagus & Eggs in Bacon Envelopes ... 159
358. Strawberry Spinach Smoothie ... 159
359. Strawberry Milkshake ... 160
360. Avocado Coconut Smoothie ... 160
361. Fried Spaghetti ... 160
362. Classic Mozzarella Sticks ... 161
363. Grilled Onion & Goat Cheese Flatbread ... 161
364. Pumpkin Spaghetti with Meatballs ... 162
365. Pepperoni Pizza ... 163
366. Cauliflower Pizza ... 163
367. Cauliflower Puree ... 164
368. Tofu Fries ... 164
369. Almond Butter Bread ... 164
370. Zucchini Lasagna ... 165
371. Coconut Almond Flour Bread ... 165
372. Cauliflower Tortillas ... 166
373. Cauliflower Macaroni & Cheese ... 166
374. Keto Zucchini ... 167
375. Zucchini Curry ... 167
376. Zucchini Brunch Spaghetti ... 167
377. Zucchini Puffs ... 168
378. Air Fryer Zucchini & Mushroom ... 168
379. Zucchini Melanzane Spread with Hazelnuts ... 168
380. Spinach & Vegetables ... 169
381. Fried Egg on Green Salad ... 169
382. Sautéed Mushrooms ... 169
383. Scrambled Eggs with Ham & Mushrooms ... 170
384. Roast Beef ... 170
385. Turkey Steak with Vegetables ... 170
386. Turkey Sliced with Karfiolpüree ... 171

387. Omelet Roll with Cream Cheese & Salad . 171
388. Marinated Zucchini 172
389. Salmon Fillet with Rice & Beans 172
390. Honey Glazed Salmon 173
391. Herbed Scrambled Eggs 173
392. Chicken & Potato Cubes 173
393. Hokkaido Sticks 174
394. Gurktaler Bacon Chips 174
395. Stuffed Sage Bacon Roulade 174
396. Fried Fish with Garlic 174
397. Baked Zucchini 175
398. Vegetables with Turmeric & Fennel 175
399. Fine Roast Beef with Porcini Mushrooms 175
400. Minced Roast with Egg 176
401. Asian Salmon Cubes with Broccoli 176
402. Basic Vegetables 177
403. Filled Melanzani 177
404. Salmon Fillet on Zucchini 177
405. Salmon Fillet with Zucchini Gratin 178
406. Marinated Fish In Wok 178
407. Vegetable Soup 179
408. Roast Beef Salad 179
410. Char with Mushroom Polenta 180
411. Sesame Salmon with Asian Broccoli 180
412. Zoodles with Paprika & Almond Sauce 181
413. Tandoori Cauliflower 181
414. Eggplant Yogurt Casserole with Meatballs
.... 182
415. Artichoke Omelet 182
416. Honey Chicken with Fennel & Mushrooms
.... 183
417. Braised Young Vegetables with Stir-Fried Ham 183
418. Paprika Turkey Schnitzel with Peas 183
420. Chicken Schnitzel with Olive Fig Salsa & Whole Meal Pasta 184
421. Tarragon Turkey with Sugar Peas 184

422. Keto Schlemmerlädchen 185
423. Cucumber Salad with Pomegranate Seeds, Cottage Cheese & Radicchio 185
424. Sliced Turkey with Spring Vegetables 185
425. Chicken Fillets with Spinach & Date Filling
.... 186
426. Keto Cauliflower Tacos 186
427. Quinoa Salad with Tuna, Arugula & Pomegranate 187
428. Salmon in Cream Sauce with Peas & Lemon
.... 187
429. Salmon Fillet with Almond Crust & Pea & Parsnip Puree 188
430. Asian Air Fryer with Shrimp & Vegetables 188
431. Grilled Salmon with Pumpkin & Steamed Beans 189
432. Air Fryer Chinese Shrimp Salad 189
433. Butternut Squash with Tomatoes & Harissa
.... 190
434. Stuffed Pumpkin with Cauliflower Rice & Mushrooms 190
435. Pumpkin Au Gratin 191
436. Roasted Pork Chop with Vegetables 191
437. Quinoa with Roasted Pumpkin 192
438. Roast Duck with Orange-Date Stuffing 192
439. Vegetables with Beans, Peppers & Carrots
.... 193
440. Roasted Avocado with Bacon 193
441. Fried Cauliflower with Fresh Herbs 193
441. Fried Liver with Onion & Herbs 194
442. Green Asparagus with Salmon Fillet & Dill Butter 194
443. Chicken Breast Strips with Asian Asparagus
.... 195
444. Salmon Fillet On Green Asparagus & Kohlrabi 195
445. Roasted Trout with Butter & Lemon 195
446. Steak on Spring Onions with Cherry Sauce
.... 196

447. Peppers Au Gratin 196
448. Shrimp on Salad 197
449. Entrecôte Steak 197
450. Salmon Fillet with Dill 197
451. Chicken Breast with Julienne Vegetable Salad 198
452. Beef Fillet with Tomatoes 198
453. Duck Breast with Wok Vegetables 198
454. Roasted Chicken Breast with Tomato Salsa 199
455. Colorful Salad with Fried Mushrooms 199
456. Chicken with Chanterelles 200
457. Shashlik 200
458. Lamb Meatballs with Salsa 201
459. Roasted Orange & Rosemary Chicken 201
460. Chicken Breast Fillet with Vegetables 202

© Copyright 2020-Dr. Elise Robson-All rights reserved.

The content in this book may not be reproduced, duplicated or transmitted without direct written permission from the author or the publisher.

Under no circumstances will any blame or legal responsibility be held against the publisher or author for any direct or indirect damages, reparation, or m1tary loss due to the information contained in this book.

Legal Notice:

This book is copyright protected. This book is only for personal use. You cannot amend, distribute, sell, use, quote or paraphrase any part of the content of this book without the written consent of the author or publisher.

Disclaimer:

The information contained in this document is for educational and entertainment purposes only. We have made every effort to present accurate, up-to-date, reliable and complete information. No warranties of any kind are declared or implied. Readers acknowledge that the author is not engaged in the rendering legal, financial, medical or professional advice.

The content within this book has been derived from various sources. Please consult a licensed professional before attempting any techniques outlined in this book.

By reading this document, the reader agrees that under no circumstances is the author responsible for any losses, direct or indirect, which are incurred as a result of the use of the information contained within this document, including, but not limited to, errors, omissions, or inaccuracies.

KETOGENIC NUTRITION AT A GLANCE

WHAT IS THE KETOGENIC DIET?

The ketogenic diet is a type of low-carb diet characterized by the body learning a new way of producing energy with food.

By eating many healthy fats and very few carbohydrates, the body enters the state of ketosis.

In this condition, the body burns fat instead of sugar as fuel for cell energy. Due to the lack of sugar molecules, the liver is forced to convert fatty acids into ketone bodies.

These ketone bodies are anti-inflammatory and can help you lose weight.

A successfully conducted ketogenic diet must fulfill the following criterion: The liver produces ketone bodies as an alternative fuel to glucose.

WHAT CAUSES KETOSIS?

A ketogenic diet always pursues the goal of bringing the body into ketosis. In this state, many people experience advantages compared to normal sugar burning.

But what are the benefits, and what is the ketogenic diet used for?

BENEFITS OF KETOGENIC NUTRITION AND KETOSIS

Anti-inflammatory: The ketogenic diet and resulting ketosis has a strong anti-inflammatory effect. This is likely to reduce the risk of degenerative diseases such as Alzheimer's and cancer.

Energy-enhancing: The state of ketosis helps cells, especially in the brain, to produce more mitochondria. These mitochondria are the energy powerhouses of your body, making you alert and focused from morning to night.

Fat Burning: The ketogenic diet can help you lose weight in a quick and healthy way. The ketone bodies ensure longer-term satiety and reduce hunger hormones (such as ghrelin). This means that you no longer get food cravings and are no longer dependent on snacks.

Concentration-enhancing: Ketone bodies are an ideal source of energy for the brain. Once the body has adapted to ketosis, the brain can gain up to 75% of its energy from ketone bodies. The brain also benefits from the high consumption of healthy fats, as it consists of a large quantity of fat and omega-3 fatty acids that support the health of the brain.

Lowering Blood Sugar: We have received many testimonials in which people with diabetes report significant improvements in their symptoms. When the ketogenic diet is properly performed, insulin and blood glucose levels stabilize.

Where is the ketogenic diet used therapeutically?

Historically, the ketogenic diet was first used and scientifically documented for the treatment of childhood epilepsy in 1921.

Since the beginning of the 21st century, more and more studies have been demonstrating the treatment options and benefits of the ketogenic diet. Thus, this form of nutrition is increasingly becoming the focus of medicine, professional athletes, and nutritionists.

It is still one of the most effective treatments for childhood epilepsy.

KETOGENIC DIET: CONS

Are there any disadvantages?

As with any diet, there are also downsides. To understand this, one must always see nutrition in the context of the situation.

1. Keto Flu / low-carb Influenza: Switching to the ketogenic diet can cause "Keto flu." Symptoms include mental and physical loss of power, weakness, insomnia, nausea and digestive problems.

These symptoms originate from the great change in metabolism and usually last only 3-4 days. In order to help the body with the conversion and to lower the symptoms, there are various possibilities.

2. Food Selection: Another challenge is the choice of food. Those who are not careful to consume enough vegetables and animal products from a species-appropriate attitude may favor a shortage of vitamins and minerals.

HOW DO YOU GO ON A KETOGENIC DIET?

We've learned about the ketogenic diet and its benefits. But how do you implement it?

The most important point is the ratio of macronutrients. The goal is to consume so little carbohydrates and so much healthy fat that the body begins to produce ketone bodies.

WHAT TO EAT ON THE KETO DIET? MACRONUTRIENTS

Before we go into the specific food and the nutrition plan, let's learn about the distribution of macronutrients.

1. Carbohydrates (Few)

On the ketogenic diet, lower your carbohydrate consumption greatly to promote ketogenesis. The number of carbohydrates to consume cannot be generalized, as it varies greatly from person to person. The amount of carbohydrates that can be consumed depends on various factors such as age, gender, physical activity, stress, and diseases such as Hashimoto.

For example, a young, athletic person with good metabolism can often consume up to 50g carbohydrate per day and get into ketosis.

Recommendation: To start a ketogenic diet, do not consume more than 30g of carbs per day. These should come from natural and unprocessed products.

2. Proteins (Moderate)

Unlike what is often stated, ketogenic nutrition is not a high-protein diet in which only meat is consumed. In fact, too much protein can hinder the formation of ketone bodies.

This is due to gluconeogenesis. In this process, the body transforms the excess supply of protein into its components, amino acids. These amino acids are converted to glucose to produce energy from them.

Recommendation: 20% of your calories can come from protein. That's about 0.8g-1.4g protein per kg body weight.

3. Fats (Lots)

Now we come to the most important source of energy in a ketogenic diet: fat. By consuming low-carb calories and modest amounts of protein, the body begins to gain energy from fat reserves or dietary fats.

For a long-term healthy diet, it is important that you cover all your energy needs from the diet. Therefore, it is important that you consume enough healthy fats.

On the contrary, it is important that you eat enough fats so that the body can produce a sufficient amount of energy. Otherwise, your body slips into a calorie deficit that will slow your metabolism in the long term.

If you consume nutritious, unprocessed foods and healthy fats, you will feel great. Eventually, you will intuitively know how much fat you should consume.

Ketogenic food

Before we get to the actual recipes, we want to look at another important point: food quality.

To avoid consuming large quantities of antibiotics, heavy metals, medicines, or chemical preservatives, be sure to purchase organic vegetables and animal-friendly products from a species-appropriate attitude.

RECIPES

1. Spinach Cheddar Eggs

INGREDIENTS

- 25 g of cheddar cheese
- 100 g fresh spinach shredded
- 100 g tomatoes
- 150 g eggs
- 30 g fresh cream
- 19 g olive oil
- 1 tsp chili flakes
- salt
- pepper

INSTRUCTIONS

1. Stir eggs and fresh cream
2. Shred or purée fresh spinach and add.
3. Chop the tomatoes, add and stir
4. Season with chili flakes, salt and pepper to taste
5. Brush an air fryer with olive oil and heat
6. Put the mass in the air fryer.
7. Let it set, then stir again and again.
8. Sprinkle cheddar cheese over it, let it melt and mix.

2. Gaucho Keto Burger

INGREDIENTS

PATTIES

- 450 g ground beef
- 250 g sausage meat
- 30 g shallots, chopped
- 5 g garlic clove
- 1/4 tsp pepper black
- 1 tsp salt

EGG SALAD

- 4 fried eggs
- 100 g lettuce

SAUCE
100 ml burger pesto (

INSTRUCTIONS

PREPARING PATTIES

1. Mix all patty ingredients and shape into patties with a hamburger press
2. Grill patties for about 15 minutes
3. Heat a greased air fryer
4. Place the egg shaper in the air fryer, add an egg and finish cooking.
5. Put patties on lettuce leaves, place the egg on top and add the burger pesto.

3. Frozen Mocha Almond Fat Bombs

INGREDIENTS

- 35 g coconut oil
- 115 g almond puree, white
- 30 g butter
- 10 g cocoa powder (baking cocoa, unsweetened)
- 10 drops of Mocha Flavdrops
- Almond chips to garnish

INSTRUCTIONS

1. Liquefy butter and coconut oil in the microwave for 40 sec. Mix half the butter and half the coconut oil with the almond paste. If it becomes too sticky, heat for 45 sec in the microwave on medium and then mix.
2. Fill the mass in silicone cups.
3. Put in the freezer for 30 min.
4. Mix the remaining butter, coconut oil and cocoa powder together.
5. Fold in the Flavdrops.
6. Put in the cooled cups and then sprinkle almonds over them.
7. Put back in the freezer and let it harden.
8. Remove the Frozen Fat Bombs from the silicone molds.

4. Berries with Coconut

INGREDIENTS

- 50 g blueberries
- 38 g raspberries
- 30 g coconut
- 3 g vanilla extract
- Mint leaves

INSTRUCTIONS

1. Mix the berries with the coconut.
2. For a more intense taste, add vanilla extract.
3. Optionally garnish with mint leaves.

5. Mini Meatballs

INGREDIENTS

- 500 g minced meat
- 1 egg
- 1 tsp Dijon mustard
- 1 tbsp MCT oil
- 1/2 tsp cayenne pepper
- 1/4 tsp ground cumin
- salt
- pepper

INSTRUCTIONS

1. Mix all ingredients except the MCT oil

2. Brush air fryer with oil and heat. Form small meatballs and place in the hot air fryer
3. Sear on both sides
4. Cook at low heat (about 10-15 minutes)

6. Cloud Buns (Keto Rolls)

INGREDIENTS

- 150 g eggs
- 90 g cream cheese

INSTRUCTIONS

1. Preheat air fryer to 150° C. Cover two baking trays with parchment paper (or bake one sheet at a time, one at a time).
2. Now separate the eggs and beat the egg whites until stiff.
3. In a bowl, mix the cream cheese with the yolk and then carefully remove from the egg whites.
4. with a spoon, spread about 8 large buns on the sheets and bake for 15 min in the air fryer.
5. When the Cloud Buns have turned very brown, take them out of the air fryer and let them cool.

7. Crunchy Cinnamon Flaxseed

INGREDIENTS

- 80 g ground almonds
- 2 tsp cinnamon
- Ground 30 g flaxseed
- 2 ml Xucker light erythritol
- 80 g butter (cold)

INSTRUCTIONS

1. Preheat air fryer to 200 C and line the baking tray with parchment paper.
2. Mix the ground almonds, flaxseed flour, cinnamon and Xucker in a Food Processor.
3. Sprinkle pieces of butter over the mixture and mix again until the dough becomes roughly crumbly.
4. Spread the dough on the baking sheet and bake for 20 to 25 min.

8. Keto Jalapeño Cheddar Waffle

INGREDIENTS

- 80 g cream cheese
- 3 eggs
- 1 ml coconut flour
- 1 tsp of psyllium husk
- 1 tsp baking powder
- 30 g of cheddar
- 1 jalapeño
- salt
- pepper

INSTRUCTIONS

1. Put all the ingredients in a bowl.
2. Mix with a blender into a uniformly fine waffle dough.
3. Turn on waffle iron. Once the waffle iron is hot enough, pour in the waffle dough.

9. Gooseberry Jam

INGREDIENTS

- 1000 g gooseberries
- 330 g gelling xylitol 3: 1 mixture

INSTRUCTIONS

1. Boil jars and lids for the jam for 10 minutes.
2. Wash berries. Pour gooseberries in a blender.
3. Pour gooseberry sauce into an air fryer, add the gelling xylitol and stir. Simmer for 5 minutes.
4. Pour into jars, close and turn upside down. Turn over after 5 minutes and allow it to cool.

10. Chicken Breast Stuffed with Tomato, Mozzarella & Spinach

INGREDIENTS

- 500 g chicken breast fillet
- 125 g Mozzarella
- 125 g tomatoes
- 30 g spinach
- salt
- pepper

INSTRUCTIONS

1. Cut the chicken breast on one side and beat flat with the meat mallet. Season with salt and pepper.
2. Then fill the fillet with tomato, mozzarella and spinach.
3. Fix with toothpicks.
4. Fry in the air fryer on all sides. Turn down the heat and cook at low temperature for about 20 minutes.

11. Crispy Chicken Thighs

INGREDIENTS

- 650 g chicken thighs
- 20 g olive oil
- 1 tsp curry spice
- 1 tsp cumin spice
- 1 tsp paprika spice
- 1 tsp salt
- 1/2 tsp coriander spice
- 1/2 tsp cayenne pepper seasoning
- 1/2 tsp cardamom spice
- 1/2 tsp pepper seasoning
- 1/2 tsp baking powder
- 1/4 tsp baking soda
- 1/4 tsp allspice spice

INSTRUCTIONS

1. Preheat the air fryer to 180 C (circulating air).
2. Mix all powdered ingredients with the olive oil to make marinade.
3. Marinate the thighs, place on a baking sheet and put in the air fryer.
4. Cook for 50 min. in the air fryer.

12. Keto Cheeseburger with Egg & Bacon

INGREDIENTS

- 2 eggs
- 200 g beef mince
- 2 slices of bacon
- 25 g mozzarella
- 50 g of cheddar
- 1 tbsp butter
- 1 tsp salt
- 1/2 tsp pepper

INSTRUCTIONS

1. Season the minced meat and make meatballs filled with mozzarella.
2. Prepare 2 air fryers. Heat 1/2 tbsp butter in an air fryer and liquefy.
3. Fry burger meatballs in an air fryer.
4. Fry the bacon crispy in the second air fryer and set aside.
5. Put the silicone molds (Round Egg Ring Forms) in the air fryer. Crack one egg at a time and place in an egg-shaped ring.
6. While the fried eggs finish cooking, put the bacon on the roasted burger meat.
7. Add the cheddar cheese and let it melt.
8. Remove from the air fryer and serve on a plate. Put the fried egg on top and season with pepper and salt to taste.

13. Asparagus Wrapped In Bacon

INGREDIENTS

- 500 g asparagus
- 100 g bacon
- 20 ml coconut oil
- 1 tsp salt
- 1/2 tsp pepper

INSTRUCTIONS

1. Preheat the air fryer to 150° C.
2. Wash and peel asparagus. Wrap 3 bars each with a slice of bacon and place on a baking tray.
3. Brush with coconut oil and season with salt and pepper.
4. Bake for approx. 20-30 minutes.

14. Mini Eggplant Mushroom Pizza

INGREDIENTS

- 1 eggplant
- 70 g mushrooms
- 100 g tomatoes
- 25 g tomato paste
- 120 g mozzarella, shredded
- 2 tbsp olive oil
- 1 chili pepper
- 1 tbsp Italian herbs
- 1 pinch of pepper
- 1 pinch of salt

INSTRUCTIONS

1. Preheat the air fryer to 180° C
2. Cut eggplant into 1cm thick slices
3. Salt the slices vigorously on both sides and place in air fryer for 10 minutes

4. Mix the tomato paste, olive oil and spices and spread on the eggplant slices
5. Chop tomatoes, mushrooms, chili peppers and mozzarella
6. Spread the ingredients on the eggplant slices and bake in the air fryer for 10 minutes

15. Keto Soft Air Fryer Cakes With Butter Syrup

INGREDIENTS

- 140 g eggs
- 15 g egg white powder
- 30 ml coconut oil
- 1 tsp vanilla extract
- 120 ml butters syrup

INSTRUCTIONS

1. Separate eggs and beat the egg whites until stiff.
2. Whisk the egg yolks and mix with the remaining ingredients.
3. Heat oil in an air fryer and add a small amount (approx. 3 tbsp) each. Roast for 2 minutes on both sides until golden brown.
4. Serve with the syrup together.

16. Egg Nest With Fresh Cream & Tomato

INGREDIENTS

- 100 g eggs
- 45 g vine tomatoes
- 25 g bacon
- 16 g fresh cream
- 28 g mozzarella grated
- 5 g macadamia nut oil
- Chili flakes for seasoning
- Dried chives to refine
- Salt for seasoning
- Pepper for seasoning

INSTRUCTIONS

1. Dice a small tomato. Beat 2 eggs and place in a bowl.
2. Put the fresh cream and tomato in the bowl and mix with the egg.
3. Coat air fryer with macadamia oil and fry bacon until crisp.
4. Put the Egg Ring Forms in the air fryer and put the bacon in them.
5. Distribute the contents of the bowl evenly in both egg rings.
6. Sprinkle the grated mozzarella cheese on top.
7. Once the egg has stabilized and the mozzarella cheese has melted, you can remove the egg nests from the air fryer.

17. Basil Quiche

INGREDIENTS

CRUST
- 30 g almond flour
- 35 g flaxseed flour
- 10 g coconut flour
- 5 g chia seeds
- 2.5 g psyllium husk
- 80 ml water
- 1/3 tsp salt

TOPPING

- 100 g basil
- 400 g ricotta
- 80 g parmesan rubbed
- 200 g eggs
- 20 g spring onion
- 5 g garlic
- 40 ml lemon juice
- salt
- pepper

INSTRUCTIONS

1. Mix all ingredients for the dough with a food processor and then wrap in cling film. Refrigerate for 30 minutes.
2. Peel the garlic and chop it into fine slithers.
3. Wash the spring onion and cut into fine rings.
4. Remove the leaves from the basil and mince.
5. Now mix all ingredients together. Season with salt and pepper as desired and set aside.
6. Grease a quiche and preheat air fryer to 180° C.
7. Remove dough from the fridge and roll out on parchment paper. Carefully place in the mold and form a border.
8. Add filling.
9. Bake in the air fryer for about 30 minutes.

18. Salmon Fillet with Low-Carb Yogurt Dip

INGREDIENTS

- 350 g salmon fillet
- 150 g Greek cream yogurt
- 1 tbsp olive oil
- 3 g Ursalz fish
- 1 tsp lemon zest
- 1 clove of garlic
- dill
- rosemary
- Dressed thyme

INSTRUCTIONS

1. Preheat the air fryer to 180ºC
2. Season salmon with Ursalz Fisch
3. Brush casserole dish with oil; put in the salmon fillet
4. Chop garlic and herbs and sprinkle over the salmon
5. Rub the lemon peel and mix in the Greek yogurt
6. Bake the salmon in the air fryer for 15 to 20 minutes
7. Serve the salmon fillet with the low-carb dip

19. Keto Asparagus Muffins

INGREDIENTS

- 120 g cream cheese
- 200 g asparagus fresh
- 45 ml cream
- 400 g eggs
- 20 g Parmesan
- 60 g mozzarella rubbed
- 1/2 tsp salt
- 1/4 tsp pepper

INSTRUCTIONS

1. Grease two muffin plates. Preheat the air fryer to 160° C.
2. Wash asparagus, peel and cut into pieces about 1cm long.
3. Mix cream cheese, eggs, cream, Parmesan cheese, salt and pepper into a dough. Distribute into the molds and add asparagus.
4. Sprinkle the mozzarella cheese on top and bake for about 20 minutes.

20. Keto Bolognese Sauce

INGREDIENTS

- 10 g coconut oil
- 100 g breakfast bacon
- 130 g Onion
- 5 g garlic
- 500 g ground beef
- 400 g sausage meat
- 500 g tomatoes
- 400 g pizza sauce (canned)
- 250 ml vegetable broth
- 1/2 tsp stevia extract
- 4 tbsp cream double
- 2 tbsp butter
- 2 pieces of bay leaves
- 1 tbsp of parsley fresh
- 1 tbsp of oregano fresh
- 1 tbsp thyme fresh
- 1/2 tsp cinnamon ground
- 1/2 tsp nutmeg ground
- 1/2 tsp salt
- 1/2 tsp pepper

INSTRUCTIONS

1. Peel onion and garlic and chop finely. Heat coconut oil in an air fryer and sauté the onions and garlic.
2. Cut bacon into small pieces and sauté briefly.
3. Press the sausage meat out of the peel and put it into the air fryer with the minced meat.
4. Add the spices, stevia extract, salt and pepper and mix well. Roast about 7-8 minutes.
5. Then stir in the tomato sauce, the pizza tomato and the broth. Simmer with occasional stirring for a further 10 minutes.
6. Remove the bay leaves, stir in the cream double and the butter and season to taste.

21. Keto Pork Ribs

INGREDIENTS

SPARERIBS
- 1 kg ribs peeling rib of pork
- 360 ml chicken broth
- 45 ml lime juice
- 1 tsp garlic chopped
- 1 tsp salt

SAUCE
- 180 ml mayonnaise
- 45 ml lime juice
- 40 g shallots
- 10 g garlic
- 1 handful of parsley
- 1/2 tsp salt

INSTRUCTIONS

SPARERIBS

1. Preheat the air fryer to 150° C.

2. Place ribs in the air fryer. Sprinkle with salt and add stock, lime juice and garlic.
3. Close tightly with a lid or aluminum foil and place in the air fryer for approx. 2 hours.

SAUCE

4. Peel shallots and garlic.
5. Place in a blender and add the remaining INGREDIENTS.
6. Puree and add to the ribs.

22. Keto Mini Burger

INGREDIENTS

PATTIES
- 400 g ground beef
- 50 ml coconut oil
- 1/2 tsp coriander ground
- Ground 1/2 tsp cumin
- 1/2 tsp cayenne pepper ground
- salt
- pepper

TOPPING
- 200 g tomato
- 150 g bacon
- 40 g onion
- 1 tbsp of parsley fresh
- 50 g mayonnaise bought or homemade

INSTRUCTIONS

1. Mix the minced meat with the spices and make 12 small patties.
2. Heat the coconut oil in an air fryer and fry the patties well.
3. Peel the onion and cut it into rings. Wash and slice the tomato.
4. Cut the bacon into small pieces and sauté briefly in the air fryer.
5. Add a tsp of mayonnaise and top with tomato, onion, parsley and bacon.

23. Slow Apple Low-Carb Dessert

INGREDIENTS

- 200 g low-carb applesauce
- 40 ml slow juice
- 125 g mascarpone
- 125 g Greek cream yogurt
- 2 ml erythritol
- 16 drops of Flavdrops, vanilla

INSTRUCTIONS

1. Mix mascarpone, Greek yogurt and erythritol.
2. Pour low-carb apple compote into small glasses.
3. Spread the cream over it.

24. Low-Carb Carrot Cake

INGREDIENTS

- 5 eggs
- 200 g carrots
- 200 g butter
- 170 g cream cheese
- 100 g almond flour
- 30 g of walnuts chopped
- 20 g coconut flakes
- 4 ml erythritol
- 2 tsp baking powder
- 1 tsp cinnamon, ground
- 1 vial of vanilla flavor

INSTRUCTIONS

1. Preheat the air fryer to 180° C
2. Grate carrots
3. Mix eggs, butter, 1 tbsp erythritol and vanilla flavor
4. Add the grated carrots, walnuts, almond flour, baking powder and grated coconut and mix well
5. Pour the cake dough into air fryer and bake for about 40 minutes
6. Allow to cool
7. Heat cream cheese in microwave for 20 seconds at medium power
8. Mix the cream cheese with the remaining erythritol and spread over the cake
9. Garnish with cinnamon

25. Double Chocolate Cookies

INGREDIENTS

DOUGH

- 150 g ground hazelnuts
- 1 tsp baking powder
- 1/8 tsp salt
- 20 g butter
- 45 ml walnut oil
- 60 g erythritol
- 1 egg
- 1/2 tsp vanilla flavor

FILLING

- 50 g dark chocolate 99% cocoa
- 30 g erythritol powdered sugar
- 35 g butter
- 1/4 tsp vanilla flavor

INSTRUCTIONS

COOKIES

1. Preheat the air fryer to 160° C (circulating air) and prepare a baking tray with parchment paper.
2. Knead all INGREDIENTS for the cookie dough (preferably in a food processor) to a dough.
3. Spread 16 pastry blobs on the baking sheet with a tbsp and form into a round shape.
4. Bake the cookie dough in the air fryer for about 10 minutes, remove and allow it to cool well.

FILLING

5. Melt bittersweet chocolate in a water bath.
6. Stir in butter, powdered sugar erythritol and vanilla flavor until smooth.
7. Spread the chocolate evenly over the cooled cookies.

26. Cookies With Keto Marmalade

INGREDIENTS

- 3 eggs
- 70 g erythritol
- 160 g almond flour
- 1/2 tsp baking soda
- 1/2 tsp salt
- 60 g butter
- 50 g keto jam

INSTRUCTIONS

1. reheat the air fryer to 180° C and line a baking sheet with parchment paper
2. Mix all ingredients (excluding keto jam) into a cookie dough
3. Place 12 cookies on the baking tray, flatten and press a spoon in the middle of the cookie dough
4. Fill with jam in the middle.
5. Bake the cookies and serve

27. Keto Air Fryer Cakes

INGREDIENTS

- 3 eggs
- 80 g cream cheese

INSTRUCTIONS

1. Mix the dough out of eggs and cream cheese (if available in a Food processor)
2. Bake in an air fryer (yield: 12 small air fryer cakes)

28. KETO CHOCOLATE CAKE

INGREDIENTS

PIE CRUST
- 300 g hazelnuts ground
- 60 g butter (soft)
- 3 tsp erythritol
- 1 pinch of salt

CAKE TOPPING
- 400 g mascarpone
- 200 g dark chocolate 99% cocoa
- 6 tsp erythritol
- 70 g butter (soft)
- 50 ml cream

TOPPING
- 150 ml cream

garnish / REFINEMENT

- cocoa nibs
- cocoa powder

INSTRUCTIONS

PREPARATION
1. Preheat the air fryer to 180° C (convection).

PIE CRUST
1. Mix together butter, the ground hazelnuts, salt and erythritol and knead a cake dough
2. Lay out a springform air fryer (24 cm) with parchment paper
3. Distribute the dough evenly in the mold, press it flat and form a 1cm high edge
4. Bake the cake bottom for 15 minutes in the air fryer

CAKE TOPPINGS PREPARATION WITH THE COOKING CHEF FOOD PROCESSOR
1. Heat all INGREDIENTS for the cake topping at 40º C in the Cooking Chef
2. ... and mix

CAKE TOPPING PREPARATION WITHOUT COOKING CHEF
1. Heat and liquefy mascarpone
2. Melt chocolate in a water bath
3. Mix the rest of the cake coating INGREDIENTS with mascarpone and chocolate

COMPLETE
1. Spread the mixture on the cake and chill for 2 hours in the refrigerator
2. Then beat the cream for the topping stiff and spread on the chocolate cake
3. Garnish with cocoa powder and cocoa nibs

29. BUTTERCREAM CHRISTMAS COOKIES

INGREDIENTS

COOKIES
- 20 g butter
- 35 g cream cheese
- 60 g erythritol
- 1/4 tsp baking powder
- 1 tsp vanilla flavor
- 1/2 tsp salt
- 120 g almond flour

FROSTING
- 120 g erythritol
- 40 g butter
- 20 ml almond milk
- 1 tbsp raspberry juice for coloring

INSTRUCTIONS

COOKIES
1. Preheat the air fryer (150° C convection) and line a baking tray with parchment paper.
2. Mix all INGREDIENTS into a smooth cookie dough in a food processor.
3. Roll out the dough and cut out cookies with a small mold.
4. Bake the cookies in the air fryer for about 15 minutes until light brown and then allow to cool well.

FROSTING
5. Mix all the frosting INGREDIENTS with a spoon to a creamy mass.
6. Cover the cookies with a knife.
7. For the border fill the cream in a decorative syringe and gently apply the edge.

30. LOW-CARB ZUCCHINI BREAD

INGREDIENTS

- 80 g zucchini
- 500 g eggs
- 90 g butter
- 30 g Stevia sweetener
- 10 g almond flour
- 80g coconut flour
- 1 g baking powder 1 tsp
- 2 tsp cinnamon
- 1/2 tsp ginger ground
- 1 tsp salt
- 1 tsp vanilla extract

INSTRUCTIONS

1. Preheat the air fryer to 150° C.
2. Either grease a box tin or line it with parchment paper.
3. Finely chop the zucchini with a food processor.
4. Now process all the INGREDIENTS with the food processor to a smooth dough and fill in the box shape.
5. Bake in the air fryer for about 60 minutes. Allow to cool after removal.

31. LIME MOUSSE

INGREDIENTS

- 40 g egg yolk
- 40 ml lime juice or lemon juice
- 10 g erythritol
- 8 g gelatin powder
- 90 ml cream
- 1/4 tsp orange flavor

INSTRUCTIONS

1. Beat the cream until stiff.
2. Separate the eggs and place the egg yolk in a small bowl. Use the egg white for another recipe.
3. Add erythritol to the egg yolk and stir well.
4. In a water bath, warm the lime juice and the orange flavors. Add the gelatin and stir until it dissolves. Stir in the egg yolks. Let cool down.
5. Carefully fold in the cream and spread on two glasses.
6. Put in the refrigerator for about 2 hours.

32. COCONUT CHOCOLATE FAT BOMBS

INGREDIENTS

- 90 ml coconut oil
- 20 g cocoa butter
- 15 g baking cocoa
- 12 g Whey Protein Powder neutral
- 30 g erythritol
- 1/2 tsp almond extract

INSTRUCTIONS

1. Melt the cocoa butter and coconut oil in a small air fryer on low heat.
2. Add the remaining INGREDIENTS and stir to a creamy mixture.
3. Pour these into ice cube or chocolate cases and place in the refrigerator for about 2 hours.
4. When they have become solid, squeeze out of the molds. Store in the refrigerator until consumption.

33. PRALINE FAT BOMBS

INGREDIENTS

- 40 ml coconut oil
- 20 g of almond paste
- 10 g baking cocoa
- 10 g coconut flour
- 5 g erythritol

INSTRUCTIONS
1. Heat the coconut oil in the microwave until it is liquid.
2. Add the remaining INGREDIENTS and mix well with a blender.
3. Spread the cocoa cream in chocolate molds and put everything in the fridge for about 30 minutes.

34. KETO BREAKFAST CAKE

INGREDIENTS

CRUMBLE MIXTURE

- 20 g almond flour
- 20 g stevia
- 3 ml coconut oil
- 1/2 tsp cinnamon

BASE

- 120 g almond flour
- 90 g Greek yogurt
- 80 g Stevia sweetener
- 50 g egg
- 1 tsp vanilla extract

INSTRUCTIONS
1. Preheat the air fryer to 150° C.
2. Grease a small baking tin or line it with parchment paper.
3. For the crumble, process all INGREDIENTS into a dough with your hands and set it aside.
4. Mix all INGREDIENTS for the base with a food processor and pour into the mold.
5. Spread the sprinkles on top and bake in the air fryer for about 20 minutes.

35. KETO CHOCOLATE MOUSSE

INGREDIENTS

- 200 g dark chocolate min. 85%
- 90 ml water
- 3 eggs
- 50 ml coconut milk full fat
- 1 tbsp erythritol

INSTRUCTIONS

1. Heat the chocolate together with the water and the erythritol in a water bath.
2. Stir until a smooth mass has formed. Then set aside.
3. Separate the eggs.
4. Stir the egg yolk and coconut milk into the chocolate mixture.

5. Beat the egg whites until stiff and fold gently.

36. CHICKEN CAULIFLOWER CASSEROLE WITH PESTO

INGREDIENTS

- 244 g chicken thighs without skin
- 112 g of cheddar
- 120 g cream
- 140 g cauliflower
- 45 g leek
- 56 g tomato
- 28 g unsalted butter
- 16 g of keto pesto
- 1 tsp salt
- 1/2 tsp pepper

INSTRUCTIONS

1. Preheat the air fryer to 180° C.
2. Heat butter in an air fryer.
3. Cut the chicken into pieces. Cook the chicken in the air fryer for about 6-8 minutes until golden brown.
4. Add salt and pepper to the chicken.
5. Mix pesto and cream.
6. Put the chicken in a casserole dish and add the pesto cream to the cream.
7. Chop cauliflower, tomato and leek into pieces.
8. Put the pieces of vegetables in the casserole dish.
9. Cut the cheese into small pieces and sprinkle on top.
10. Bake the casserole for 25-30 minutes.

37. SALAD WRAPS

INGREDIENTS

SALAD
- 300 g lettuce
- 150 g cucumber

DRESSING
- 110 g breakfast bacon
- 200 g mushrooms
- 60 ml chicken broth
- 10 ml coconut vinegar
- 10 ml MCT oil
- 2 tbsp of parsley
- 1/2 tsp Stevia liquid
- 1/2 tsp salt
- 1/4 tsp pepper

FILLING
- 500 g minced meat
- 80 g onion
- 7 g garlic
- 4 ml Coconut Aminos
- 1/4 tsp fish sauce
- 10 g ginger fresh
- 10 g spring onion
- 5 ml coconut vinegar

INSTRUCTIONS

DRESSING
1. Cut the bacon into 1cm pieces and fry in an air fryer until crispy in the MCT oil.
2. Cut the mushrooms into small pieces and add to the bacon. Roast 5 minutes together.
3. Add vinegar and broth and simmer for another 5 min.
4. Stir in salt, pepper and stevia. Sprinkle with parsley and set aside.

FILLING
1. Fry the minced meat in an air fryer and then remove with a ladle. The liquid should remain in the air fryer.
2. Chop the onion and garlic, grate the ginger and fry everything in the air fryer.
3. Add vinegar, coconut aminos and fish sauce.

4. Fold in the minced meat and spring onion.

SALAD
1. Wash the lettuce and pick the leaves from the stalk. Serve on a plate.
2. Distribute the minced meat mixture evenly on the lettuce leaves and add the dressing. Add the cucumber to taste.

38. SALMON CHEESE AIR FRYER CAKES

INGREDIENTS

CAKE DOUGH
- 3 eggs
- 80 g cream cheese

FILLING
- 40 g cream cheese
- 85 g smoked salmon

INSTRUCTIONS
1. Mix the dough of cream cheese and eggs
2. Bake air fryer cakes in air fryer
3. Spread air fryer cakes with cream cheese, place the salmon on it and roll up the air fryer cakes

39. GRILLED TROUT

INGREDIENTS
- 520 g trout
- 10 ml MCT oil
- 1 tsp salt
- 4 sprigs of thyme fresh
- 2 sprigs of rosemary fresh

INSTRUCTIONS
1. Preheat the air fryer (grill setting) to 160° C.
2. Thoroughly wash the trout under running water. Dab dry with kitchen towels and then salt. Make three deep cuts on both sides.
3. Put trout in an air fryer and cover with the herbs and MCT oil.
4. After 15 minutes, check the cooking level and if necessary, increase the temperature to 180° C.
5. After another 5-8 minutes, remove the fish from the air fryer.

40. EGG AVOCADO WRAPPED IN BACON

INGREDIENTS
- 330 g avocado
- 50 g egg
- 100 g bacon
- 20 g coconut oil

INSTRUCTIONS
1. Hard boil the egg.
2. Cut the avocado in half and carefully remove the core. Use a spoon to separate the flesh from the skin. If necessary, scrape out a bit more avocado from the core area, so that fits a boiled egg.
3. Place two strips of bacon horizontally and on top of a large board. Now place five more strips, beginning on the vertical strip of bacon, downwards.
4. Fill the avocado with the egg and close the halves well.
5. Put the stuffed avocado down on the bacon and roll up. Also wrap around with the length of bacon strips and press well.
6. Heat coconut oil an air fryer and fry the avocado well on all sides.

41. SALMON IN ZUCCHINI BED

INGREDIENTS
- 250 g salmon fillet
- 1 lemon
- 1 zucchini
- 2 tomatoes
- 30 g onion red
- 1 tbsp olive oil
- 1 clove of garlic
- Dressed thyme
- Dill, dried
- Fresh rosemary
- salt
- pepper

INSTRUCTIONS
1. Preheat air fryer to 150° C convection
2. Line 2 bowls with aluminum foil
3. Slice the zucchini and lemon and spread in the bowls
4. Put the salmon in the aluminum bowls and top with pieces of tomato
5. Chop the onion and garlic
6. Distribute all INGREDIENTS on the salmon
7. Season with salt and pepper
8. Put herbs in the bowls and close aluminum foil well
9. Bake in the air fryer for 20 minutes

42. KETO BREAKFAST NUT YOGURT

INGREDIENTS
- 100 ml coconut milk
- 120 g Greek cream yogurt
- 15 g pecans
- 15 g macadamia nut kernels, roasted & salted
- 1 tsp of psyllium husks
- 3 drops of Flavdrops, Peanut Butter Flavor

INSTRUCTIONS
1. Put the macadamia nut kernels and pecans in a small bag.
2. Take a meat mallet to chop the nuts with a few blows.
3. Mix coconut milk, psyllium husks, crushed nuts and 3 drops of Flavdrops with the Greek yogurt.
4. Finally stir and garnish with a few chopped nuts.

43. COCONUT CINNAMON KETO FAT BOMBS

INGREDIENTS
- 125 g almond bread light
- 25 g almond cream dark
- 55 g coconut oil
- 1 tsp cinnamon
- 20 drops of Stevia
- 1 pinch of salt

INSTRUCTIONS
1. Add almond paste, coconut oil, stevia and cinnamon to a bowl.
2. Mix with a blender.
3. Place in aluminum molds (1 tbsp. each).
4. Put the Fat Bombs in the freezer for about 1 hour.

44. BLUEBERRY KETO ICE CREAM

INGREDIENTS

KETO ICE CREAM
- 300 g blueberries
- 300 g cream cheese
- 60 ml MCT oil

FOR garnish
- blueberries

- 40 g powdered Xucker erythritol
- 1 tsp vanilla flavor
- 15 drops of stevia

- mint leaves

INSTRUCTIONS
1. Pre-freeze 300g blueberries for 4 hours (or overnight).
2. Put frozen blueberries in a blender with cream cheese, vanilla flavor, MCT oil and stevia.
3. Sieve powdered Xucker (100% erythritol) into it.
4. Purify the whole thing.
5. Pour into the ice cream machine.
6. When the ice cream machine has turned the mass into ice garnish with mint leaves and a few blueberries and serve.

45. GOOSEBERRY RASPBERRY KETO ICE CREAM

INGREDIENTS
- 540 ml cream
- 225 g Xucker light erythritol
- 70 g egg yolk
- 240 g cream cheese

- 210 g gooseberries
- 300 g raspberries
- 360 ml coconut milk

INSTRUCTIONS
1. Heat the cream in an air fryer.
2. As soon as the cream begins to simmer, stir in the Xucker and dissolve.
3. Remove the pot from the heat and let it cool for about 5 minutes.
4. Add the coconut milk and cream cheese, then stir in the egg yolk slowly.
5. Allow the mass to cool for about 5 minutes.
6. Place in a blender with the gooseberries and raspberries and blend well.
7. Pour into the ice cream machine.

46. SHRIMP SPIESSE

INGREDIENTS
- 225 g of shrimp
- 1/2 tbsp of lemon juice
- salt

- pepper
- Chili flakes

INSTRUCTIONS
1. Thaw shrimp and stick on 5 wooden skewers
2. Fry in an air fryer coated with olive oil
3. Drizzle with lemon juice
4. Season to taste with salt, pepper and chili flakes

47. STUFFED CHICKEN BREAST FILLET

INGREDIENTS
- 600 g chicken breast fillet
- 120 g mozzarella
- 80 g of cheddar grated
- 1 tomato
- 30 g Keto Pesto
- salt
- pepper

INSTRUCTIONS
1. Heat the air fryer to 180º C (convection).
2. Brush a casserole dish with oil, clean the meat with water and then dab it dry.
3. Slice the tomato and mozzarella cheese.
4. Cut the poultry meat transversely every 2 cm (do not cut through).
5. Alternating, place mozzarella and tomato slices in the cuts.
6. Season with pepper, place in a baking dish and sprinkle Cheddar over it.
7. Bake for 40 minutes and serve.

48. LOW-CARB PIZZA ROLL

INGREDIENTS
- 180 g Edam cheese, shredded
- 180 g quark (40% fat)
- 60 g Passed tomatoes
- 3 eggs
- 1 slice of cooked ham
- 2 bars of spring onion
- 10 g arugula
- salt
- pepper

INSTRUCTIONS
1. Preheat air fryer to 180 C (circulating air) and line a baking sheet with parchment paper
2. Knead the cottage cheese, eggs and 2/3 of the Edam cheese to a dough
3. Spread the dough on the parchment paper and then bake for about 10 minutes
4. In the meantime, cut the spring onions into small rings
5. Cut the ham into pieces
6. Flake arugula
7. Season the chopped tomatoes with salt and pepper, remove the tin from the air fryer and spread the sauce on the dough
8. Spread the spring onions and the boiled ham on top
9. Sprinkle the remaining Edam over it and bake for another 10 minutes in the air fryer
10. Then remove from the air fryer and let cool for 2 minutes
11. Spread the arugula over it, roll up everything carefully and wrap it firmly in an aluminum foil (this makes it easier to cut pieces)

49. ZUCCHINI SHRIMP

INGREDIENTS
- 2 zucchini
- 215 g of shrimp
- 45 ml white wine, sweet
- 2 tbsp of lemon juice
- 8 g garlic
- 1/4 tsp red pepper flakes
- salt
- pepper
- 2 tbsp olive oil

INSTRUCTIONS

1. If you have bought fresh shrimp, scratch the back with a sharp knife and remove the black intestinal threads. For ready-to-cook shrimp, this step is eliminated.
2. Cut zucchini with a spiral cutter into long strips (zucchini spaghetti)
3. Chop garlic and juice half a lemon
4. Heat the oil in the air fryer
5. Roast the shrimp and garlic for about 8 minutes, season with salt and set aside
6. Add the wine, lemon juice and pepper flakes to the air fryer and bring to a boil
7. Add the zucchini and simmer for about 2 minutes
8. Garnish with a slice of lemon

50. SMOKED PORK CHOPS WITH PICKLED CABBAGE

INGREDIENTS
- 150 g Kassel
- 150 g sauerkraut
- 1/4 onion
- 1 bay leaf
- Black peppercorns, optional
- 3 cloves, optional
- Juniper berries, optional

INSTRUCTIONS
1. Moisten a coated air fryer with a little oil.
2. Roast Kassel on both sides until it turns a bit brownish on the outside.
3. Then season with pepper.
4. Drain the herbs and heat in an air fryer.

51. KETO CHICKEN CAULIFLOWER CASSEROLE

INGREDIENTS
- 1000 g chicken thighs
- 1 1/2 tsp chili powder
- 2 tbsp olive oil
- 150 g cream cheese
- 120 g of cheddar grated
- 160 g tomatoes
- 20 g Parmesan
- 40 g fresh cream
- 550 g cauliflower
- 30 g jalapeño
- salt
- pepper

INSTRUCTIONS
1. Preheat the air fryer to 200º C (recirculation setting).
2. Cook the chicken for about 30 minutes and remove the meat from the bones.
3. Then fry the meat in a roasting air fryer until it turns brownish.
4. Add cream cheese and cheddar and stir.
5. Cut tomatoes into small pieces, add to them.
6. Mix everything well, season to taste with salt and pepper and then set aside.
7. Chop the cauliflower and jalapeño into small pieces.
8. Add the cauliflower, fresh cream and jalapeño over the meat and cheese mixture.
9. Sprinkle Parmesan over it, put it in the air fryer and bake for 20 minutes.

52. HOT CHILI SOUP

INGREDIENTS

- 2 tbsp olive oil
- 2 pieces of chili peppers fresh
- 360 ml chicken broth
- 360 ml water
- 1/2 tsp Ground cumin
- 32 g tomato paste
- 350 g chicken meat
- 30 g butter
- 1 avocado
- 60 g cream cheese
- 15 ml lime juice
- salt
- pepper

INSTRUCTIONS

1. Core chili peppers and cut into small pieces.
2. Cut the chicken into small pieces.
3. Coat an air fryer with olive oil and sauté the meat and set aside.
4. Heat 2 tbsp of olive oil in air fryer, add the coriander seeds and wait until they develop their aroma.
5. Do the pieces of chili peppers.
6. Pour chicken stock and water into the pot and let it boil.
7. Season with cumin, salt and pepper.
8. Bring the soup to a boil briefly.
9. Then stir in the tomato paste and butter.
10. Now simmer the soup for another 5 to 10 minutes.
11. Add lime juice.
12. Put 1/4 of the meat in a soup plate (or bowl), fill with soup and refine with 1 spoon of cream cheese.
13. garnish with coriander.
14. If necessary, season with salt and pepper.
15. Slice the avocado and place 1/4 of each in a soup plate.

53. PAPRIKA CAULIFLOWER SOUP

INGREDIENTS

- 360 g bell peppers, red or green
- 320 g cauliflower
- 23 g olive oil
- 18 g spring onion
- 4 g garlic
- 90 g feta
- 90 ml pastry cream
- 540 ml chicken broth-3 cups
- 1/2 tsp paprika spice seasoning
- 1/2 tsp thyme
- 1/2 tsp red pepper flakes
- salt
- pepper

INSTRUCTIONS

1. Set the air fryer to "grill" and preheat to 200º C.
2. Cut the peppers in half and core them.
3. Then moisten with olive oil inside and outside.
4. Put the peppers on the baking tray (use parchment paper) and grill for 10-15 minutes.
5. While the peppers are cooking, cut the cauliflower into florets.
6. Remove the ready-grilled peppers from the air fryer and place in zip-closed freezer bags or a container with a lid.
7. Now place the cauliflower florets on the baking sheet.

8. Mix 1 tbsp olive oil with salt and pepper. Use it to coat the cauliflower.
9. Put the plate in the air fryer and cook the cauliflower for 30 to 35 minutes at 200° C with circulating air (do not forget to switch from "grilling" to "convection").
10. Remove the skin from the peppers.
11. Dice the spring onions. Heat 2 tbsp of olive oil in the pot and sauté the onions.
12. Once the spring onions are seared, add the spices. Mix everything well and let the spices release their aroma.
13. Now add the peppers. Let them fry for a moment.
14. Now add the chicken broth, red pepper and cauliflower.
15. Simmer for another 10-20 minutes at low temperature.
16. Pour the pastry cream into it.
17. Take the soup from the hob and purée with a blender for about 2 minutes.
18. Season to taste.
19. Before serving, dice the feta cheese, spread on top and garnish with thyme and spring onions.

54. KETO SALAMI PIZZA

INGREDIENTS
PIZZA DOUGH
- 30 g almond flour
- 35 g flaxseed flour
- 10 g coconut flour
- g psyllium husk
- 5 g chia seeds
- 1/3 tsp salt
- 80 ml water

PIZZA TOPPINGS
- 20 g Passed tomatoes
- 40 g salami
- 35 g tomatoes
- 12 g pepper
- 20 g of cheddar
- Italian herbs

INSTRUCTIONS
PIZZA DOUGH
1. Mix almond flour, flaxseed, coconut flour, psyllium husk, chia seed, salt in a bowl.
2. Add water.
3. Knead with a KitchenAid (if available) to a dough.
4. Then refrigerate for 30 minutes.
5. Preheat the air fryer (180º C circulating air).
6. Then make a ball out of the dough. Place the dough ball on parchment paper, roll it out thinly and form a rim.
7. Bake the keto pizza dough for about 10 minutes.

PIZZA TOPPINGS
1. Wash the peppers, core them and cut them into small pieces.
2. Slice tomatoes and distribute them on the pizza base.
3. Spread salami slices, peppers and tomatoes on the pizza base.
4. Sprinkle the cheddar cheese over it.
5. Bake in the air fryer for 10 to 15 minutes until the pizza crust is nice and crispy.
6. Take the keto pizza out of the air fryer and enjoy.

55. LOW-CARB PESTO CHICKEN ROULADE

INGREDIENTS
- 500 g chicken breast fillet 4 pieces
- 150 g halloumi-grilled cheese
- 250 ml Keto Pesto
- 1 tbsp olive oil
- 5 g a lemon peel
- 1 tsp garlic

- 1 tsp salt
- 1 tsp pepper
- 2 tbsp of olive oil for frying

INSTRUCTIONS
1. Wash the chicken breast under running water. Dry well with paper towels.
2. Fillet the chicken breast as thinly as possible.
3. Knock the chicken breast fillets flat with a meat mallet (flat side).
4. Mix 250ml pesto (1/4 cup) with 1 tbsp of olive oil.
5. Distribute your pesto on the chicken breast.
6. Grate a bowl of 1 lemon over the chicken.
7. Cut the Halloumi cheese into small pieces and spread the cheese on the chicken.
8. Roll the fillets together as much as possible and fix them with chopsticks (maybe a toothpick).
9. Preheat the air fryer to 230 C.
10. Take a cast iron skillet (roast casserole too) and sprinkle with 2 tbsp olive oil.
11. Now fry the roulades in the air fryer, so that all sides are a little brown.
12. Then put everything in the air fryer and let it cook for 6-7 minutes.
13. Once clear juices run out of the roulade, remove from the air fryer, let rest briefly for 5-6 minutes and serve.

56. LOW-CARB TOMATO SOUP

INGREDIENTS
- 800 g tomatoes
- 20 g butter
- 1/4 onion (red onion)
- 1 clove of garlic
- 250 ml vegetable broth
- 4 tsp olive oil
- 8 g erythritol
- 1 pinch of salt
- 1 pinch of pepper

INSTRUCTIONS
1. Carefully slice into the tomatoes in a crosswise pattern
2. Put the tomatoes briefly in boiling water and then quench with cold water
3. Skin tomatoes with a knife and chop tomatoes
4. Chop onions, garlic and basil
5. Sauté with butter
6. Broth to give and boil briefly
7. Add the tomatoes and simmer for 10 minutes
8. Transfer to a blender and puree

57. CAULIFLOWER PIZZA

INGREDIENTS
- 700 g cauliflower
- 200 g mozzarella, shredded
- 30 g parmesan, shredded
- 1 egg
- 1 handful of basil fresh
- 1/2 tbsp Italian herbs

INSTRUCTIONS
1. Preheat air fryer to 180º C (circulating air)
2. Place cauliflower in food processor until it is the size of rice grains
3. Mix the cauliflower with parmesan, egg, herbs and half of the mozzarella cheese
4. Bake the mixture in the air fryer for 10 minutes
5. Then sprinkle the remaining mozzarella cheese over it and bake for another 10 minutes until the cheese turns brown

58. KETO LASAGNA

INGREDIENTS
- 900 g eggs
- 40 g butter
- 400 g sausage coarse
- 400 g cream cheese
- 350 ml beef broth
- 100 g cooked ham
- 100 g bacon
- 125 g grated Parmesan
- 125 g Mozzarella
- 1 tsp salt
- 1/2 tsp pepper

INSTRUCTIONS
1. Preheat the air fryer to 160° C. Grease well.
2. Whisk all eggs in a large bowl and pour half into the air fryer. Now let it set like an omelet. After about 4 minutes, reduce the heat. Season with salt and pepper. Flipping is not necessary. Do the same with the rest of the egg mass. Set aside.
3. Press the sausage meat out of the peel and place in the air fryer approximately 5-6 min. Then stir in the cream cheese and add the broth. Simmer the sauce with constant stirring for 2 minutes until it thickens. Season with salt and pepper.
4. Now grease a square, high casserole dish and add the first layer of the canned egg mass. Spread the bratwurst sauce on top and top with cooked ham.
5. Fill in the second layer of egg and again spread a portion of the sauce on it.
6. Cover with the ham and the sliced mozzarella.
7. Add the remaining sauce and sprinkle with Parmesan cheese.
8. Bake in the air fryer for 30 min.

59. AVOCADO TUNA SALAD

INGREDIENTS
- 85 g tuna in water
- 15 g olive oil
- 18 g green olives
- 158 g avocado
- 85 g red oak leaf lettuce
- 10 g onion fresh
- 16 g balsamic vinegar
- 2 eggs cooked

INSTRUCTIONS
1. Hard boil the eggs for 10-15 minutes.
2. Rip up the lettuce leaves and place them in a large salad bowl.
3. Chop the avocado and place it in the salad bowl.
4. Chop onion and add together with the olives.
5. Drain the tuna and put it into the bowl with a fork. Use the fork to break the tuna into small pieces.
6. When the eggs are done, peel, cut into small pieces and add to salad.
7. Drizzle with olive oil and balsamic vinegar and mix well.

60. KETO MUFFIN ROLLS

INGREDIENTS
- 3 eggs
- 60 g cream cheese
- 15 g psyllium husk
- 10 g coconut flour

INSTRUCTIONS
1. Preheat the air fryer to 150° C.
2. Separate the eggs and beat the egg whites until very stiff.
3. Mix the egg yolk with the remaining INGREDIENTS and carefully remove from the egg whites.

4. Now fill the dough in twelve muffin tins and bake in the air fryer for about 20 minutes.

61. MEATLOAF PIZZA

INGREDIENTS

BASE

- 500 g mixed minced meat
- 50 g liver, optional
- 1 egg
- 50 g grated mozzarella cheese
- 0.5 onion, optional
- Spices: pepper, salt; chili pepper, oregano, parsley

TOPPING

- 100 g mushrooms
- 75 g fresh leaf spinach
- 30 ml full cream
- 75 g feta cheese
- Spices: pepper, salt, oregano
- 1 tsp coconut oil

INSTRUCTIONS

1. Heat the air fryer to 175° C.
2. Add all spices, mozzarella and egg to the minced meat in a large bowl. Mix thoroughly (with your hands).
3. Take a large enough piece of parchment paper and place the dough on it.
4. Make a nice round pizza shape from the mixture. Try not to make it thicker than 1 centimeter.
5. Place in the air fryer for 30 minutes. Keep an eye on your pizza.
6. Meanwhile, cut the mushrooms into equal parts. Melt some coconut oil in the air fryer and stir-fry the mushrooms for 3 minutes. Then add the herbs and the freshly washed leaf spinach.
7. As soon as the spinach starts to shrink, add the full cream. Let it cook for another 1 minute and remove from the heat.
8. Once the dough is ready, you can add the toppings. Place in the air fryer for 7 minutes (possibly on grill setting) so that the top is warmed up faster.

62. STEWED CABBAGE & MINCED MEAT

INGREDIENTS

- 500 g mixed minced meat
- 500 g pointed cabbage
- 2 large spring onion
- 2-3 cm of fresh ginger
- Spices: salt, pepper, chili peppers to taste
- 1 tbsp sesame seeds
- 1 tbsp sesame oil
- 1 tbsp coconut oil

INSTRUCTIONS

1. Cut the cabbage and the spring onion into pieces. Chop the ginger.
2. Meanwhile, melt the coconut oil in a large enough air fryer.
3. Add the mixed minced meat. Keep stirring until well cooked.
4. Now add the pointed cabbage, fresh ginger and spring onion.
5. Stir fry for 5 minutes.
6. Add all herbs and mix well.
7. Finish with (roasted) sesame seeds and sesame oil.

63. KETO STROMBOLI SNACKS

INGREDIENTS

- 25 g coconut flour
- 175 g grated mozzarella cheese
- 100 g cream cheese
- 1 large egg
- 1 tsp of baking powder
- Spices: pepper, salt and other spices based on your filling keto Stromboli

INSTRUCTIONS

1. Take a small air fryer and let the cream cheese and mozzarella melt on a low heat. Keep stirring continuously so that the cheese does not turn brown.
2. Beat the egg. Add the melted cheese, coconut flour and all herbs.
3. Mix well together (with your hands).
4. Place the dough on wax paper and roll out with a rolling pin. If necessary, place an extra piece of wax paper on top to make the rolling easier.
5. Make small shapes of the dough (circles with a large glass, squares with a knife).
6. Place your favorite fillings in the middle and fold the packages nicely.
7. Place in the air fryer for 8-10 minutes or until golden brown.

64. CUCUMBER GAZPACHO

INGREDIENTS

- 1 clove of garlic
- 0.5 onion optional
- 0.5 (small) red pepper optional
- 1 cucumber
- 0.5 avocado
- 0.5 lemon, juiced
- Spices: salt, pepper
- 3 tbsp olive oil
- 4-6 tbsp water

INSTRUCTIONS

1. Crush the look. & cut all the vegetables into pieces (don't have to look too small if you have a good mixer).
2. Put all the INGREDIENTS together in a food processor.
3. Mix until you have a smooth gazpacho. If necessary, add a little more water if the soup is too firm.
4. Finish with some extra olive oil and a string cucumber.
5. Garnish with avocado

65. FISH STICKS

INGREDIENTS

- 500 g cod
- 2-3 eggs

BREAD-CRUMBS

- 30 g almond flour
- 30 g coconut flour
- 50 g grated Parmesan cheese
- 4 tbsp coconut oil
- 1 tbsp basil
- 0.5 tbsp cayenne pepper

INSTRUCTIONS

1. Take a jar and beat the eggs well with a fork.
2. In another bowl, mix all the INGREDIENTS for the breadcrumbs well together. Add any additional spices to taste.
3. Cut the cod into strips slightly wider than your finger. Place them first in the bowl with the beaten eggs and then in your homemade breadcrumbs.
4. Bake the fish sticks for two minutes along each can on a low fire with a good amount of coconut oil.
5. Serve with some (homemade) mayonnaise, tzatziki or another sauce of your choice.

66. SIMPLE SPAGHETTI

INGREDIENTS

- 750 g mixed minced meat
- 1 tbsp coconut oil
- 2 small peppers
- 50 g parmesan cheese
- 350 g zucchini
- 125 ml full cream
- Spices: salt, oregano, cayenne pepper, pepper, garlic

INSTRUCTIONS

1. Melt the coconut oil in an air fryer.
2. Add the mixed minced meat and keep stirring.
3. Meanwhile, cut the bell pepper into small pieces. Once the minced meat has been baked, add the pepper pieces. Keep stirring occasionally and add all herbs.
4. Let the peppers boil a little and let the cream boil at the end.
5. Meanwhile, make strings of your zucchini with your spiralizer.
6. Arrange the raw zucchini on a plate and top with the warm sauce. Finish with some Parmesan cheese.

67. SAUSAGE ROLLS

INGREDIENTS

- 4 long sausages
- 2 eggs
- Spices: salt, pepper, oregano
- 2 tsp coconut oil or butter

INSTRUCTIONS

1. Take a small bowl and beat one egg (with some herbs) together with a fork.
2. Heat air fryer and melt a tsp of coconut oil.
3. Place the air fryer on low. Now pour the egg mixture into the air fryer. Turn the air fryer gently so that the egg mixture covers the entire bottom.
4. Let it bake for two minutes. Since this is paper thin, you don't even have to turn them over! Then do the same again with the other egg.
5. Meanwhile, heat the sausage in another air fryer until it is ready.
6. Then roll the sausage into the omelet.

68. PIZZA WITH SOUR CREAM & BACON

INGREDIENTS

- 300 g almond flour
- 2 tbsp of olive oil
- 1 tbsp of salt and oregano
- 1 egg
- 5 large tbsp of sour cream
- 1/2 onion

INSTRUCTIONS

1. Preheat the air fryer to 180 C.
2. Combine all INGREDIENTS. Mix everything well until a large ball is formed.
3. Place the ball on a baking tray lined with parchment paper. Place another parchment paper on top to facilitate rolling. The dough can be sticky.
4. Roll out as evenly as possible. Place in the air fryer for 15 minutes.
5. In the meantime, fry the bacon and the onions in another air fryer.
6. Once the 15 minutes are up, remove the pizza from the air fryer. Cover with sour cream, add the bacon and the onion on top.
7. Place in the air fryer for another 5 minutes-under the grill.

69. POPPY SEED BREAD

INGREDIENTS

- 0.5 cauliflower +/- 250 g
- 5 eggs
- 175 g almond flour
- 25 g psyllium
- 75 g butter
- 2-3 tbsp poppy seeds
- 1 tbsp baking powder
- 0.5 tbsp of salt

INSTRUCTIONS

1. Heat the air fryer to 175° C.
2. Cut (or grate) the cauliflower into small pieces. Steam the cauliflower until it is completely flat. Place the butter on the cauliflower and mix until you have a smooth mass.
3. Meanwhile, take a large bowl and mix all dry INGREDIENTS together (poppy seeds, baking powder, almond flour, salt, psyllium).
4. Beat the eggs briefly and mix them with the cauliflower through the dry INGREDIENTS.
5. Garnish with extra poppy seeds (or sesame seeds, if desired).
6. Cook 35-40 minutes in the air fryer.

70. RHUBARB PECAN PIE

INGREDIENTS

- 300 g fresh rhubarb
- 80-100 g pecans
- 250 g almond flour
- 1/2 tsp baking powder
- 1/4 tsp sea salt
- 120 g erythritol
- 1/2 tsp xanthan gum
- 75 ml cream

- 3 eggs
- 45 g butter
- 1 tsp cinnamon

INSTRUCTIONS

1. Heat the air fryer to 175° C.
2. Wash the rhubarb stalks and cut them into even pieces.
3. Take a large bowl and mix well the erythritol, xanthan gum and a pinch of salt. Add the pieces of rhubarb and pecans and mix well.
4. Add this mixture to a baking air fryer covered with parchment paper. Make sure that the pieces of rhubarb and pecans are nicely spread over the cake.
5. Place the mixture in the middle of your shape and make sure that you remain 1 cm away from the edge. This way you will have some space for the dough and your cake will get a nice shape.
6. Meanwhile, melt the butter.
7. In another bowl, mix almond flour, pinch of salt, cinnamon, baking powder.
8. In another small bowl, mix eggs, cream and melted butter. Add the almond flour mixture. Mix well.
9. Spread the dough on top of your rhubarb-pecan mixture.
10. Place in the air fryer for 30 minutes. Test with a skewer to be sure.
11. Once the cake is ready, let it cool down and remove the edge of your spring form.
12. Take a large serving plate, place it on top and turn your cake over.

71. SPINACH & MUSHROOM QUICHE

INGREDIENTS

- 450 g version spinach
- 200-250 g feta cheese
- 200-250 ml full cream
- 500 g mushrooms
- 4 eggs beaten
- 200 g grated mozzarella cheese
- Spices: pepper, salt, oregano
- 3 cloves of garlic
- pork chop

INSTRUCTIONS

1. Preheat the air fryer to 175° C.
2. Wipe the mushrooms clean and cut into equal parts.
3. Stir fry the finely chopped (or crushed) pieces of garlic in a generous amount of coconut fat. Keep stirring.
4. Add the mushrooms after 1-2 minutes. In the meantime, keep stirring well for 5 minutes. Meanwhile, take a large baking dish and grease the undersides and sides well.
5. Place the fresh (washed) spinach spread on the bottom. Add the garlic and the mushrooms on top.
6. In the meantime, take a separate scale. Mix the eggs and the cream well together and add all the herbs.
7. Now add the crumbled feta cheese on top of the mushrooms. & pour the egg-cream mixture in between.
8. Add some extra grated mozzarella cheese on top. Place everything in the air fryer for 35-45 minutes.

72. CHEESE SAUCE

INGREDIENTS

- 60 ml whipped cream
- 30 g hard butter
- 60 g cream cheese
- 60 g grated cheddar (or other hard cheese)
- pinch of salt
- Additions to taste

- cayenne pepper
- garlic powder
- paprika powder
- fresh chopped herbs to taste

INSTRUCTIONS

1. Heat cream and butter in the air fryer. In the meantime, start grating the cheese.
2. Once the butter has melted, add the cream cheese. Stir everything well until you have a smooth whole. As soon as you see bubbles appear, remove the air fryer from the heat.
3. Add the grated cheese and keep stirring until you have a smooth sauce.
4. If you want thicker sauce, leave it on the fire for a few minutes. If it is too thick, you can add a tbsp of water or cream.

73. CHEESE & HAM OMELET

INGREDIENTS

- 2 eggs
- 2 slices of ham of your choice.
- 1 tbsp grated mozzarella cheese A slice of cheese is also a good option.
- 1 tsp butter
- 1 pinch of salt and pepper
- 1 tsp oregano

INSTRUCTIONS

1. Melt butter melt in the air fryer.
2. Take a small bowl and beat the eggs and herbs together with a fork. Chop the onion and add to the mixture.
3. Place in an air fryer on low heat.
4. When the egg is almost completely solidified, place the ham and cheese on top.
5. Roll the omelet, and leave on the fire for another 30 seconds.

74. HOMEMADE GRANOLA

INGREDIENTS

- 75 g sunflower seeds
- 75 g pumpkin seeds
- 50 g sesame seeds
- 25 g linseed
- 50 g macadamia nuts
- 50 g pecan nuts
- 50 g almond nuts
- 2 tbsp coconut oil
- 1 tbsp cinnamon
- 1 egg whites, beaten

INSTRUCTIONS

1. Mix all the seeds in a bowl. Break the nuts into smaller pieces if desired, and add them to the bowl.
2. Heat the coconut oil. Mix in with nut and seed mixture. Add cinnamon.
3. Beat the egg whites with a hand blender. Spatula this gently through the granola. The protein ensures that the whole is a little crisper.
4. Spread the granola on a baking tray lined with parchment paper. Place this in your preheated air fryer at 170° C (150° if hot air) for 20 to 25 minutes. Mix well every 10 minutes, so that everything turns brown and crispy.

75. SPINACH & CHEESE FLATBREAD

INGREDIENTS

- 200 g grated mozzarella
- 100 g cream cheese
- 2 tbsp almond flour
- 200 g spinach
- 0.5 white onion optional
- 1 clove optional
- Herbs: chives, salt

INSTRUCTIONS

1. Heat the air fryer to 175° C.
2. Bring a pot of water to the boil. Let the spinach cook well for 3 minutes. Drain and let cool.
3. Chop the clove and onion into small pieces.
4. Add mozzarella cheese and the cream cheese in an air fryer. Put on a low heat and keep stirring until it is melted well.
5. Add the almond flour in a separate bowl. Mix everything well.
6. Cut the spinach into small pieces and mix with the garlic and onion to the mixture.
7. Spread out on a baking tray lined with parchment paper.
8. Place in the air fryer for ten minutes or until it has turned golden brown.

76. CRACKERS

INGREDIENTS

- 6 tbsp Flax seeds
- 2 tbsp Mixed seeds
- 2 tbsp Sesame seeds
- 6 tbsp Water

INSTRUCTIONS

1. Mix all seeds and water in a large bowl.
2. Then spread the mix over a sheet of parchment paper.
3. Cut it into 6 pieces.
4. Then place the parchment paper on a glass plate.
5. Place the plate in preheated air fryer and make sure the crackers are baked at the highest setting for 4 minutes.

77. LOW-CARB BREAD

INGREDIENTS

- 30 g almond flour
- 20 g low-carb potato fibers
- 30 g butter
- 1 egg
- 1 pinch of salt

INSTRUCTIONS

1. Melt butter and mix all INGREDIENTS together to form a dough
2. Press the bread dough into shape
3. Bake the low-carb bread at the highest level for 2 minutes in the microwave
4. Your micro low-carb bread is now ready to serve

78. KETO ZUCCHINI BOATS WITH TUNA

INGREDIENTS

- 2 zucchini
- 150 g tuna (in water / can)
- 200 g tomatoes
- 12 g onion
- 70 g Cheddar (shredded)
- 1 clove of garlic
- salt
- pepper

INSTRUCTIONS

1. Preheat the air fryer to 180º C (circulating air)
2. Cut the zucchini longitudinally in half, remove the cores and hollow out
3. Season with salt & pepper and set aside
4. Drain the tuna
5. Chop tomatoes, onions and garlic
6. Divide all INGREDIENTS into the zucchini boats
7. Sprinkle with cheese and bake for 20 minutes in the air fryer

79. TOMATO-MOZZARELLA EGGPLANT FAN

INGREDIENTS

- 2 eggplants
- 2 tomatoes medium
- 1 mozzarella cheese
- 2 tbsp olive oil
- 1 pinch of salt
- Italian Herbs

INSTRUCTIONS

1. Preheat the air fryer to 150ºC.
2. Slice the eggplants, add salt and set aside
3. Slice mozzarella and tomatoes
4. Tomato and mozzarella alternately stuck in the eggplant fan
5. Put a leaf of basil on each mozzarella bills
6. Season with Italian herbs
7. Put everything in a greased dish and brush with olive oil
8. Cook for 40 minutes in the air fryer (top / bottom heat).

80. PECAN ICE CREAM

INGREDIENTS

- 160 ml cream
- 20 g butter
- 1/3 cup of erythritol
- 1 pinch of Stevia liquid
- 1 tsp vanilla flavor
- 80 g egg yolk
- 100 g pecans

INSTRUCTIONS

1. Bring the cream in the air fryer to the boiling point and remove from heat.
2. Stir in butter and erythritol and allow it to cool.
3. In the meantime, mince the pecans. For example, you can put the nuts in a small bag and smash them with a meat mallet.

4. Then add in the nuts, as well as the remaining INGREDIENTS in the pot and mix.
5. Now add everything in the ice machine. After about 30 minutes, the ice cream is ready to serve.

81. LOW-CARB VANILLA ICE CREAM

INGREDIENTS

- 450 ml whipped cream, 30%
- 5 egg yolks
- 150 g erythritol
- 1 tsp bourbon vanilla
- 1 vial of vanilla flavor

INSTRUCTIONS

1. Mix erythritol and egg yolks in a water bath until the erythritol has dissolved
2. Mix the mass with the cream

WITH ICE MAKER

1. Put everything in the ice cream machine and let it sit for 30 minutes

WITHOUT ICE MAKER

1. Put everything in a bowl and place in the freezer
2. After 20 minutes, stir the mixture and repeat every half an hour until the mass has solidified

82. CAULIFLOWER HASH BROWNS

INGREDIENTS

- 1 small head grated cauliflower (about 3 cups)
- 1 large Egg
- 3/4 cup Shredded Cheddar Cheese
- 1/4 tsp Cayenne Pepper (optional)
- 1/4 tsp garlic powder
- 1/2 tsp Pink Himalayan Salt
- 1/8 tsp black pepper

INSTRUCTIONS

1. Grate the entire head of the cauliflower.
2. Microwave for 3 minutes and let cool. Place on paper towels or cheesecloth and ring out the excess water.
3. Place cauliflower in a bowl, add rest of INGREDIENTS and combine well.
4. Form into six square shaped hash browns on a greased baking tray.
5. Place in a 400 F air fryer for 15-20 minutes.
6. Let cool for 10 minutes and hash browns will firm up.

83. EGG WRAP WITH SALMON & SPINACH

INGREDIENTS

- 3 medium eggs
- dash of almond milk
- 100 g baby spinach
- 2 tbsp olive oil
- salt and pepper to taste
- 25 g cream cheese
- 20 g arugula
- 50 g smoked salmon
- 4 cherry tomatoes
- 1/4 tsp salt

- optional: handful of pine nuts

INSTRUCTIONS

1. Cut the baby spinach into small pieces on a large board.
2. Heat a tbsp of olive oil in air fryer and fry the baby spinach approximately 2 minutes. Mix the eggs, almond milk and salt in a large bowl with a whisk. After frying the spinach, drain the excess from the air fryer and add the spinach to the bowl and mix well with the eggs.
3. Fry the spinach omelet over a low heat for 5-10 minutes until cooked. If possible, carefully turn the omelet halfway through baking with a spatula.
4. Allow the omelet to cool for a minimum of 30 minutes and then cut the cherry tomatoes into small slices. When the omelet has cooled, spread the cream cheese over the omelet and coated with the arugula, smoked salmon, cherry tomatoes and pine nuts. Roll the omelet tightly, cut in half and enjoy!

84. SALMON WITH LEMON & CAPERS

INGREDIENTS

- 4 salmon fillets (150 g each)
- 60 ml olive oil
- 1/2 tsp salt
- 1/2 tsp freshly ground black pepper
- 1 tbsp fresh rosemary, finely chopped
- 8 slices of lemon
- juice of 1 lemon
- 100 ml white wine
- 4 tsp capers

INSTRUCTIONS

1. Coat the top and bottom of salmon fillets with olive oil and season with salt, pepper and rosemary. Place each piece of seasoned salmon on a piece of foil that is large enough to cover the salmon.
2. Now place 2 lemon slices, 1 tbsp lemon juice, 2 tbsp wine and 1 tbsp capers on top of each piece of salmon. Then close the aluminum foil tightly.
3. Turn on a grill air fryer over medium-high heat. Place the salmon packets in the air fryer and bake for 8-12 minutes.

85. LOW-CARB PUMPKIN SQUASH

INGREDIENTS

- 350 g pumpkin lasagna sheets or 1 bottle gourd
- 1 onion
- 1 clove of garlic
- 1 tbsp olive oil
- 500 g (lean) ground beef
- 400 g tomato pulp
- 1 tbsp Italian herbs
- 1 tbsp tomato puree
- 200 g ricotta
- 35 g grated Parmesan cheese
- 120 g grated cheese for air fryer gratin
- optional: Italian stir-fry vegetable

INSTRUCTIONS

1. Preheat the air fryer to 180 C. Carefully remove the skin from the bottle gourd and cut into thin slices. It is also possible to use ready-made pumpkin lasagna sheets.
2. Then cut the onion and garlic clove into small pieces. Heat a tbsp of olive oil in a large frying air fryer and add the finely chopped onion and garlic. Fry the onion and garlic until the onions turn glassy. Then add the ground

beef and fry it, stirring for about 3-5 minutes. Optional: add a little Italian stir-fry vegetable to the minced meat.
3. Then add the tomato pulp, tomato puree and Italian herbs, salt and pepper. Reduce the heat to low and let the mixture simmer for 10 minutes.
4. Meanwhile, make the sauce by mixing the ricotta with Parmesan cheese. When the minced meat is ready, take a baking dish and grease it with a little oil.
5. Spoon some of the minced meat mixture into the baking dish and place a few pumpkin lasagna sheets over it. Then spread the slices with the ricotta sauce. Repeat this until all your INGREDIENTS are used up. Finally, sprinkle the lasagna with the remaining grated cheese.
6. Bake the pumpkin lasagna 30-35 minutes in the preheated air fryer. After baking, allow the lasagna to cool down and cut into four equal-sized pieces.

86. LOW-CARB CHEESE TACOS

INGREDIENTS

Cheese tacos:

- 180 g grated cheese (Cheddar or Gouda)

Minced meat filling:

- 500 g ground beef
- 1 tbsp olive oil
- 1 onion, cut into pieces
- 1 clove of garlic, crushed
- 1 tbsp tomato puree
- 1 tsp chili powder
- 1 tsp cumin powder
- 1 tsp paprika powder
- 1 tsp garlic powder
- 1/2 tsp black pepper
- 1/2 tsp salt
- 1/2 tsp oregano
- hand iceberg lettuce
- handful of cherry tomatoes, cut into pieces
- grated cheese to taste
- fresh cream to taste

INSTRUCTIONS

1. Preheat the air fryer to 180 C. Then take a large baking sheet and line it with a sheet of parchment paper. Divide the grated cheese into 6 portions for 6 cheese tacos. Place each portion of cheese in a heap on the baking sheet with enough space between the heaps. Bake the cheese heaps 8-10 minutes in the preheated air fryer.
2. When the cheese is melted, remove the cheese tacos and pat the excess fat from the cheese with a paper towel. Then form a taco from the melted cheese by placing it on the spatula. Allow the taco to cool down in this position and repeat this until you have formed a taco of all heaps of cheese.
3. Then heat an olive oil in air fryer. Add the sliced onions and crushed garlic and fry for 2-3 minutes until golden brown. Then add the minced meat and cook for another 5-6 minutes.
4. In the meantime, mix all the herbs together in a small bowl and add to the air fryer with the tomato puree. Stir well and fry for 3-4 minutes.
5. Fill the cheese tacos with the seasoned meat and garnish with iceberg lettuce, cherry tomatoes, fresh cream and grated cheese.

87. BELL PEPPER NACHOS WITH MINCED MEAT & AVOCADO

INGREDIENTS

Spice mix:

- 1 tsp chili powder
- 1 tsp cumin powder
- 1 tsp paprika powder
- 1 tsp garlic powder
- 1/2 tsp black pepper
- 1/2 tsp salt
- 1/2 tsp oregano
- 1/4 dried chili flakes

Nachos:

- 500 g (lean) ground beef
- 1 tbsp olive oil
- 500 g mini peppers (outsiders)
- 150 g grated (melted) cheese
- 2 large tomatoes
- 1 avocado, cut into pieces
- optional: sour cream, olives, jalapeños

INSTRUCTIONS

1. In a small bowl, mix the herbs well. Then heat a tbsp of olive oil in an air fryer over medium-high heat. Add the minced meat to the air fryer and cook for 7-10 minutes. Then add the spice mix to the minced meat and briefly stir-fry it.
2. Then preheat the air fryer to 190 C. Then cut the mini peppers in half on a large cutting board and the tomatoes in small pieces.
3. Divide the bell pepper and tomato pieces on a baking sheet lined with parchment paper and then add the minced meat from the air fryer. Finally sprinkle the grated cheese over paprika nachos.
4. Put the bell pepper nachos in the preheated air fryer and bake for 10-12 minutes, until the cheese has melted.
5. After baking, garnish the nachos with avocado pieces, sour cream, olives and jalapeños. Serve hot and enjoy!

88. BIG MAC SALAD

INGREDIENTS

Salad:

- 500 g ground beef
- 400 g finely chopped iceberg lettuce
- 40 g sliced onion
- 80 g grated cheese
- 80 g pickle cubes
- 1 tbsp olive oil
- salt and pepper to taste

Big Mac sauce:

- 100 ml mayonnaise
- 2 tsp mustard
- 2 tbsp finely chopped pickle cubes
- 1 tbsp white wine vinegar
- 1 tbsp finely chopped onion
- 1/2 tsp paprika powder
- 1/2 tsp onion powder
- 1/4 tsp garlic powder

INSTRUCTIONS

1. Heat a tbsp of olive oil in air fryer. Add half of the sliced onions and fry. Then add the ground beef and fry it for 5-8 minutes until done. Season the minced meat with salt and pepper.

2. In a large bowl, mix mayonnaise, mustard, white wine vinegar, paprika, onion powder, and garlic powder. Finely chop the onions and pickle cubes and add this to the sauce. Let the sauce sit in the refrigerator so that the flavors can absorb well.
3. Drain the liquid from the air fryer after frying the minced meat. Then mix the iceberg lettuce, sliced onion, pickle cubes, grated cheese and minced meat in a large bowl.

89. SUGAR-FREE CRÈME BRÛLÉE

INGREDIENTS

- 500 ml whipped cream
- 5 egg yolks
- 1 vanilla pod
- 45 g Stevia Crystal
- 4 tbsp Stevia Ery-Bronze for the topping
- pinch of salt

INSTRUCTIONS

1. Preheat the air fryer to 150 C. Then cut the vanilla pod in half lengthwise. Use the blunt side of your knife to remove the seeds from the stick.
2. Pour the whipped cream into air fryer and add the vanilla and vanilla pod. Heat the cream over a medium heat to just below the boiling point and then let cool for 5 minutes.
3. Then split the eggs and beat the yolks together with a pinch of salt and Stevia crystal.
4. Remove the vanilla pod from the whipped cream and add the whipped cream to the egg yolk bowl while stirring. Then pour the mixture into 4 ramekin dishes.
5. Place the dishes in a baking dish and pour in half of the boiling water. Bake the crème brûlée 40-45 minutes in the preheated air fryer.
6. Allow the crème brûlée to cool in the fridge for at least 2 hours. Before serving, sprinkle the top of the crème brûlée with Stevia Kristal Sweet and caramelize with a gas burner to put in the air fryer briefly under the grill.

90. LOW-CARB CREPES

INGREDIENTS

- 3 eggs
- 85 g cream cheese
- 10 g coconut flour
- 5 g Stevia Crystal
- 1 tsp cinnamon
- 50 g strawberries
- optional: sugar-free chocolate from Stevia Frost
- butter or oil

INSTRUCTIONS

1. In a large bowl, whisk together the eggs, coconut flour, and Stevia crystal. Then heat the cream cheese in an air fryer. Add the cream cheese to the egg mixture and mix well. Let the batter rest for a few minutes.
2. Then heat a tbsp of butter or oil. Do by using a tbsp 1/4 of the batter in the air fryer and turn the air fryer to divide the batter.
3. Bake the crepe over low heat and turn it over when the bottom is golden brown. Repeat this until the batter runs out. In the meantime, cut the strawberries into slices and place on top of the baked air fryer cakes.
4. Garnish the crepes with melted sugar-free chocolate from Stevia Frost powdered sugar.

91. HAMBURGER SALAD WITH AVOCADO

INGREDIENTS

- 4 burgers
- 200 g sliced romaine lettuce
- 4 pickles, cut into pieces
- 1/2 red onion, cut into rings
- 1 avocado, diced
- 175 g cherry tomatoes, cut in half
- 50 g grated cheese

Dressing:

- 50 g light mayonnaise or yogurt
- 1 tsp mustard
- 1 tbsp juice from pickles
- 4 tsp ketchup
- 1/4 tsp onion powder
- 1/4 tsp garlic powder
- 1/4 tsp paprika powder

INSTRUCTIONS

1. In a large bowl, mix the sliced lettuce, pickles, avocado, cherry tomatoes, and grated cheese. Put the bowl in the fridge for a while and then heat up the electric grill or barbecue.
2. Cook the hamburger together with the onion rings on the barbecue or electric grill. Grab a bowl during baking and mix the mayonnaise, mustard, pickle juice, ketchup and herbs to make the dressing.
3. Cut the hamburgers into 16 pieces after baking and let cool.
4. Then take the bowl with the salad and add the hamburgers, onion rings and dressing.

92. LETTUCE WRAPS WITH ASIAN MINCED CHICKEN

INGREDIENTS

- 500 g natural minced chicken
- 2 tbsp sesame seed oil or wok oil
- 110 g mushrooms
- 6 g fresh basil
- 2-3 tbsp hoisin sauce
- 1 tsp fresh ginger, chopped
- 1 tbsp soy sauce
- 2 tsp chopped garlic
- 1 tsp rice vinegar
- 1 tsp corn flour
- 1 head of romaine lettuce
- 3 stems of spring onion

INSTRUCTIONS

1. On a large cutting board, cut the mushrooms, spring onion and basil into small pieces. Then heat the wok oil in an air fryer over medium heat. Put the minced chicken in the air fryer and fry it for about 5 minutes. Then add the mushrooms and basil and fry for another 5 minutes.
2. In the meantime, grab a small bowl and mix with a whisk the soy sauce, hoisin sauce, ginger, garlic, rice vinegar and corn flour. Add the sauce to the minced chicken and let it simmer for a few minutes. Finally add the spring onion to the air fryer.
3. Grab the head of romaine lettuce and carefully remove the leaves. Clean the leaves with water and place on four plates. Fill the salad leaves with the minced chicken and serve with soy sauce.

93. LOW-CARB CHICKEN MEATBALLS

INGREDIENTS

Chicken meatballs:

- 450 g minced chicken
- 1 small zucchini (300 gr)
- 2–3 spring onion stems
- 3 tbsp parsley
- 1 clove of garlic
- 1/2 tsp black pepper
- 1/2 tsp cumin
- 2 tbsp olive oil

Avocado dip:

- 1 avocado
- 1/4 red onion
- 1/2 tomato
- salt and pepper to taste

INSTRUCTIONS

1. Grate the zucchini above a large bowl using a hand grater. Then grab a clean tea towel and place it on a large bowl. Spoon the grated zucchini into the tea towel. Lift your clean tea towel with the zucchini in it and squeeze out all the moisture. Drain the water in the bowl and dry it. Then put the zucchini in the bowl.
2. On a large cutting board, cut the spring onion into small pieces and add to the zucchini with the chicken mince, parsley and herbs. Mix everything well with a fork. Form about 20 balls of the minced meat mixture.
3. Then heat two tbsp of olive oil in an air fryer over medium-high heat. Add the chicken meatballs to the air fryer and fry for 5 to 6 minutes. Then turn the balls over and bake for another 5 minutes. Reduce the heat to low and fry the chicken meatballs for a few minutes with the lid on the air fryer. It is also possible to bake the chicken meatballs in the air fryer. Preheat the air fryer to 205 C and bake the chicken meatballs for 15-20 minutes.
4. Chop an avocado in a medium-sized bowl. Then cut the red onion and tomato into small pieces and add this to the bowl together with the lemon juice. Season with salt and pepper and the dip is ready!

94. LOW-CARB HAMBURGER STICKS

INGREDIENTS

- 450 g ground beef (lean)
- 50 g bacon
- 1 tbsp mustard
- 1/4 tsp salt
- 1/4 tsp onion powder
- 1/4 tsp black pepper
- 1 head of butter lettuce
- 15 cherry tomatoes
- 15 slices of pickle
- mayonnaise, ketchup or mustard as a dip

INSTRUCTIONS

1. Cut the bacon into small pieces on a large cutting board. Now mix the bacon, ground beef, mustard and herbs with your hands in a large bowl. Form of the minced meat mixture 15 small meatballs.
2. Then heat an air fryer and fry the meatballs for 3 minutes per side until done.
3. In the meantime, cut the cherry tomatoes in half and the pickles into slices. When the meatballs are ready, take the skewers and place a meatball, lettuce, slice of pickle and half a cherry tomato on each skewer. Repeat this until you have 15 filled sticks. Enjoy your meal!

95. LOW-CARB BREAKFAST PORRIDGE

INGREDIENTS

- 140 ml almond milk, unsweetened
- 25 g almond flour
- 2 tbsp coconut chips
- 1 tbsp linseed flour
- 1 tbsp chia seed
- 1/2 tbsp erythritol or crystal sweet
- 1/2 tsp cinnamon
- 1/2 tsp vanilla aroma
- pinch of salt

INSTRUCTIONS

1. In a medium bowl, mix almond flour, coconut chips, linseed flour, chia seed, erythritol, cinnamon and salt.
2. Then pour the almond milk and vanilla aroma into air fryer and add the dry INGREDIENTS from the bowl. Boil the contents of the air fryer over high heat.
3. Reduce the heat as the porridge boils and let it simmer for 1 minute. Remove the air fryer from the heat after boiling and let it cool down for 3 minutes.
4. Put the porridge in a small bowl and garnish with nuts, fruit and coconut juice.

96. CREAM PUFFS

INGREDIENTS

Profiteroles:

- 4 medium eggs
- 1 tsp baking powder
- 1 tsp vanilla aroma
- 1 tbsp Stevia crystal
- pinch of salt
- optional: Stevia Frost

Whipped cream filling:

- 250 ml fresh whipped cream
- 2 tbsp Stevia crystal
- 1 tsp vanilla aroma

INSTRUCTIONS

1. Preheat a convection air fryer to 180° C. Then cover a baking sheet with parchment paper and grease it with baking spray or butter. Now take two medium sized bowls and separate the eggs in them.
2. Then add the vanilla flavor, baking powder, salt and the Stevia crystal to the bowl. Now take an electric mixer and beat the egg whites.
3. Shape the batter using a large tbsp of 15 balls and place these balls on the baking sheet. Bake the puffs 15-20 minutes in the preheated air fryer. Keep an eye on the air fryer, because the puffs can easily burn.
4. Then add the fresh whipped cream, Stevia crystal and vanilla aroma to a medium-sized bowl. Beat the whipped cream with an electric mixer and scoop the whipped cream into a piping bag with a small, smooth nozzle. Put the piping bag in the fridge until the puffs are ready.
5. After baking, allow the puffs to cool down and then puncture a hole in the bottom of each puff with a knife and fill them with the whipped cream. Garnish the whipped cream puffs with a little Stevia Frost powdered sugar.

97. CHOCOLATE COCONUT PUDDING

INGREDIENTS

- 200 ml light or full-fat coconut milk
- 1 medium-sized egg yolk
- 50 g dark chocolate, at least 70% cocoa
- 1/2 tsp vanilla aroma

INSTRUCTIONS

1. Heat air fryer over a low heat containing the coconut milk and the egg yolk. Let it simmer for 10 minutes with constant stirring (no boiling).
2. Then break the chocolate into small pieces and put the pieces in a medium bowl. Then place the vanilla pod on a cutting slice or plate and cut the pod lengthwise with a sharp knife. Then unfold the baton. Inside the stick you see all small black seeds. Now take a small spoon or a blunt knife and scrape out the vanilla marrow (the small black seeds) and add it to the bowl.
3. Then add the warm coconut milk to the bowl and let it stand for a while, until the chocolate is completely melted. Then stir in the bowl and divide the chocolate pudding into 3 dessert glasses or bowls.
4. Put the dessert glasses or bowls in the fridge for at least 2 hours so that it can solidify properly. Serve with fresh fruit or a little light whipped cream.

98. LOW-CARB CHEESE CRACKERS

INGREDIENTS

- 170 g grated mozzarella
- 85 g almond flour
- 30 g cream cheese
- 1 egg
- 1/2 tsp sea salt
- 1/2 tsp dried rosemary or to taste

INSTRUCTIONS

1. Preheat the convection air fryer to 220 C. Then put the mozzarella, cream cheese and almond flour in a large microwave-safe bowl.
2. Put the bowl in the microwave for about 1 minute, until the cheese is partially melted. Stir the contents of the bowl well.
3. Allow the cheese and almond flour mixture to cool for 1-2 minutes. After cooling, add the herbs and egg to the bowl and knead with the hands through the dough for at least 1 minute.
4. Then place the dough between two sheets of parchment paper and roll the dough to the desired thickness with a rolling pin. Remove the top sheet of parchment paper and cut the crackers into small squares (30 pieces) with a pizza slicer. You can also make large crackers if you want.
5. Bake the cheese crackers for 10-12 minutes in the preheated air fryer. Keep an eye on the air fryer, thin crackers will be ready faster. After baking, allow the cheese crackers to cool on a cooling rack for at least 5 minutes.

99. COCONUT MACAROONS

INGREDIENTS

- 4 eggs
- 100–150 g unsweetened grated coconut
- 1 tsp vanilla aroma
- 40 g Stevia Crystal or to taste

INSTRUCTIONS

1. Preheat the air fryer to 180 C.
2. Then take a large clean bowl and mix the 4 eggs and the sweetener. Beat the whites stiff with the help of a whisk hand mixer.
3. Add the grated coconut and vanilla and mix it through the protein mixture.
4. Then shape 20 balls with your hands and place them on a baking sheet with a sheet of parchment paper on top. Bake the low-carb coconut macaroons for 10 to 14 minutes in the preheated air fryer.

100. LOW-CARB CABBAGE SALAD

INGREDIENTS

- 200 g white cabbage, finely chopped
- 150 g red cabbage, finely chopped
- 100 g grated carrot
- 10 radishes
- 1 stem spring onion
- 150 g sour cream
- 65 ml mayonnaise
- 1 tbsp lemon juice
- 1/8 tsp onion powder
- 1/4 tsp black pepper

INSTRUCTIONS

1. On a large cutting board, cut the radishes into strips and the spring onion into small pieces. Then mix the white cabbage, red cabbage, grated carrot, spring onion and radishes in a large bowl.
2. Grab another bowl and mix in the mayonnaise, sour cream and the herbs. Then stir the dressing into the coleslaw. Divide into 6 portions and serve with lemon juice.

101. LOW-CARB RÖSTI

INGREDIENTS

- 150 g celeriac
- 1 tbsp olive oil
- 1 tbsp butter
- 15 g bacon, cut into small pieces
- 20 g grated Parmesan cheese
- 1/2 tsp salt
- 1/8 tsp ground black pepper
- 1/4 tsp garlic powder
- handful of lamb's lettuce

INSTRUCTIONS

1. Start with the celeriac. Place the celeriac on a large cutting board and cut the tuber in half. Then place the flat can of the celeriac on the shelf and carefully cut away the peel until you only have the white flesh.
2. Then take a large grater and grate a piece of celeriac over a bowl. Grate the celeriac until you have 150 g of grated flesh. Add the Parmesan cheese and the herbs and mix well.

3. Then heat the olive oil and butter in a frying air fryer over medium heat. Add the bacon and fry it until crispy. Then add the celeriac mixture to the air fryer and press the mixture into the spell with the back of a large spoon to form a large air fryer cake.
4. Bake the rösti over medium to low heat for about 5 minutes, until the bottom is golden brown and crispy. When the rösti is ready, remove the air fryer from the heat and hold it upside down above a plate and carefully drop the rösti.

102. CHICKEN CORDON BLEU

INGREDIENTS

- 4 chicken fillets (150 g)
- 170 ml whipped cream
- 70 ml dry white wine
- 40 g butter
- 4 slices of Swiss cheese
- 4 slices of ham
- 15 g flour
- 2 tsp corn flour
- 3/4 block of chicken stock
- 3/4 tsp paprika powder
- salt and pepper to taste

INSTRUCTIONS

1. Place the chicken fillets on a clean surface and smash them with a meat hammer. Place the ham and cheese slices on the chicken fillets and roll the chicken fillets. Secure the chicken fillets well with skewers.
2. Mix the flour, paprika, salt and pepper in a bowl. Sprinkle the chicken fillets with the flour and paprika powder mixture.
3. Heat the butter in an air fryer over medium heat and fry the chicken fillets until brown on all sides. Add the wine and chicken stock. Reduce the heat to low and cover the air fryer and let it cook for about 15 to 30 minutes, until the chicken is no longer pink on the inside.
4. Remove the skewers and place the chicken fillets on a warm dish. Mix the corn flour with the whipped cream in a small bowl and beat slowly in the frying air fryer. Cook this and keep stirring until the sauce is thick. Pour the sauce over the chicken fillets and serve.

103. MUSHROOM PIZZA

INGREDIENTS

- 2 XXL mushrooms (portobello)
- 30 ml pasta sauce
- 75 g grated mozzarella
- 6 slices of spicy salami
- 2 black olive, cut into pieces
- 1 clove of garlic, crushed

INSTRUCTIONS

1. Preheat the air fryer to 190 C. Remove the mushroom stem and place the mushroom "hat" on a baking sheet and bake the mushroom for 5 minutes in the preheated air fryer.
2. Remove the mushroom from the air fryer after baking and spread the pasta sauce over the mushroom. Then put the mozzarella, olives, salami and garlic on top of the sauce.
3. Bake the mushroom for another 15-20 minutes in the preheated air fryer.

104. Stuffed Peppers with Chorizo & Egg

INGREDIENTS

- 3 peppers
- 100 g chorizo
- 1/2 small onion
- 4 medium eggs
- splash of milk or whipped cream
- 50 g fresh cream
- 75 g grated mozzarella
- 1 clove of garlic
- salt and pepper to taste
- dried parsley to taste

INSTRUCTIONS

1. Preheat the air fryer to 180 C. Cut the chorizo, onion and garlic into small pieces on a large cutting board. Remove the top of the peppers and carefully cut away the seeds.
2. Then bake the chorizo in an air fryer. Add the onion and garlic and stir well in the air fryer. Bake for another 3 minutes.
3. In a bowl, beat the eggs, milk, parsley, and salt and pepper together.
4. After baking, set the chorizo aside and bake the eggs in the air fryer over a low heat until done.
5. Remove the air fryer from the heat and add the chorizo to the air fryer with the fresh cream and parsley. Stir everything well and scoop the mixture into the peppers. Place the peppers in a shallow baking dish. Bake the peppers in the preheated air fryer for 30-35 minutes. Remove the peppers from the air fryer, sprinkle with mozzarella and bake for another 10-15 minutes.

105. Egg & Bacon Breakfast Muffins

INGREDIENTS

- 4 medium eggs
- 4 slices of bacon or bacon
- 4 tsp melted butter
- 1 slice of cheese
- 2 slices of cheese
- 4 paper aluminum muffin tin
- salt and pepper to taste

INSTRUCTIONS

1. Preheat the air fryer to 175 C. Put the bacon slices in a frying air fryer and cook over medium heat. Bake until the slice is equally brown everywhere. Remove the bacon from the air fryer and wrap the bacon slices in the muffin molds.
2. Place a tsp of melted butter in the bottom of each mold. Beat the eggs in a bowl and add salt and pepper to taste. Now put the eggs in the muffin molds.
3. Place the molds on a rack and place in the air fryer. Bake the bacon and egg muffins for 10 to 15 minutes in the preheated air fryer. When the muffins are almost ready, place the 1/2 slice of cheese on top of each muffin and bake them in the air fryer for a few minutes until the cheese has melted.

106. Air Fryer Scrambled Eggs

INGREDIENTS

- 12 medium eggs
- 300 ml milk
- 50 g butter or margarine, melted
- salt and pepper to taste

INSTRUCTIONS

1. Preheat the air fryer to 175 C. Pour the melted butter into a 33 cm x 22 cm baking dish.
2. In a large bowl, beat the eggs with the salt and pepper. Add the milk little by little while you are beating the eggs.
3. Pour the mixture into the baking dish. Bake the egg mixture for 10 minutes in the preheated air fryer. Take the baking dish out of the air fryer and stir the egg mixture well.
4. Bake for another 10 to 15 minutes and serve.

107. Cheddar & Bacon Stuffed Mushrooms

INGREDIENTS

- 8 large mushrooms
- 3 slices of bacon
- 85 g cheddar cheese
- 1/2 small onion, cut into pieces
- 15 g butter

INSTRUCTIONS

1. Bake the bacon in an air fryer over medium heat until the slices turn brown. Rinse the excess fat from the bacon and cut the slices into cubes. Then preheat the air fryer to 200 C.
2. Now take the mushrooms and remove the stems. Put the mushroom 'hats' aside and then cut the stems into small pieces. Heat the butter in air fryer over medium heat. Add the stems and onions and let it simmer until the stems and onions are soft.
3. In a medium bowl, mix 30 g of grated cheddar cheese and the bacon cubes. Add the mushroom stems and onion and stir well. Then scoop the mixture into the mushroom "hats".
4. Bake the stuffed mushrooms in the preheated air fryer for 15 minutes. After 12 minutes, remove the mushrooms from the air fryer and sprinkle the remaining cheddar cheese over the mushrooms. Then bake for another 3 minutes, until the cheese has melted.

108. Savory Ham & Cheese Muffins

INGREDIENTS

- 340 g ham cubes
- 150 g grated cheese
- 3 medium eggs
- 45 g green pepper
- 1 stalk of celery
- 1 tbsp chives, finely chopped
- 1 tbsp parsley, finely chopped
- 1/4 tsp onion powder
- 1/4 tsp pepper

INSTRUCTIONS

1. Preheat the air fryer to 180 C. Cut the bell pepper and celery into small pieces on a large cutting board. Finely grind the ham in a food processor. Then mix all INGREDIENTS in a large bowl.
2. Divide the mixture from the bowl among the twelve aluminum muffin tins. Place the aluminum muffin tins on an air fryer rack lined with parchment paper.
3. Bake the muffins in the preheated air fryer for about 30-35 minutes until golden brown. Allow the muffins in the can on the rack to cool for 10 minutes. Remove the muffins from the tin and serve.

109. Broccoli in Almond-Lemon Butter

INGREDIENTS

- 1 large broccoli, cut into florets
- 60 g butter
- 2 tsp lemon juice
- 1 tsp lemon zest
- 30 g planed almonds

INSTRUCTIONS

1. Cook the broccoli florets for about 4 to 8 minutes, then drain the florets.
2. Melt the butter in air fryer over medium heat. When the butter has melted, remove the air fryer from the heat and add the lemon juice, lemon zest and almonds.
3. Stir this well and pour over the broccoli.

110. Grilled Salmon with Avocado Sauce

INGREDIENTS

Avocado sauce:

- 2 avocados, diced
- 2 cloves of garlic, crushed
- 1 tbsp lemon juice
- 3 tbsp Greek yogurt

Salmon:

- 900 g salmon fillet
- 2 tsp dried dill
- 2 tsp lemon pepper
- salt and pepper to taste

INSTRUCTIONS

4. Heat the grill device or the barbecue and grease the grid with oil. Puree the avocado with the garlic, yogurt and lemon juice in a bowl. Season the sauce with salt and pepper.
5. Rub the salmon fillets with dill, lemon pepper and salt. Place them on the hot barbecue or grill and bake for 15 minutes. The salmon fillets are ready when the salmon falls apart easily if you poke it with a fork. Serve the salmon fillets with the avocado sauce.

111. Baby Spinach Omelet

INGREDIENTS

- 2-3 eggs
- 30 g baby spinach, cut into pieces
- 10 g Parmesan cheese, grated
- 1/4 tsp onion powder
- 1/8 tsp nutmeg
- salt and pepper to taste

INSTRUCTIONS

1. Beat the eggs in a large bowl and add the spinach and Parmesan cheese while stirring. Season with onion powder, nutmeg, salt and pepper.
2. Grease an air fryer with butter or oil and heat the air fryer over a medium heat.

3. Fry the omelet for about 3 minutes on one side. Then turn the omelet with a spatula and bake for another 3 minutes. Reduce the heat to low and cook for another 2 minutes.

112. BLUEBERRY BOWL WITH FIG, POMEGRANATE, CHIA AND BANANA

INGREDIENTS

- 200 g quark, lean stage
- 20 g blueberries, frozen
- 30 g pomegranate, raw
- 1 fig
- 30 g banana
- 5 g chia seeds
- 2 tbsp tap water

INSTRUCTIONS

1. Put the berries with 2 tbsp of tap water in a mixing bowl and finely puree with the hand blender.
2. Put the quark in a bowl and stir in the berry puree.
3. Wash and dry the fig, then slice
4. Peel and slice the banana
5. Carefully remove the pomegranate seeds.
6. Spread the fig and banana slices, pomegranate seeds and the chia seeds on the berry quark and serve.

113. Salmon in Cream Sauce with Peas & Lemon

INGREDIENTS

- 500 g salmon fillet, without skin
- 150 g peas, green, raw
- 200 ml whipped cream 30%
- 2 small shallots
- 1 toe garlic
- 20 g Parmesan
- 40 g butter
- 1 medium lemon
- 1 pinch of nutmeg
- 1 pinch of pepper, white
- 1 pinch of sea salt

INSTRUCTIONS

1. Wash the salmon and pat dry, then cut into bite-sized pieces. Peel the shallots and finely dice. Peel the garlic and finely chop.
2. Heat the butter in the air fryer, add shallots and garlic and fry the salmon pieces in it. Add the cream and stir. Add the peas and simmer briefly over medium heat.
3. Halve the lemon and squeeze out the juice.
4. Add grated Parmesan, lemon peel and a little nutmeg to the air fryer and stir. Season with lemon juice, salt, and pepper.

114. Air Fryer Steamed Vegetables

INGREDIENTS

- 100 g broccoli
- 50 g paprika, red, fresh
- 50 g paprika, yellow, fresh
- 50 g onion
- 100 g snow peas, fresh
- 2 medium carrots, fresh
- 1 pinch of sea salt
- 1 tbsp olive oil

INSTRUCTIONS

1. Wash the broccoli and cut the florets from the stalk. Remove the seeds from the peppers and cut into strips.
2. Peel the onion and cut into rings.
3. Wash and drain the pears
4. Peel the carrot and cut into thin sticks.
5. Heat the olive oil in the air fryer. Put the prepared vegetables in the air fryer and fry them all over, stirring several times. Season everything with salt and serve.

115. Chicken Breast with Air Fryer Vegetables

INGREDIENTS

- 180 g chicken breast, without skin
- 80 g Brussels sprouts
- 120 g carrot, fresh
- 120 g onion
- 1 pinch of sea salt
- 1 pinch of pepper, black
- 1 tbsp olive oil
- 1 stalk of parsley, fresh

INSTRUCTIONS

1. Wash chicken breast and pat dry
2. Remove the dry stem and withered leaves from the sprouts, then halve each time.
3. Peel carrot and slice. Peel the onion and cut into pieces. Wash the parsley and shake dry, then chop.
4. Heat the olive oil in the air fryer and fry the chicken breast on both sides until golden brown until the meat is cooked. Season the chicken breast with salt and pepper.
5. Add the vegetables to the hot air fryer and fry, then season with salt and pepper.

116. Mushroom with Cream Sauce & Herbs

INGREDIENTS

- 250 g mushrooms, brown, fresh
- 100 g whipped cream 30%
- 10 g butter
- 2 toes of garlic
- 1 pinch of sea salt
- 1 pinch of pepper, black
- 1 pinch of nutmeg
- 1 shallot
- 1 stalk of oregano, fresh

INSTRUCTIONS

1. Brush the mushrooms, then cut off the dry ends of the stems. Slice the mushrooms. Peel the garlic and cut into thin slices.
2. Peel the shallot and dice finely.
3. Heat the butter in the air fryer and sauté the shallot with garlic
4. Add mushrooms and fry everything for a few minutes.
5. Add the cream and season everything with salt, pepper, and freshly grated nutmeg. Wash the oregano and shake it dry.
6. Serve with cream sauce and herbs.

117. Yogurt with Cereal & Persimmons

INGREDIENTS

- 150 g Greek yogurt
- 20 g oatmeal
- 60 g kaki, fresh
- 30 ml tap water

INSTRUCTIONS

1. Roast oats in the air fryer while stirring until golden brown, then place on a plate and allow to cool briefly
2. Peel the khaki and add to a blender jar with water.
3. Purée the persimmon with the hand blender.
4. Layer yogurt, toasted oatmeal, and khaki in a glass jar.

118. Chicken Breast with Peppered Vegetables

INGREDIENTS

- 1 chicken breast, without skin
- 50 g paprika, red, raw
- 50 g paprika, green, raw
- 50 g paprika, yellow, raw
- 1 onion, red
- 4 stems of coriander, fresh
- 1 pinch of sea salt
- 1 pinch of pepper, black
- 1 tbsp olive oil

INSTRUCTIONS

1. Wash the chicken breast and dab it dry. Remove chili from cores and partitions and cut into strips. Peel onion and cut into rings. Wash the coriander and shake dry.
2. Heat the olive oil in the air fryer and fry the chicken breast on both sides until golden brown-the roasted chicken breast is served in a grill air fryer. Season the meat with salt and pepper, then remove from the air fryer.
3. Add the pepper strips and onions to the hot air fryer and fry briefly. Season the vegetables with salt and pepper.
4. Cut the chicken breast into strips and serve with the vegetables on a plate.

119. Fresh Cucumber Salad with Onions & Herbs

INGREDIENTS

- 200 g cucumber with shell, raw
- 15 g spring onion
- 2 stems of parsley, fresh
- 1 pinch of sea salt
- 1 pinch of pepper, black
- 1 tbsp olive oil

INSTRUCTIONS

1. Wash cucumber and dry, then slice into thin slices.
2. Clean the spring onion and cut them into thin rings. Wash the parsley and shake it dry, then peel off the leaves and chop.
3. Put cucumber, spring onion and parsley with olive oil in a bowl and season with salt and pepper.

120. Beef Pot Roast

INGREDIENTS

- 800 g beef stew
- 150 ml red wine
- 3 garlic (toes)
- 1 tbsp tomato concentrate
- 400 ml beef stock
- 1-star anise
- 1 tsp Ras el hanout
- 2 bay leaves, dried
- 6 stems thyme, fresh
- 1 tsp of sea salt
- 1 tsp pepper, black
- 1 tbsp olive oil

INSTRUCTIONS

1. Wash beef stew and pat dry, then chop into cubes. Wash thyme stalks and shake dry. Peel and crush the garlic with the flat side of the knife.
2. Heat the olive oil in the braised air fryer. Add the beef, garlic, and thyme to the air fryer and sauté the meat all around. Add the tomato puree and sauté.
3. Douse everything with red wine and cook it briefly. Fill up with cattle stock, then add sternalis, bay leaves, and a little salt and pepper. Simmer meat with lid closed for 10 minutes.
4. Place in the 160° C preheated air fryer and cook the beef for about 2 hours. After half of the cooking time, turn the pieces of beef or stir once.
5. Remove the finished beef stew from the air fryer and let it rest briefly. Add fresh herbs as desired and serve with a salad.

121. ORANGE CARROT POWER DRINK

INGREDIENTS

- 1 orange, fresh (small)
- 1 carrot
- 50 g apple
- 1 g ginger (grated)
- 1 pinch of cinnamon, ground
- 100 ml tap water

INSTRUCTIONS

1. Halve orange and squeeze • Peel the carrot and cut into pieces • Apple, wash, quarter and remove the core casing, then cut into pieces Peel ginger and cut small.
2. Pour orange juice, carrot, apple, ginger, and cinnamon into a blender jar with the water and puree with a hand blender. • Pour the carrot and orange power drink into a glass and serve.

122. Beef Steak with Arugula & Cherry Tomatoes

INGREDIENTS

- 1 beef steak hip, sliced
- 100 g cherry tomatoes
- 20 g arugula, fresh
- 1 stalk of rosemary, fresh
- 1 pinch of sea salt
- 1 pinch of pepper, black
- 30 g butter
- 1 tbsp olive oil

INSTRUCTIONS

1. Wash beef and pat dry. Wash rosemary and shake dry.
2. Heat the butter and oil in the air fryer, then add the beef steak with the sprig rosemary.
3. Fry the steak for a few minutes, then turn over and roast on the other side for a few minutes, depending on the desired cooking level. Season the steak with salt and pepper and serve on a plate.
4. Meanwhile, wash the arugula and dry in the salad spinner. Wash tomatoes and drain, then cut in half.
5. Add arugula and tomatoes to the steak and then season everything with salt and pepper.

123. Fried Sea Bream with Mango Salsa

INGREDIENTS

- 4 small bream, fillet
- 100 g mango, raw
- 100 g cucumber with shell, raw
- 100 g paprika, red, raw
- 50 g spinach, raw
- 30 g Parmesan, grated
- 1 pinch of sea salt
- 1 pinch of pepper, black
- 1 g lemon
- 1 tbsp olive oil

INSTRUCTIONS

1. Wash bream and dab it dry. Peel the mango and cut the pulp into small slices. Wash the cucumber and cut into small pieces. Free the peppers from the seeds and partitions and cut into small cubes.
2. Wash the spinach and dry it in the salad spinner. Remove long stalks from the spinach.
3. Wash and dry the lemon, then make lemon zest with the grater. Halve the lemon and squeeze out the juice.
4. Mix mango, cucumber, paprika and a little lemon juice in a bowl and season with salt and pepper. Put spinach leaves on two plates.
5. Heat olive oil in air fryer and fry the fillets on both sides. Season the fillets with salt and pepper and sprinkle with freshly grated Parmesan.
6. Add the fish fillets to the spinach and serve with the mango salsa.

124. Red Cabbage Salad with Nuts & Seeds

INGREDIENTS

- 150 g red cabbage, raw
- 20 g walnut kernels, fresh
- 1 tbsp balsamic vinegar (balsamic vinegar)
- 1 tsp agave syrup
- 1 pr sea salt
- 1 pinch pepper, black
- 5 g chard, raw

INSTRUCTIONS

1. For red cabbage, remove the outer leaves, then quarter with a knife, remove the stalk and cut into wonderful strips with the knife. Or a plane with the vegetable slicer in very narrow strips.
2. Add the balsamic, agave syrup, salt, and pepper to the bowl and mix. Rinse chard and dry.
3. Put the red cabbage and chard in the bowl and mix with the dressing. Finely chop walnut kernels.
4. Arrange red cabbage salad on a plate or in a bowl and serve with the chopped walnut kernels.

125. Eggplant Tomato Omelet

INGREDIENTS

- 4 eggs
- 100 g cherry tomatoes
- 50 g eggplant, raw
- 1 stalk of basil, fresh
- 1 tbsp whipped cream
- 1 pinch of sea salt
- 1 pinch of pepper, black
- 1 tsp olive oil

INSTRUCTIONS

1. Wash the tomatoes, drain and slice. Slice and lightly salt eggplant.
2. Put and beat the eggs in a bowl and whisk with cream, a little salt, and pepper.
3. Heat the oil in the air fryer and add the egg mass. Spread the eggplants and place tomato slices on top.
4. Season with salt and pepper and sprinkle with basil. Fold the omelet carefully in half and place on a plate.

126. Chickpea & Halloumi Salad

INGREDIENTS

- 200 g chickpeas
- 200 g Halloumi
- 1 shallot
- ½ spring onion
- 30 g radish
- 50 g tomatoes
- 50 g paprika
- 50 g cucumber
- 20 g canned corn
- 4 stems of parsley
- 4 tbsp olive oil
- sea salt
- pepper

INSTRUCTIONS

1. Place chickpeas in a sieve and rinse under running water, then drain
2. Heat air fryer and fry halloumi on both sides until roast strips are recognizable
3. Season halloumi with salt and pepper, then remove from the air fryer and cut into pieces.
4. Meanwhile, clean the radishes and cut into thin slices. Wash tomatoes and cut into pieces. Deseed peppers and cut into pieces. Wash the cucumber and cut into small cubes.
5. Peel the shallot and cut it into fine rings. Clean the spring onion and cut into rings at an angle
6. Wash the parsley and shake it dry, then pluck the leaves and chop them • Remove the corn from the can and drain.
7. Put all prepared salad INGREDIENTS in a bowl, and mix • Add olive oil and some salt and pepper and stir again.

127. Chard, Avocado, Nut & Feta Salad

INGREDIENTS

- 20 g baby chard
- 60 g avocado
- 50 g dried tomatoes
- 30 g feta
- 30 g of walnuts
- 20 g red onion
- 2 tbsp olive oil
- sea salt
- pepper

INSTRUCTIONS

1. Wash the chard and drain well. Halve the avocado and remove the seed, then peel the pulp and cut into small pieces.
2. Cut the dried tomatoes into pieces.
3. Crumble feta by hand. Chop walnuts. Peel onions and cut into rings.
4. Put all the INGREDIENTS and the olive oil in a salad bowl and mix. Finally, season the salad with salt and pepper and place on a plate.

128. Tuna with Vegetables & Avocado

INGREDIENTS

- 150 g tuna, canned
- 1 avocado
- 100 g paprika
- 100 g tomatoes
- 50 g cucumber
- 1 spring onion
- 30 g corn, from the tin
- ½ bunch of parsley
- 50 g radish
- ½ chili pepper
- 1 lime
- 2 tbsp olive oil
- nutmeg
- sea salt
- pepper

INSTRUCTIONS

1. Open the tuna can a piece and drain the juice, then open the tin completely and tuck the tuna into pieces with the fork • Halve the avocado and remove the kernel • Halve the lime and squeeze the juice • Sprinkle both avocado halves with a little lime juice.
2. Peel the cucumber and then cut it into pieces. • Remove the peppers from the seeds and partitions and cut into small cubes. • Wash the tomatoes and cut into pieces. • Clean the spring onion and cut into rings.
3. Pour corn into a sieve and drain • Wash the parsley and shake it dry, then peel and chop the leaves • Chop the chili lengthwise and core lengthwise, then chop finely • Clean the radish and cut into small pieces.
4. Put the tuna, cucumber, peppers, tomatoes, spring onions, corn, parsley, radishes and chili pepper in a bowl. • Add the olive oil and some lime juice and season with grated nutmeg, salt, and pepper. • Mix the salad well, then serve together with the avocado.

129. Colorful Vegetable Salad

INGREDIENTS

- 1 eggplant, approx. 200g
- 150 g tomatoes
- 140 g paprika
- 50 g salad (endives, Roman, arugula)
- 1 small red onion
- ½ red chili pepper
- 2 cloves of garlic
- 4 tbsp olive oil
- cumin
- sea salt
- pepper

INSTRUCTIONS

1. Wash eggplant and dry, then cut into pieces. Peel garlic and squeeze with garlic press. Mix eggplant with 1 tbsp olive oil, garlic, salt, and pepper in a bowl and spread on a baking sheet lined with parchment paper
2. Cook eggplant for about 10 minutes at 160° C in a preheated air fryer.
3. Meanwhile, wash and quarter the tomatoes. Cut peppers into thin sticks. Wash lettuce leaves and shake dry, then cut into thin strips. Peel the onion and cut into strips. Cut chili pepper into thin rings.
4. Mix tomatoes, peppers, lettuce, onion, and chili pepper in a salad bowl. Add the olive oil, cumin, salt, and pepper and mix well.
5. Take the eggplant out of the air fryer, allow it to cool briefly and add to the salad. Mix everything and place on two plates.

130. Smoothie Bowl with Spinach, Mango & Muesli

INGREDIENTS

- 150 g yogurt
- 30 g apple
- 30 g mango
- 30 g low-carb cereal (alternatively nuts, chopped)
- 10 g spinach
- 10 g Chia seeds

INSTRUCTIONS

1. Wash spinach leaves and drain • Peel mango and cut into strips • Core the apple and cut into pieces.
2. Put the spinach, apple pieces and half of the mango strips with yogurt in a shaker • Puree everything with the hand blender.
3. Put the spinach smoothie into a bowl • Add low-carb cereal, chia seeds, and mango and serve.

131. CHICKPEA TOMATO & CUCUMBER SALAD

INGREDIENTS

- 100 g tomatoes
- 50 g chickpeas
- 60 g cucumber
- 10 g spring onion
- 1 tbsp olive oil
- sea salt
- pepper

INSTRUCTIONS

1. Wash tomatoes and cut into pieces • Chickpeas in a colander and rinse under running water, then drain • Wash cucumber and cut into pieces • Clean spring onion and cut into rings.
2. Place tomatoes, chickpeas, cucumber, and spring onion in a salad bowl. • Add olive oil and season with salt and pepper. • Mix the salad and put in a bowl.

132. Beef Steak with Broccoli

INGREDIENTS

- 120 g beef fillet or steak
- 60 g broccoli
- 30 g paprika
- ½ red onion
- 2 cloves of garlic
- 1 stalk of basil
- 1 sprig rosemary
- 2 tbsp olive oil
- sea salt
- pepper

INSTRUCTIONS

1. Wash the peppers and cut into strips • Peel the onion and cut into rings • Peel and finely chop the garlic • Wash the herbs and shake dry, peel the leaves from the basil and chop.
2. Wash the broccoli and cut the florets from the stalk • Add the broccoli to a pot of water and steam, bring the water to a boil and cook the vegetables with the lid closed for 5 to 8 minutes.
3. Wash beef fillet and pat dry • Heat the olive oil in the air fryer and add the fillet with rosemary together • Fry the fillet for 3-5 minutes, depending on the thickness and desired cooking point, then remove, salt and pepper and let rest briefly.
4. Meanwhile, add the peppers, onion, and garlic to the hot air fryer and sauté. • Season with salt and pepper.
5. Arrange broccoli, pate, and beef fillet on a plate. • Pour basil over the meat and serve.

133. Chicken Thighs with Vegetables

INGREDIENTS

- 4 chicken legs, ready to cook
- 100 g cherry tomatoes
- 60 g mushrooms or other mushrooms
- 1 onion
- 6 tbsp olive oil
- 4 cloves of garlic
- 2 stalks of rosemary
- paprika
- sea salt
- pepper

INSTRUCTIONS

1. Wash the chicken drumsticks and pat dry • Peel the onion and cut into rings • Wash the rosemary and shake it dry • Crush the garlic cloves with the flat side of the knife.
2. Rub the chicken drumsticks all over with olive oil, paprika, salt, and pepper. • Then place the thighs together with onion and garlic in a fireproof mold and place the rosemary on them. • Boil thighs in a preheated air fryer at 200° C for 30 minutes.
3. While doing so, wash and halve the tomatoes • Clean and slice the mushrooms • Add both after 30 minutes to the thighs and cook everything for another 10-15 minutes until the thighs are cooked.

134. Green Smoothie with Avocado, Spinach & Banana

INGREDIENTS

- 60 g avocado
- 30 g young spinach leaves
- 70 g banana
- 2 dates
- Water as needed

INSTRUCTIONS

1. Halve the avocado and remove the kernel, then peel the pulp out of the bowl and place in a shaker • Wash leafy spinach • Peel the banana and break into pieces.
2. Put the spinach, banana and pitted dates into the blender jar • Puree everything with the hand blender, add a little water if necessary. • Pour the green smoothie into a glass and serve.

135. Sweet Pear, Pomegranate & Nuts Salad

INGREDIENTS

- 1 small pear (about 100 g)
- 5 g baby spinach
- 30 pomegranate seeds
- 20 g walnuts

INSTRUCTIONS

1. Wash and dry the pear, then cut in half and remove the core • Cut the pear into thin slices • Wash the spinach and drain well • Chop the nuts roughly.
2. Layer the pear, spinach, pomegranate seeds, and walnuts alternately into a glass until all the INGREDIENTS have been consumed. • Close the glass and refrigerate until ready to eat.

136. Avocado & Mozzarella Salad Bowl

INGREDIENTS

- 60 g avocado
- 50 g tomatoes, colorful mixture
- 40 g mozzarella
- 30 g mixed salad
- 2 tbsp olive oil
- 1 stalk of basil
- sea salt
- pepper

INSTRUCTIONS

1. Wash lettuce leaves and drain well, then chop into pieces and place in a bowl • Wash tomatoes and slice • Slice mozzarella • Wash basil and shake dry, then peel off the leaves.
2. Halve the avocado and remove the core. • Remove the avocado flesh from the skin and cut into strips. • Add the avocado, tomatoes, mozzarella, and basil to the salad. • Sprinkle with olive oil and season the salad bowl with salt and pepper.

137. Chicken Breast with Arugula & Tomatoes

INGREDIENTS

- 140 g chicken breast fillet
- 50 g tomatoes
- 30 g arugula
- 10 g pine nuts
- 3 tbsp olive oil
- sea salt
- pepper

INSTRUCTIONS

1. Wash the arugula and drain well, then remove long stalks

2. Wash and quarter the tomatoes • Brown the pine nuts in an air fryer without oil until golden brown, then remove and set aside • Arrange the arugula, tomatoes and pine nuts on a plate and drizzle with 1 tbsp of olive oil.
3. Wash chicken breast and dab dry • Heat 2 tbsp of olive oil in the air fryer and roast the meat on each side for about 6 to 10 minutes.
4. Remove the chicken breast from the air fryer, cut into strips and season with salt and pepper.

138. Zucchini Chips

INGREDIENTS

- 400 g zucchini
- Bamboo salt
- pink pepper
- 2 tbsp olive oil

INSTRUCTIONS

1. Wash the zucchini, dry them and cut off the ends • Cut into very thin slices.
2. Place the zucchini slices on a baking sheet lined with parchment paper and salt.
3. Brush with olive oil.
4. Sprinkle the slices with paprika powder and lightly salt again.
5. Heat the zucchini slices in a 200° C preheated the air fryer for 8-12 minutes until golden brown.

139. Fried Egg & Bacon

INGREDIENTS

- 2 eggs
- 30 g bacon
- 2 tbsp olive oil
- sea salt
- pepper

INSTRUCTIONS

1. Heat the oil in the air fryer and fry the bacon slices. Then reduce the heat and add the eggs to the air fryer.
2. Fry the eggs over medium heat and season with salt and pepper

140. CHOCOLATE SHAKE WITH ALMOND MILK

INGREDIENTS

- 300 ml almond milk
- 2 tsp cocoa, heavily de-oiled
- 2 tbsp of agave syrup
- Water as needed

INSTRUCTIONS

1. Almond milk-best, of course, tastes homemade-with cocoa and sweetener of your choice in a blender jar or shaker and mix all INGREDIENTS by mixing or shaking well, add some water as needed.
2. tip: instead of almond milk, soy or rice drink, any other nut milk or cow's milk can be used. Try the Chocolate Shake cold or hot!

141. Kebab Skewers with Chicken & Tzatziki

INGREDIENTS

For the skewers
- 500 g chicken meat, preferably thighs
- 200 g zucchini
- 200 g cherry tomatoes
- 150 g paprika
- 1 onion
- 2 tbsp olive oil
- 3 tsp kebab seasoning

For the Tzatziki
- 250 g Greek yogurt
- 100 g cucumber
- 2 tbsp olive oil
- 3 cloves of garlic
- sea salt
- pepper

INSTRUCTIONS

1. Wash meat and pat dry • Cut meat into pieces • Wash and slice zucchini • Wash and halve tomatoes • Peel the onion and cut into pieces, then separate each layer.
2. Stir meat and vegetables alternately on wooden skewers • Mix the olive oil, kebab seasoning and a little salt and pepper in a small bowl and brush the skewers all around with it.
3. Heat the air fryer and grill the skewers on all sides.
4. While doing so, wash and dry the cucumber, then finely grate with the grater • Peel garlic cloves and press into a bowl
5. Add yogurt, cucumber and olive oil and season the Tzatziki with salt and pepper.

142. Steamed Veggies

INGREDIENTS

- 100 g broccoli
- 50 g paprika, red, fresh
- 50 g paprika, yellow, fresh
- 50 g onion
- 100 g snow peas, fresh
- 2 medium carrots, fresh
- 1 pinch of sea salt
- 1 tbsp olive oil

INSTRUCTIONS

1. Wash the broccoli and cut the florets from the stalk • Remove the peppers from the seeds and partitions and cut into strips.
2. Peel the onion and cut into rings • Wash and drain the pears • Peel the carrot and cut into thin sticks.
3. Heat the olive oil in the air fryer • Put the prepared vegetables in the air fryer and fry them all over, stirring several times.
4. Season everything with salt and serve.

143. Spinach & Cream Cheese Frittata

INGREDIENTS

- 4 eggs
- 30 g spinach, raw
- 3 tbsp whipped cream 30%
- 50 g Parmesan
- 100 g granular cream cheese
- 1 pinch of sea salt
- 1 pinch of pepper, black
- 1 tbsp olive oil

INSTRUCTIONS

1. Wash the spinach and drain well. • Beat the eggs and stir in a bowl with whipped cream. • Add the cream cheese and season with salt and pepper. • Stir again.
2. Heat the olive oil in the air fryer and add the egg mass. • Add the spinach leaves and let the egg mass stagnate over medium heat. • Then add freshly grated Parmesan cheese over the egg mass.
3. Place the frittata in the air fryer for 15-20 minutes in the air fryer preheated to 180° C. • Remove the finished frittata from the air fryer and cut into pieces, drizzle with freshly squeezed lemon juice and serve.

144. Fresh Cucumber Salad with Onions & Herbs

INGREDIENTS

- 200 g cucumber with shell, raw
- 15 g spring onion
- 2 stems of parsley, fresh
- 1 pinch of sea salt
- 1 pinch of pepper, black
- 1 tbsp olive oil

INSTRUCTIONS

1. Wash cucumber and dry, then slice into thin slices, alternatively cut into thin slices with a knife.
2. Clean the spring onion thoroughly and cut into thin rings, • Wash the parsley and shake it dry, then peel off the leaves and chop.
3. Put cucumber, spring onion and parsley with olive oil in a bowl and season with salt and pepper. • Stir and serve.

145. Colorful Vegetable & Chicken Skewers

INGREDIENTS

- 300 g chicken breast fillet
- 200 g bacon
- 300 g tomatoes
- 300 g zucchini
- 300 g paprika
- 2 onions
- 100 g mushrooms
- 4 sprigs of thyme
- 2 sprigs of rosemary
- 6 tbsp olive oil
- Colorful pepper
- sea salt

INSTRUCTIONS

1. Wash chicken breast and dab dry, then cut into even 2 cm cubes • Peel the onion and cut into pieces
2. Clean mushrooms and cut off the dry stem end • Wash herbs and shake dry, then pluck the leaves from the stem and chop roughly.
3. Wash and drain the tomatoes and zucchini
4. Slice the zucchini • Halve the peppers and then remove the seeds and partitions • Wash the peppers and cut into pieces • Cut the bacon into strips and roll up.
5. Place the prepared INGREDIENTS alternately on wooden skewers • Place skewers on a plate and sprinkle with oil
6. Then season with salt and pepper and sprinkle with the herbs • Grill in the air fryer.

146. Mediterranean Vegetable Omelet

INGREDIENTS

- 4 eggs
- 1 tbsp cream
- 4 cherry tomatoes
- 40 g paprika
- 50 g avocado
- 20 g peas, fresh or frozen
- 20g onion
- 20 g corn, canned
- 6 stalks of parsley
- 3 tbsp olive oil
- sea salt
- pepper

INSTRUCTIONS

1. Wash and drain the tomatoes and peppers • Slice the tomatoes, cut the peppers into thin strips • Remove the avocado flesh from the shells and cut into strips • Peel the onion and cut into thin strips.
2. Wash the parsley and shake it dry, then pluck the leaves from the stalk and chop them. • Drain the corn in a colander.
3. Wash and drain the fresh peas, put the frozen peas in a bowl to thaw.
4. Pound the eggs in a bowl and whisk with cream, a little salt and pepper. • Heat the oil in the air fryer and add the egg mass.
5. Distribute the prepared vegetables on the omelet and warm them.
6. Season with salt, pepper and sprinkle with parsley.
7. Carefully fold the omelet in half and place it on a plate.

147. Grilled Pineapple

INGREDIENTS

- 500 g pineapple
- 1 organic lemon
- 1 stalk of rosemary
- 2 sticks of mint

INSTRUCTIONS

1. Peel and slice the pineapple • Using a sharp knife or a cookie cutter, remove the hard stalk • Wash the herbs and shake them dry • Halve the lemon and squeeze out the juice.
2. Pluck the rosemary leaves from the stalk and put them on the slices
3. Put the pineapple in an air fryer and grill on both sides
4. Remove the pineapple from the grill and drizzle with lemon juice
5. Pick the mint leaves, place them on the pineapple slices and serve them warm.

148. Celery Chive Puree

INGREDIENTS

- 1 celeriac about 500 g
- 75 g soy cream, alternatively whipped cream
- ½ bunch of chives
- 1 tbsp olive oil
- nutmeg
- sea salt

INSTRUCTIONS

1. Peel, clean and dice the celeriac • Put the celery in a pot and cover the cubes with water.

2. When the pot is closed, simmer the celery cubes for 15-20 minutes over medium heat.
3. Drain the celery into a sieve and let it evaporate briefly in an empty, hot air fryer. • Add the celery dice to the mixing bowl and finely puree with the hand blender
4. Then stir in soy cream, olive oil, a little salt and freshly grated nutmeg with a spoon.
5. Wash and drain the chives, then cut into rings.
6. Serve with chives.

149. Tomato Avocado, Cucumber & Herb Salad

INGREDIENTS

- 200 g tomatoes
- 200 g cucumber
- 1 avocado
- ½ red onion
- 1 tsp. Chili pepper, finely chopped
- Juice of half a lime
- Parsley or other fresh herbs at will
- 2 tbsp olive oil
- sea salt
- pepper

INSTRUCTIONS

1. Wash the tomatoes and cucumber and drain. • Halve the tomatoes and remove the stalk, then cut into pieces. • Cut the cucumber lengthwise and cut into slices. • Peel the onion and cut it into rings.
2. Halve the avocado and remove the core. • Remove the avocado flesh from the skin and cut into pieces. • Sprinkle the avocado with lime juice to leave the flesh green and not discolored.
3. Mix tomatoes, cucumber, onion, avocado and chili pepper in a bowl
4. Wash the herbs and pluck the leaves from the stalk • Add olive oil and herbs to the salad and season with salt and pepper.

150. Broccoli Hummus with Pine Nuts

INGREDIENTS

- 200 g chickpeas (canned)
- 150 g broccoli
- 30 g pine nuts
- 1 tsp Tahini
- 2 cloves of garlic
- ½ green chili pepper
- 2 tbsp lime juice, freshly squeezed
- 40 ml olive oil
- 4-5 tbsp water
- sea salt
- nutmeg

INSTRUCTIONS

1. Wash the broccoli and cut the florets from the stalk • Bring the water to a boil in a small air fryer, add the broccoli florets and cook for 2-3 minutes.
2. Strain the broccoli with a sieve and then cool under cold water to stop the cooking process.
3. Put and roast pine nuts in a frying air fryer without oil until golden brown.
4. Put the chickpeas in a colander and rinse under running water.
5. Put the chickpeas and broccoli in a shaker. Peel the garlic and add the chili pepper and half of the pine nuts to the blender jar.
6. Add the Tahini sesame, olive oil, lime juice and water to the mixing bowl and finely puree with the blender.
7. Season the broccoli hummus with salt and nutmeg and place it in a bowl. • Sprinkle with olive oil and add the remaining pine nuts.

151. Braised Eggplant, Peppers, Olives & Capers

INGREDIENTS

- 300 g eggplant
- 100 g red pepper
- 100 g green pepper
- 1 red onion
- 1 chili pepper
- ½ bunch of basil
- 6 sprigs of thyme
- 400 ml vegetable stock
- 2 tbsp olive oil
- 1 tbsp of green olives, pitted
- 1 tbsp capers (from the glass)
- 2 tsp tomato paste
- ½ tsp tandoori
- Himalayan salt
- pepper

INSTRUCTIONS

1. Wash eggplant, peppers and chili peppers and drain • Halve eggplant lengthways and slice • Halve peppers, remove seeds and partitions and cut into pieces.
2. Peel onion and finely dice • Slice olives • Wash herbs and shake dry
3. Tear thyme leaves from stalk
4. Cut the chili into rings.
5. Heat the olive oil in the air fryer and sauté the onion.
6. Add the eggplant, paprika and chili pepper and sauté.
7. Add the tomato puree and stir in. • Douse everything with the vegetable stock and top up.
8. Add olives, capers, thyme, tandoori, salt and pepper and stir.
9. Cook the vegetables for 5-10 minutes in air fryer on medium heat. • Then season the vegetables with salt and pepper, garnish with basil leaves and serve.

152. Fresh Garden Salad with Beef

INGREDIENTS

- 180 g beef steak, organic
- 50 g mixed lettuce
- 5 cherry tomatoes
- 3 radishes
- 1 carrot
- 6 sprigs of thyme
- 1 sprig rosemary
- 3 tbsp olive oil
- sea salt
- pepper

INSTRUCTIONS

1. Wash lettuce leaves and dry them in a salad spinner • Pare large lettuce leaves • Peel the carrot and cut into thin slices with Clean peeler radish and slice • Wash tomatoes and cut in half.
2. Wash thyme and rosemary and shake dry • Wash beef steak and dry with a kitchen crepe • Heat 2 tbsp of oil in the air fryer
3. Add the herbs and steak and fry the meat on both sides for a short while.
4. Remove steak from the air fryer, season with salt and pepper and let it rest for a short while.
5. Place the prepared salad INGREDIENTS on a plate and season with salt and pepper.
6. Pour 1 tbsp of olive oil over the salad. • Slice the steak and add to the salad.

153. Herbed Zucchini Patties with Yogurt Dip

INGREDIENTS

Patties
- 400 g zucchini
- 2 eggs
- 60 g potatoes
- 50 g Parmesan
- 2 tbsp olive oil
- 2 tbsp chopped parsley
- nutmeg
- sea salt
- pepper

Dip
- 150 g yogurt
- 2 tbsp olive oil
- Juice of half a lemon
- sea salt
- pepper

INSTRUCTIONS

1. Wash and dry the zucchini, then grate with the grater • Peel and grate the potatoes • Mix both in a bowl with a little salt and leave to soak for 5 to 10 minutes.
2. Meanwhile, prepare the dip, mix yogurt, olive oil, lemon juice and some salt and pepper in a small bowl and then season again.
3. Keep the dip cold until it is consumed.
4. Whisk the eggs in a bowl and add the parsley, freshly grated Parmesan, zucchini and potatoes • Season with salt, pepper and nutmeg and mix.
5. Heat the oil in a frying air fryer and add the portions of zucchini to it with your hands. • As soon as the patties on the underside are fried crisp and golden brown, turn over and fry on the other side as well.
6. Zucchini sandwiches may be kept warm in the air fryer at 50° C while the rest are roasted.
7. Serve zucchini sandwiches with herbs and yogurt dip.

154. Salmon, Egg & Parmesan Salad

INGREDIENTS

- 200 g of salmon
- 4 eggs
- 200 g Romana salad
- 100 g arugula
- 10 cherry tomatoes
- 1 organic lemon
- 50 g Parmesan
- 5 tbsp olive oil
- Balsamic-Date & fig at the pleasure
- sea salt
- pepper

INSTRUCTIONS

1. Cook the eggs in a pot of boiling water for 8-10 minutes. • Then chill the eggs cold, peel and cut in half.
2. Wash lettuce leaves and dry in a salad spinner, then pluck small • Wash tomatoes, drain and then halve
3. Place lettuce leaves and tomatoes on two plates and drizzle with 1 tbsp of oil.
4. Wash salmon and dab it dry. • Cut the salmon into bite-sized pieces.
5. Heat 3 tbsp of oil in the air fryer and roast the salmon pieces all around. • Season the salmon with salt and pepper and add to the salad.
6. Add the eggs to the salad and sprinkle with freshly grated Parmesan cheese
7. Halve the lemon and drizzle some juice over the salmon and salad.
8. Finally, refine the salad with balsamic.

155. Fried Eggs with Bacon, Avocado & Arugula

INGREDIENTS

- 2 eggs
- ½ avocado
- 20 g arugula
- 30 g bacon-about 4 strips
- 1 tbsp olive oil
- sea salt
- pepper

INSTRUCTIONS

1. Halve the avocado and remove the kernel. • Remove the pulp from the skin and cut into strips.
2. Wash the arugula and remove long stalks.
3. Arrange the avocado and arugula on a plate.
4. Heat the oil in the air fryer and fry the bacon strips on both sides. • Place the bacon on one side in the air fryer.
5. Open the two eggs in the middle and fry over medium heat to the desired consistency.
6. Put the warm bacon slices and the two fried eggs on the plate and season with salt and pepper.

156. Chicken Breast with Green Beans

INGREDIENTS

- 1 chicken breast fillet, approx. 200 g
- 200 g green beans
- 2 tbsp olive oil
- 1 organic lemon
- sea salt
- pepper

INSTRUCTIONS

1. Clean the beans and cook in an air fryer with water. Cook for 8-10 minutes. Wash and dry the chicken breast fillet. Brush the grill air fryer with oil and fry the meat on each side for 3 to 5 minutes, depending on the consistency of the meat.
2. Wash the lemon hot and dry, then rub the bowl with the grater.
3. Drain the beans and season with salt, pepper and lemon.
4. Halve the grated lemon in half and add some juice over the beans.
5. Season the fried chicken breast with salt and pepper and cut into strips • Add the beans to the meat and serve everything together.

157. Grilled Salmon with Green Beans

INGREDIENTS

- 1 salmon fillet, approx. 300 g
- 500 g green beans
- 2 tbsp butter
- 1 organic lemon
- 1 clove of garlic
- 4 sprigs of thyme
- 1 sprig rosemary
- 4 tbsp olive oil
- sea salt
- pepper

INSTRUCTIONS

1. Wash the salmon fillet and pat dry • Peel and finely chop the garlic • Wash and dry the herbs, then pluck the leaves from the stalk and chop finely.

2. Mix the garlic, herbs and oil in a flat shape, then marinate the fish and leave to infuse.
3. Clean the beans and cook in a pot of water for about 8 minutes until they are cooked
4. Drain the beans and drain.
5. Cut the lemon into pieces.
6. Heat the grill air fryer and grill the salmon fillet until it has the roast strips, then turn and grill on the second side. • The salmon fillet can also be prepared on the grill as desired.
7. In the meantime, melt the butter in a second air fryer and stir in the beans.
8. Then season the beans with a little lemon juice, salt and pepper and divide them into two plates.
9. Season the salmon fillet with salt and pepper. • Halve the fillet piece and arrange half of each on the beans.
10. Add the lemon pieces, then sprinkle some lemon juice over the fish and serve.

158. ASIAN CHICKEN SALAD

INGREDIENTS

- 300 g chicken meat
- 40 g rice noodles
- 1 carrot
- 100 g cucumber
- 1 red pepper
- ½ red onion
- 1 lime
- 1 clove of garlic
- 1 green chili pepper
- 2 tbsp cashew kernels or peanuts
- 2 sprigs of lemon basil or basil
- 200 ml vegetable broth
- 50 ml teriyaki sauce
- 2 tbsp of sesame oil
- Bamboo salt
- Pepper

INSTRUCTIONS

1. Peel the carrot and cut into thin, short sticks. • Wash the cucumber and cut into thin slices.
2. Cut the peppers in half and remove the kernels and partitions, then cut into thin strips.
3. Wash the lime hot and rub the skin, then halve the lime and squeeze out the juice.
4. Peel the onion and cut into tiny strips • Peel and chop the garlic • Halve the chili along and remove the seeds, then chop
5. Wash the basil and shake dry, roughly chop the large leaves.
6. Heat the stock in a pot and heat the pasta in it. • After the cooking time, drain the pasta and drain.
7. Place the carrot, cucumber, paprika, onion and noodles in a salad bowl, season with salt and pepper and mix.
8. Wash chicken meat and pat dry
9. Heat the oil in an air fryer and fry the meat with garlic and chili all around golden brown. • Add the teriyaki sauce, lime rub and some lime juice to the meat in the hot air fryer.
10. Turn the meat into it and allow to simmer briefly, then season with salt and pepper.
11. Pour noodles with vegetables in two bowls
12. Add coarsely chopped nuts and basil • Remove meat from the air fryer, cut into strips and serve warm on the salad.

159. ZOODLES WITH SHRIMP & CHERRY TOMATOES

INGREDIENTS

- 500 g zucchini
- 200 g shrimp, without the head, with shell

- 200 g cherry tomatoes
- 2 shallots
- 2 cloves of garlic
- 1 organic lemon
- 200 ml vegetable broth
- 50 ml sesame oil
- sea salt
- pepper

INSTRUCTIONS

1. Wash and dry the zucchini • Cut into long thin noodles with the spiral cutter • Wash the tomatoes and drain them, then quarter them • Peel the shallots and finely dice • Peel the garlic and finely chop.
2. Wash the lemon hot and dry, then grate the skin with the grater • then halve the lemon and squeeze out the juice • Remove shrimp from the shell, do not throw the bowl aside, but set aside for frying- this gives a great flavor.
3. Heat the sesame oil in the air fryer and fry the garlic, shallots, shrimp and shrimp shells. • Add the tomatoes and stir everything. • Remove the shrimp and set aside. Take out the shrimp shells as well. These can now be disposed of.
4. Put the zucchini noodles in the hot air fryer and fill with stock. • Sauté the zucchini noodles for 3-4 minutes. • Add the grated lemon peel and a little lemon juice and season with salt and pepper.
5. Stir everything again, then add the shrimp again and briefly warm.

160. Low-Carb Bread with Cream Cheese & Avocado

INGREDIENTS

- 2 slices of walnut bread from the cookbook: low-carb To Go
- ½ avocado
- 50 g cream cheese
- 4 cherry tomatoes
- 4 mini mozzarella balls
- 1 tsp lime juice, freshly squeezed
- Sesame, black
- Basil shredded
- sea salt
- pepper

INSTRUCTIONS

1. Place the two walnut bread slices on a platter and sprinkle with cream cheese.
2. Wash and slice the tomatoes. • Drain mozzarella mini balls.
3. Halve and core the avocado, remove the pulp with a tbsp and slice • Drizzle the lime juice onto the avocado slices so that they do not turn brown.
4. Spread the avocado and tomato slices on both slices of bread.
5. Put the mozzarella on top and sprinkle with sesame. • Season with basil, salt and pepper and then serve.

161. Salad with Avocado & Chicken

INGREDIENTS

- 1 avocado
- 1 chicken breast fillet, 150 g each
- 200 g cucumber
- 100 g radicchio red
- 100 g corn salad
- 6 cherry tomatoes
- Herbs at will
- 2 tbsp olive oil
- sea salt
- pepper

INSTRUCTIONS

1. Wash radicchio and dry in a salad spinner. • Cut the radicchio into pieces.
2. Wash cucumber, dry and slice. • Wash and halve tomatoes. • Wash herbs and shake dry, peel off leaves and finely chop.
3. Put all the prepared salad INGREDIENTS in a bowl and season with salt and pepper
4. Drizzle 1 tbsp of olive oil over the salad, mix again and place on two plates
5. Halve the avocado and remove the kernel • Remove avocado flesh from the skin and cut into thin slices • Put an avocado half on the plate.
6. Wash chicken breast and dab dry
7. Heat 1 tbsp of olive oil in the air fryer and fry the meat until golden brown, turning it several times
8. Season the chicken breast with salt and pepper, then place on a platter and cut into thin slices
9. Add the meat to the salad and serve.

162. Cheese Stuffed Mushrooms

INGREDIENTS

- 500 g mushrooms, organic
- 150 g cream cheese
- 1 organic lemon
- 2 spring onions
- 150 g Parmesan
- 2 tbsp olive oil
- 1 clove of garlic
- parsley
- nutmeg
- sea salt
- pepper

INSTRUCTIONS

1. Brush the mushrooms as needed with a soft brush, then cut off the dry ends of the stems
2. Carefully unscrew the mushroom stalks • Chop the stalks and place in a bowl • Place the mushrooms on a baking sheet lined with parchment paper so that they can be filled well.
3. Clean the spring onions and cut into rings
4. Peel the garlic and chop finely • Wash the parsley and shake it dry, then finely chop
5. Grate the parmesan • Wash the lemon hot and dry, then rub the peel off.
6. Heat the oil in the air fryer and fry the spring onions, garlic and mushroom stalks.
7. Add the cream cheese and mix everything.
8. Mix in the lemon, then season with salt, pepper and nutmeg.
9. Pour the warm stuffing into the mushrooms and sprinkle with Parmesan. • Mushrooms in the preheated air fryer at 200° C. Bake on the medium rack for 15-20 minutes. • Place mushrooms on a large plate, sprinkle with parsley and serve hot.

163. Pea Soup with Roasted Asparagus & Feta

INGREDIENTS

- 500 g frozen peas
- 100 g green asparagus
- 200 g feta
- 2 shallots
- 4 spring onions
- 100 g potatoes, floury
- 800 ml vegetable broth
- Ginger, freshly grated
- 3 tbsp olive oil
- ½ bunch of basil
- nutmeg
- sea salt

- pepper

INSTRUCTIONS

1. Peel the shallots and finely chop them
2. Clean the spring onions and cut into rings • Peel and cut the potatoes • Peel the asparagus in the lower third, then cut the bars into 3 cm long piece
3. Wash the basil and shake dry, four beautiful stems for the garnish set aside, chop the rest.
4. Heat 2 tbsp of oil in a frying air fryer and sauté potatoes with shallots and spring onions. • Deglaze everything with the stock and then simmer for about 10 minutes. • Add frozen peas, bring to a simmer and simmer for another 5 minutes.
5. Add the ginger and basil to the soup
6. Remove the pot from the stove and finely puree everything with the hand blender • Season the soup with freshly grated nutmeg, salt and pepper and set aside, set aside.
7. Season the asparagus with salt and pepper • Fill the soup with four bowls and add the asparagus pieces
8. Crumble the feta and add to the soup • Garnish with basil.

164. Swiss Chard Salad with Feta & Dried Tomatoes

INGREDIENTS

- 50 g chard
- 50 g arugula
- 50 g young spinach
- 50 g feta
- 50 g dried tomatoes
- 1 tbsp hemp seed, peeled
- 8-10 black olives, pitted
- 2 tbsp olive oil
- sea salt
- pepper

INSTRUCTIONS

1. Wash the chard, arugula salad and spinach and dry in the salad spinner
2. Remove long stalks from the leaves and pluck large leaves • Arrange lettuce leaves on a plate.
3. Cut the feta into cubes and pour over the salad with the dried tomatoes, olives and hemp seeds.
4. Sprinkle everything with olive oil and season with salt and pepper.

165. Broccoli & Quinoa Salad

INGREDIENTS

- 100 g broccoli
- 50 g quinoa colorful
- 40 g paprika
- 4 cherry tomatoes
- 20 g arugula
- 1 tbsp lime juice, freshly squeezed
- 1 tbsp olive oil
- sea salt
- pepper

INSTRUCTIONS

1. Put the quinoa in a colander and rinse under running water to remove the bittering substances.
2. Cover the quinoa with water in a small air fryer. Cook for 5-10 minutes until the granules are firm. • Drain the water and season the quinoa with lemon juice, salt and pepper.

3. Cut and wash broccoli florets from the stalk.
4. Cut the broccoli into bite-sized pieces, place in a pot with stew-pot and cook covered for about 5 minutes.
5. Then take the broccoli out and let it cool down.
6. Wash the peppers, tomatoes and arugula and drain well.
7. If necessary, remove the cores and partitions from the pepper, then cut into cubes.
8. Tear the arugula, remove long stalks. • Halve the tomatoes.
9. When the quinoa and broccoli have cooled, place in a glass one after the other
10. Add the peppers and tomatoes in portions.
11. Sprinkle the olive oil over the vegetables and finish with the arugula leaves.

166. Grilled Chicken Breast with Fresh Herbs
INGREDIENTS

- 4 chicken breast fillets
- 1 garlic bulb
- 1 organic lemon
- 2 sprigs of rosemary
- 3 dill blossoms
- 5 sprigs of thyme
- 4 tbsp olive oil
- sea salt
- pepper

INSTRUCTIONS

1. Wash chicken breasts and pat dry • Halve the lemon and squeeze out the juice • Wash the herbs and shake dry, pluck the leaves off the stems.
2. Mix the herbs, oil, lemon juice and a little salt and pepper in a bowl and marinate the meat. • Cut the garlic bulb unpeeled in the whole across with a large knife.
3. Heat the grill air fryer and add the marinated chicken breast fillets and the halved garlic bulb. • Pour the remaining marinade over the meat. • Turn the fillets several times until they are cooked.

167. Arugula, Radish & Couscous Salad
INGREDIENTS

- 100 g arugula
- 50 g couscous
- 5 radishes
- 6 cherry tomatoes
- 200 g cucumber
- 1 celery stick
- 4 tbsp olive oil
- 1 tsp cumin
- nutmeg
- pepper
- sea salt

INSTRUCTIONS

1. Wash the arugula and remove long stalks • Wash and halve the tomatoes • Clean, wash and slice the radishes • Clean and wash the celery stalk, then cut into small pieces • Wash the cucumber and cut it into pieces.
2. Cook the couscous, then season with cumin, nutmeg, salt and pepper. • Put all the INGREDIENTS in a salad bowl and drizzle with olive oil. • Season the salad with salt and pepper, mix and divide into two small bowls.

168. Grilled Chicken Skewers with Onions & Peppers

INGREDIENTS

- 800 g chicken breast fillet
- 3 peppers
- 4 onions
- 4 tbsp olive oil
- Paprika, pink
- cumin
- sea salt
- pepper

INSTRUCTIONS

1. Wash the chicken and pat dry, then cut the fillets into cubes of about 3 cm. • Cut the peppers in half and remove the seeds and partitions.
2. Wash the paprika halves and drain, then cut into 3 cm pieces.
3. Peel and quarter the onions, cut the individual layers into equal pieces.
4. Put the chicken, peppers and onions alternately on the skewers until all the INGREDIENTS have been consumed. • Sauté the skewers with olive oil and season with cumin, paprika, salt and pepper.
5. Grill in an air fryer and serve hot.

169. Vegetables with Egg & Parsley

INGREDIENTS

- 3 eggs
- ½ red pepper
- ½ green pepper
- ½ onion
- 1 stalk of parsley
- 6 cherry tomatoes
- 1 tbsp olive oil
- pepper
- sea salt
- chili pepper

INSTRUCTIONS

1. Wash the peppers, tomatoes and parsley and drain • Remove the cut-offs and seeds from the pepper and cut into pieces • Halve the tomatoes
2. Chop the parsley • Peel the onion and finely dice.
3. Heat the olive oil in the air fryer and sauté the onion. • Add the paprika and tomatoes and fry them.
4. Whisk the chopped chili with the eggs, salt and pepper in a bowl and add everything to the vegetables in the air fryer.
5. Mix everything with the spatula several times so that the egg is fried from all sides.
6. Season with salt and pepper; add parsley.

170. Fried Egg with Green Beans & Paprika

INGREDIENTS

- 2 eggs
- 150 g green beans
- 50 g red pepper
- 50 g Brussels sprouts, fresh or frozen
- 30 g peas, fresh or frozen
- 1 shallot
- 1 tbsp olive oil
- sea salt
- pepper

INSTRUCTIONS

1. Wash and clean the beans, then cut into bite-sized pieces.
2. Bake beans in a pot of boiling water for 5-6 minutes. • Drain the beans and drain in the strainer.
3. Clean, fresh Brussels sprouts, remove the withered leaves and then halve • Thaw frozen Brussels sprouts and then halve • Remove fresh peas from the pod, thaw frozen peas.
4. Halve the peppers and remove the seeds and partitions. • Cut the peppers into bite-sized pieces. • Peel the shallot and finely dice it.
5. Heat the olive oil in the air fryer and sauté the diced shallots • Add the beans, Brussels sprouts, peas and paprika and roast. • Season the vegetables with salt and pepper.
6. Make some space in the middle of the air fryer and add the eggs • Season the fried eggs and serve.

171. ASIAN BROCCOLI SALAD

INGREDIENTS

- 400 g broccoli
- 2 carrots
- 1 tomato
- 200 ml water, warm
- 50 ml organic soy sauce
- 2 tbsp of sesame oil
- 1 tbsp honey
- 1 tsp sesame
- sea salt
- pepper

INSTRUCTIONS

1. Split the broccoli florets from the stalk, wash and drain. • Peel and slice the carrots.
2. Wash the tomato, halve and cut out the stalk, then cut the halves into pieces.
3. Heat the sesame oil in the air fryer and roast the broccoli with carrots
4. Add the tomato pieces, season with salt and pepper and stir • Mix the soy sauce, honey and warm water in a small bowl, then add to the vegetables in the air fryer.
5. Simmer over medium heat for several minutes.
6. Add salt and pepper. • Season the salad with sesame seeds and serve.

172. Jaair Fryerese Salad with Shrimp

INGREDIENTS

- 8 shrimp, without skin and head
- 100 g Chinese cabbage
- 50 g red cabbage
- 10 cherry tomatoes
- 2 spring onions
- 1 carrot
- 1 lime
- ½ yellow pepper
- ½ red pepper
- 6 stems of coriander
- 2 cloves of garlic
- 200 ml water, warm
- 50 ml organic soy sauce
- 4 tbsp olive oil
- 20 g honey
- 2 tsp sesame
- sea salt
- pepper

INSTRUCTIONS

1. Wash shrimp and drain, then cut lengthwise with a knife in the middle of the stomach side. • Peel the garlic and press it into a bowl with the garlic press. • Add the olive oil and shrimp to the garlic, stir and leave to stir.

2. Wash vegetables and herbs and drain • Remove the withered leaves and hard stalk from China and red cabbage • Cut Chinese and red cabbage into thin strips • Halve tomatoes • Clean spring onions and cut them into oblique strips.
3. Peel the carrot and cut into thin sticks • Remove seeds from the pepper, then cut into rings or narrow strips • Pick coriander leaves from the stalk and chop • Place all prepared salad INGREDIENTS in a large bowl.
4. Halve the lime and squeeze out the juice. • Mix the soy sauce, lime juice, honey and water in a small bowl and add to the salad. • Add to the salad with salt and pepper and mix everything.
5. Put shrimp with garlic and oil in the hot air fryer and fry for a few minutes, then add to the salad and mix again. • Sprinkle with sesame seeds and serve.

173. Veal Skewers with Vegetables

INGREDIENTS

- 600 g veal
- 1 yellow pepper
- 1 red pepper
- ½ red onion
- 100 g green olives, pitted
- 100 g cherry tomatoes
- 2 tbsp olive oil
- sea salt
- pepper

INSTRUCTIONS

1. Wash and drain the vegetables • Halve the peppers, core and cut them into 2-3 cm pieces • Peel and quarter the onion, place the individual layers of the onion pieces on a plate • Wash the meat, dab dry and cut into 2-3 cm cubes.
2. Place pieces of meat, peppers and onions alternately on the skewers • Start and finish each with a piece of meat, do not slip off the skewer when grilling
3. Season the skewers with salt and pepper and place them on the hot grill, turn them several times to allow meat and meat, grilling vegetables evenly.
4. Cut the cucumber into thin slices with the vegetable slicer or peeler
5. Halve the tomatoes and place them together with the cucumber strips in a bowl • Season both with salt and pepper and drizzle with olive oil.
6. Serve with cucumber and tomato salad and olives

174. Salmon Steak with Green Asparagus

INGREDIENTS

- 1 salmon steak about 200 g
- 6 bars of green asparagus
- 4 tbsp olive oil
- ½ organic lemon
- sea salt
- pepper

INSTRUCTIONS

1. Wash the salmon steak and dab it dry.
2. Heat the grill air fryer and brush with olive oil. Place the salmon steak in the hot air fryer.
3. Cut the lemon into small boats.
4. Peel the asparagus spears in the lower third and cut off the dry ends
5. Wash and drain the asparagus, then place it in the grill air fryer.
6. Turn the salmon steak and grill on the other side until the strips of roast are visible.

7. Season with salt and pepper.
8. Put the salmon and asparagus on a plate and serve with lemon.

175. RATATOUILLE

INGREDIENTS

- 200 g eggplant
- 300 g zucchini
- 400 g tomatoes
- 1 red pepper
- 1 yellow pepper
- 2 cloves of garlic
- 2 shallots
- 4 stems of basil
- 3 stems of thyme
- 2 sprigs of rosemary
- 200 ml vegetable broth
- 4 tbsp olive oil
- 2 tbsp tomato paste
- sea salt
- pepper

INSTRUCTIONS

1. Wash and drain the vegetables • Slice the eggplant, zucchini and tomatoes
2. Halve the peppers, core them and cut into strips • Wash the herbs and shake them dry, then pluck the leaves from the stalk • Finely chop the thyme and rosemary.
3. Peel and smoothly chop the shallots and garlic • Heat the oil in an air fryer and fry the shallots and garlic.
4. Add the tomato purée and fry it.
5. Add the vegetable stock and douse.
6. Bring the sauce to a boil, then season with salt and pepper and stir in the chopped herbs.
7. Eggplant, zucchini, tomatoes, peppers alternately in a baking dish layers
8. Then add the sauce and cook everything in a preheated air fryer at 175° C for 15-20 minutes •
9. Garnish ratatouille with basil leaves and serve.

176. Red Cabbage & Apple Salad

INGREDIENTS

- 100 g red cabbage
- 3 radishes
- 30 g apple
- 20 g red onion
- 3 stems of coriander
- 2 tbsp olive oil
- 2 tsp of agave syrup
- 1 tsp sesame
- 1 dash of lime juice, freshly squeezed
- Sea salt

INSTRUCTIONS

1. Remove the withered leaves from the red cabbage
2. Cut a thick slice from the red cabbage and finely grate it with the vegetable slicer.
3. Alternatively, cut it into thin strips with a knife. • Peel the onion and cut into thin slices.
4. Wash the radishes, clean and cut into thin slices. • Wash the apple, core it and cut it into thin slices.
5. Wash the coriander and shake it dry, then pluck the leaves. • Place the red cabbage, onion, apple and radish on a plate.
6. Mix the oil with lime and agave syrup in a bowl to dressing and season with salt
7. Drizzle the dressing over the salad • Add the coriander leaves and sesame seeds and serve.

177. Eggplant Tomato Frittata

INGREDIENTS

- 6 eggs
- 150 g eggplant
- 100 ml cream
- 50 g of cheddar
- 6 cherry tomatoes
- ½ red onion
- 3 stalks of parsley
- 2 tbsp olive oil
- nutmeg
- sea salt
- pepper

INSTRUCTIONS

1. Whisk eggs in a bowl with cream • Wash eggplant and tomatoes and drain
2. Slice eggplant • Wash parsley and shake dry • Peel onion and cut into rings.
3. Heat the oil in the air fryer and fry the onion. • Add eggplant and tomatoes and fry briefly.
4. Add the egg-cream mixture and season with salt and pepper. • Chop the cheddar or cut into small pieces and place over the vegetable-egg-air fryer.
5. Bake for 20-25 minutes in a preheated air fryer at 200° C.
6. Remove frittata from the air fryer. • Chop parsley.
7. Sprinkle frittata with freshly grated nutmeg and parsley and serve

178. Low-Carb Bread with Arugula & Trout

INGREDIENTS

- 2 slices of nut and oat bread
- 60 g trout, smoked
- 20 g arugula
- 1 egg
- 2 cherry tomatoes
- 20 g butter
- sea salt
- pepper

INSTRUCTIONS

1. Cook the egg in a small air fryer for 8-10 minutes. • Place the low-carb bread slices on a work board and butter them. • Wash the arugula and shake it dry, then remove the long stems.
2. Wash tomatoes and quarter • Put the arugula on the two slices of bread • Chill the egg and peel, then slice • Place the egg, trout and tomatoes on the bread and season with salt and pepper.

179. Grilled Chicken Breast with Avocado, Salad & Cheese

INGREDIENTS

- 2 chicken breast fillets, 250 g
- 200 g mixed salad
- 1 avocado
- 10 cherry tomatoes
- 50 g dried tomatoes
- 100 g feta
- 50 g Parmesan
- ½ bunch of parsley
- ½ bunch of basil
- 2 tbsp olive oil
- sea salt
- pepper

INSTRUCTIONS

1. Wash chicken breasts and pat dry • Cut meat into strips • Wash lettuce leaves and dry in a salad spinner • Wash and halve tomatoes • Wash herbs and shake dry, then peel off the leaves and finely chop.
2. Halve and remove the avocado, remove the flesh from the skin • Slice the flesh • Place the salad on two plates • Crumble the feta with your fingers and add to the salad along with the avocado slices and dried tomatoes.
3. Arrange fresh tomatoes on the salad plate • Finely grate the Parmesan • Mix the Parmesan with the chopped herbs and add to the salad • Season with salt and pepper.
4. Heat the oil in the air fryer and fry the chicken breast fillets. • Add to the meat with salt and pepper and serve hot on the salad.

180. Chicken Curry with Green Beans

INGREDIENTS

- 500 g chicken breast fillet
- 500 g green beans
- 400 ml coconut milk
- 2 tbsp olive oil
- 2 tsp green curry paste
- 2 spring onions
- 2 shallots
- 3 cloves of garlic
- Juice of a lime
- 4 stalks of parsley
- sea salt
- pepper

INSTRUCTIONS

1. Wash chicken meat and dab dry • Cut meat into bite-sized pieces • Wash beans, clean and cut into pieces about 3 cm long • Boil beans in boiling, slightly salted water 8-10 minutes.
2. Peel the shallots and finely dice • Peel and chop the garlic • Clean the spring onions and cut into rings or mince them • Wash the parsley and shake it dry, then chop it • Halve the lime and squeeze out the juice.
3. Heat the oil in the air fryer and fry the chicken breast fillet with shallots. • Add the curry paste and sauté. • Add the garlic and deglaze with coconut milk. • Reduce the heat and simmer for several minutes.
4. Drain the beans and then add to the meat in the air fryer • Stir in lime juice and season everything with salt and pepper • Add parsley and spring onions, mix everything and serve in a large mold.

181. Smoked Salmon Salad

INGREDIENTS

- 100 g smoked salmon, wild catch
- 50 g salad
- 4 cherry tomatoes
- ½ organic lemon
- 2 stalks

INSTRUCTIONS

1. Wash lettuce leaves, shake dry and pluck small
2. Wash and halve tomatoes • Wash dill and shake dry, then peel off the tips of the stalk • Cut the lemon into small boats.
3. Arrange lettuce, tomatoes and salmon on a plate

4. Drizzle lemon juice on the salmon • Finally, spread the dill over the salmon and serve.

182. Avocado Quinoa Buddha Bowl

INGREDIENTS

- 50 g avocado
- 40 g Gouda, young
- 30 g lamb's lettuce
- 30 g organic carrot
- 30 g organic cucumber
- 30 g paprika
- 15 g quinoa, colorful
- ½ lime
- 1 egg
- sea salt
- pepper

INSTRUCTIONS

1. Boil an egg in boiling water for 8-10 minutes. • Rinse quinoa under running water in a fine sieve. • Simmer the quinoa in water in a small air fryer for 5-10 minutes, drain and season with salt and pepper.
2. Wash vegetables and corn salad and drain
3. Cut paprika and cucumber into pieces • Peel carrot and grate • Squeeze out lime • Cut avocado into cubes and drizzle with lime juice so that the flesh does not turn brown • Cut Gouda into cubes.
4. Add the lamb's lettuce and season the vegetables and cheese. • Mix the quinoa and a dash of lime juice in the middle of the bowl.
5. Peel the egg, halve and place on the bowl. • Salt, pepper and serve the Buddha Bowl.

183. Smoked SALMON WITH LEMON

INGREDIENTS

- 500 g smoked salmon, wild catch
- 1 organic lemon
- 2-3 stems of parsley
- Sea salt

INSTRUCTIONS

1. Wash lemon, dry and cut in half. • Squeeze out one half, cut the other into small shuttles.
2. Carefully separate the salmon slices, roll them up one by one and arrange them on a large plate.
3. Wash the parsley, then shake it dry and pluck it from the stalk. • Pour lemon juice over the salmon.
4. Add lemon boat, salt, and parsley to the salmon and serve.

184. AVOCADO WITH GRAPEFRUIT

INGREDIENTS

- 1 avocado (hate)
- ½ grapefruit
- ½ grapefruit
- 2-3 stalks of mint
- Juice of half a lime
- sea salt

INSTRUCTIONS

1. Halve the avocado, remove seed and remove the flesh from the skin.

2. Cut the avocado halves into strips and sprinkle with lime juice to prevent the flesh from turning brown.
3. Fillet grapefruit
4. Wash and dry mint, then finely chop • Arrange avocado, grapefruit, and grapefruit on two plates and sprinkle with sea salt each time.

185. GREEK YOGURT WITH CHIA AND BLUEBERRIES

INGREDIENTS

- 150 Greek yogurt
- 50 g blueberries
- 2 tbsp chia seeds
- ½ tsp agave syrup, optional

INSTRUCTIONS

1. Put the Greek yogurt and chia seeds in a bowl and mix.
2. Add yogurt to taste with some agave syrup.
3. Wash blueberries and drain in the strainer.
4. Pour yogurt into a glass or bowl and layer blueberries on top.

186. Avocado Cream & Poached Egg Sandwich

INGREDIENTS

- 2 slices of low-carb bread
- 1 egg
- ½ avocado
- 1 handful of corn salad or arugula
- 1 tbsp fresh lime juice
- 8-10 stems of coriander
- 1 tbsp organic apple cider vinegar
- Thyme rubbed
- nutmeg
- Sea salt
- pepper

INSTRUCTIONS

1. Wash lettuce and coriander and drain. • Remove the avocado flesh from the skin and crush with the fork. • Chop the coriander and add to the avocado with the lime juice and mix. • Season the avocado cream with salt and pepper.
2. For the poached egg first, bring water to a boil. • Pour the cider vinegar into the water and remove the pot from the heat. • Beat the egg, put it in a cup, and pour it into the water. • Put the pot back on the heat and egg simmer over low heat for 2-3 minutes • Remove the poached egg from the pot with a skimmer and drain.
3. Toast low-carb bread and let cool briefly • salad set on the discs and spread with avocado cream •
4. Place poached egg in the center of the slice of bread and sprinkle with thyme and freshly grated nutmeg • Fold into a sandwich

187. MARGHERITA OMELET

INGREDIENTS

- 3 eggs
- 50 g Parmesan
- 2 tbsp cream
- 1 tbsp olive oil

- 1 tsp oregano, rubbed
- nutmeg
- Sea salt
- pepper

For topping
- 1 tomato
- 100 g mozzarella, grated
- 3-4 stems of basil

INSTRUCTIONS

1. Put the eggs and cream in a bowl
2. Add grated Parmesan, nutmeg, oregano, pepper and salt and stir again with the whisk
3. Heat the oil in an air fryer and pour in half of the egg mixture.
4. Heat omelet over medium heat, then turn and remove • Prepare the second omelet in the same way • Slice tomato and cover with omelet • Sprinkle mozzarella on tomatoes.
5. Place the omelet on a baking tray and cook for 5-10 minutes in the air fryer at 180° C.
6. Once the cheese has melted, remove the omelet from the air fryer and sprinkle with basil leaves.

188. SPINACH AND GINGER SMOOTHIE

INGREDIENTS

- 50 g spinach
- 2 tbsp soy yogurt
- 1 tsp grated ginger
- ½ banana
- ½ avocado
- 2 tsp maple syrup alternatively a little Xucker
- Water as needed

INSTRUCTIONS

1. Rinse and read the spinach
2. Rub the ginger
3. Cut the avocado in half and spoon out the pulp and place in a blender together with the other INGREDIENTS
4. Mix everything briefly and gradually fill with water until the desired consistency is achieved.

189. ROLLMOPS

INGREDIENTS

- 10 herrings
- 800 ml water
- 60 ml vinegar
- 5 tbsp of Xucker
- 2 small red onions
- 2 bay leaves
- 1 tbsp of mustard seeds
- 1-2 tbsp of sea salt
- Colorful pepper

INSTRUCTIONS

1. Shake pegs, cut off and remove the head. • Cut out the backbone with a sharp filleting knife. • Peel the onions, chop one of them, cut the other into rings.
2. Bring half of the chopped onion, water, vinegar, salt and Xucker to a boil for simmering in an air fryer. • Add the bay leaves and simmer on a low heat for about 30 minutes. • Let the brew cool to room temperature.

3. Place fish on a board with the skin down and pepper • fillets with the remaining chopped onion and roll up • fix herring with wooden skewers • layer the rollmops in a tall container and place the onion rings in between.
4. Pour rolling pots over in cold brew until they are completely covered with liquid • Close the container well and let the fish soak in the fridge for at least 2 days • Remove the Rollmops with pliers so that the brew does not start to mold • Dill goes well with the Rollmops.

190. CAPRESE SALAD WITH PARMA HAM

INGREDIENTS

- 2 tomatoes
- 2 handful of arugula
- 1 mozzarella
- 100 g Parma ham
- 30 g Parmesan
- 4 stems of basil
- 1 tbsp olive oil
- sea salt
- White pepper

INSTRUCTIONS

1. Wash and drain the tomatoes, basil and arugula • Slice the tomatoes • Remove the stems from the arugula
2. Stir the basil leaves from the stalk • Slice the mozzarella • Slice the ham into pieces.
3. Divide the arugula, tomatoes, mozzarella, and prosciutto into two plates, and cover with basil leaves
4. Parmesan over the salad • Season the salad with salt and pepper and drizzle with olive oil
5. Add a little bit of balsamic and serve.

191. Avocado Melon Coconut Smoothie

INGREDIENTS

- 1 avocado
- 100 g honeydew melon
- 2 tbsp of coconut oil
- 2 stalks of mint
- Water, at will

INSTRUCTIONS

1. Halve the avocado in half and remove the pulp with a spoon. • Cut the melon off the skin and place it in the blender together with the avocado and coconut oil.
2. Wash mint, drain and pour into the blender.
3. Puree everything, add some water as needed and make it more tender.

192. Low-Carb Almond Bar

INGREDIENTS

- 40 g almond flakes
- 30 g almonds
- 15 g ground almonds
- 1 tbsp honey
- 1 tbsp agave syrup
- 30 g butter
- 15 g oatmeal
- 10 g organic chia seeds
- 10 g coconut flakes
- ½ tsp cinnamon
- ½ tsp bourbon vanilla, ground
- 1 pinch of sea salt

INSTRUCTIONS

1. Melt butter, agave syrup and honey in an air fryer over low heat. • Chop almonds roughly. • Add cinnamon and vanilla to the pot and stir.
2. Crush almond leaves by hand and place them in a bowl. • Add oatmeal, ground and chopped almonds, chia seeds, coconut flakes and a pinch of sea salt and mix.
3. Pour the butter mixture into the bowl and stir it up. • Using the spatula, add the mixture of bars to a baking sheet lined with parchment paper. • Divide the dough into a rectangle approximately 1 cm in height.
4. Bake mix for 10-15 minutes in a preheated air fryer at 175° C.
5. Remove from the air fryer and allow the mass to cool slightly. • Cut the lukewarm dough into a 9 mm bar with a large knife. • Let the bar cool down on a grate and then store it in an airtight container.
6. A low-carb bar with almonds equals one serving and weighs about 15 g.

193. FRIED EGGS AND BACON

INGREDIENTS

- 2 eggs
- 2-3 slices of bacon
- ¼ red pepper
- ¼ green pepper
- 2 stems of parsley
- Bamboo salt
- pepper
- Sweet peppers
- 1 tbsp butter
- 1 tsp olive oil

INSTRUCTIONS

1. Chop the peppers roughly chop the parsley • Heat the butter and oil in an air fryer and fry the bacon crispy on both sides • Remove the bacon from the air fryer and drain on a kitchen towel.
2. Beat the eggs in the same air fryer and add the peppers.
3. Season the eggs and fry over medium heat. • Place the bacon on a plate, add the fried eggs on top and sprinkle with parsley.

194. Green Kiwi & Ginger Smoothie

INGREDIENTS

- 1 apple
- 2 kiwi
- grated ginger (as needed)
- 6-8 grapes
- Juice of a lime
- 2 tsp of agave syrup
- water

INSTRUCTIONS

1. Wash, quarter and core the apple • Peel and halve the kiwi • Peel and grate the ginger • Pick the grapes from the stalk, rinse and allow them to dry.
2. Put all the INGREDIENTS in a blender and finely puree. • Divide the green smoothie into three glasses and serve.

195. Tomato & Spring Onion Omelet

INGREDIENTS

- 6 eggs
- 1 shallot
- 2 spring onions
- 2 tomatoes
- 1 pinch of nutmeg
- 2 tbsp butter
- 1 tbsp olive oil
- Sea salt
- pepper

INSTRUCTIONS

1. Beat the eggs into a bowl, mix with the hand blender and salt and pepper • Peel the shallot and finely chop it • Clean the spring onion and cut into rings • Wash the tomatoes and cut them into pieces.
2. Melt butter and oil in an air fryer and sauté half of the shallots. • Add half of the egg mixture and cook over medium heat. • Add a few tomatoes and spring onions to the omelet.
3. Prepare the second omelet in the same way • To prevent the first omelet from cooling; it can be kept warm in the air fryer at 100° C. • Add freshly grated nutmeg to both omelets and serve.

196. Coconut Chia Pudding with Berries

INGREDIENTS

- 60 g chia seeds
- 500 ml coconut milk (alternatively almond or soy milk)
- 150 g raspberries and blueberries (fresh or frozen)
- 1 tsp agave syrup
- 1/2 tsp bourbon vanilla, ground

INSTRUCTIONS

1. Chia seeds, agave syrup and vanilla in a bowl and add coconut milk • Mix everything and let it swell for at least 30 minutes • Wash berries and drain well.
2. Divide the coconut-chia pudding into two glasses, • Halve the berries that are too large and then add them to the pudding.

197. Eel with Scrambled Eggs & Low-Carb Bread

INGREDIENTS

- 200 g smoked eel
- 4 slices of low-carb bread
- 4 eggs
- 1 shallot
- 2 stalks dill
- 1 tbsp oil
- sea salt
- White pepper

INSTRUCTIONS

1. Put the eggs in a bowl and add salt and pepper • Peel the shallot and finely chop it • Chop the dill roughly. • Remove the eel skin and cut into pieces of the same size.
2. Heat the oil in air fryer and simmer the shallot. • Pour the eggs in, let them stand, and pull them through the air fryer several times with the spatula, reducing the heat slightly. • Add the dill and stir again briefly.
3. Split the scrambled eggs into four slices of low-carb bread and top with the pieces of eel. • Add some fresh dill and serve.

198. PARMESAN, PEPPER AND OLIVE OMELET

INGREDIENTS

- 2 eggs
- 1 tomato
- 1 handful of arugula
- 2 tbsp of black olives, pitted
- 50 g Parmesan
- 50 g Gouda
- ¼ red pepper
- 1 tbsp olive oil
- Sea salt
- White pepper

INSTRUCTIONS

1. Put the eggs in a bowl and season with salt and pepper • Wash the tomatoes and peppers, drain briefly and then cut into pieces • Wash the arugula and leave to dry on a kitchen towel.
2. Grate Parmesan and Gouda • Heat the oil in an air fryer and add the eggs • Once the eggs have stabilized, add the tomato, pepper, olives, Gouda and Parmesan
3. Bake the omelet for 10 minutes in a preheated air fryer at 170° C.
4. Remove the air fryer out of the air fryer and add the arugula.

199. Fried Egg with Broccoli & Paprika

INGREDIENTS

- 3 eggs
- 3-4 broccoli florets
- ½ red pepper
- 1 tsp butter
- 1 tsp of coconut oil
- some parsley
- Sea salt
- White pepper

INSTRUCTIONS

1. Cut the peppers into small cubes • Halve broccoli florets if necessary. • Wash parsley and drain.
2. Heat coconut oil and butter in an air fryer and sauté paprika with broccoli in it. • Beat the eggs and add to the hot air fryer. • Reduce the heat and fry for several minutes.
3. Season the fried eggs with salt and pepper • Pluck the parsley from the stalk and pour over the eggs and the vegetables.

200. Mushroom & Onion Omelet

INGREDIENTS

- 6 eggs
- 2 tbsp cream
- 10-12 mushrooms
- ½ small onion
- 2 tbsp butter
- 1 tbsp olive oil
- 8-10 stems of chives
- Sea salt & pepper

INSTRUCTIONS

1. Beat eggs in a bowl • Add cream, salt, and pepper and whisk • Cut onion into strips • Clean mushrooms and slice • Cut chives into rings.
2. Melt the butter and olive oil in an air fryer and fry the mushrooms. • Remove the mushrooms and set aside. • Pour half of the mixture into the hot air fryer and fry over medium heat, then • Prepare the second omelet in the same way.

3. Put the mushrooms and onions on an omelet and fold them together. • Sprinkle the omelet with chives and serve.

201. Chia Coconut Pudding with Raspberries
INGREDIENTS

- 60 g chia seeds
- 500 ml coconut milk (alternatively almond or soy milk)
- 150 g raspberries (fresh or frozen)
- 1 kiwi
- 2-3 stems of fresh mint
- 1 tsp agave syrup

INSTRUCTIONS

1. Wash the raspberries and puree about 2/3 of them in the blender. • Add the chia seeds to the milk and stir until no more lumps are visible. • Mix the raspberry puree and agave syrup to the chia pudding.
2. Swell the chia pudding for at least 30 minutes, preferably in the refrigerator overnight. • Peel and chop the kiwi. • Chop mint roughly and mix with the kiwi. • Put fruit on the chia pudding and garnish with mint leaves.

202. Grilled Eggplant with Feta & Cherry Tomatoes
INGREDIENTS

- 1 eggplant
- 10-12 cherry tomatoes
- 100 g feta
- 2-3 stems of basil
- 3 tbsp olive oil
- 1 tbsp pine nuts
- 1 dash of lemon juice
- Himalayan salt
- pepper

INSTRUCTIONS

1. Wash eggplant, clean it, cut it into slices of about 5 mm thick and sprinkle it with salt • Leave eggplant slices to soak for 30 minutes, then dab dry.
2. Wash tomatoes and halve • Crumble feta • Wash basil leaves and pluck from the stem • Fry the pitted seeds in a hot air fryer without oil.
3. Season each eggplant slice, pepper, and drizzle with a little olive oil. • Grill the slices in an air fryer until golden brown. • Arrange with tomatoes, feta, pine nuts, and basil and serve.

203. Tomatoes, Peppers, & Ham Omelet
INGREDIENTS

- 2-3 eggs
- 1 tomato
- 2 gherkins
- ¼ red pepper
- ¼ green pepper
- 2 slices of ham
- 1 tsp oregano, rubbed
- Sea salt & pepper
- 1 tbsp olive oil

INSTRUCTIONS

1. Cut the tomato, cucumber, and pepper into small pieces • Dice the ham • Beat the eggs, place in a bowl and whisk • Season the egg mixture with salt and pepper.
2. Heat the oil in an air fryer • Sauté the vegetables with ham . Pour egg mass into the air fryer and fry over medium heat.
3. Add the vegetables and ham to the omelet and season with oregano, salt, and pepper • Fold over one half of an omelet, place gently on a plate and enjoy.

204. Melon Salad with Ham & Herbs
INGREDIENTS

- 1 cantaloupe
- 4 slices of cooked ham
- 3-4 small mozzarella balls
- 1-2 stalks of mint
- 1-2 stems basil
- 1-2 stems of parsley

INSTRUCTIONS

1. Halve the melon and use the ball cutter to remove the melon balls. • Wash and chop the herbs.
2. Arrange melon and herbs in two bowls and add mozzarella • Place the ham on the salad and serve.

205. Arugula Salad with Colorful Tomatoes
INGREDIENTS

- 1 red tomato
- 1 yellow tomato
- 60 g mozzarella
- 50 g arugula
- 1 tsp roasted sesame
- 1 tbsp balsamic

INSTRUCTIONS

1. Wash the arugula, let it dry and remove stalks that are too long • Wash the tomatoes and cut into small pieces • Slice the mozzarella.
2. Roast sesame in a hot air fryer until golden-brown. • Arrange the arugula, tomatoes, and mozzarella on a plate and sprinkle with sesame seeds. • Add balsamic as desired.

206. Raspberry Banana Coconut Smoothie
INGREDIENTS

- 50 g raspberries, fresh
- 70 g banana
- 250 ml soy drink, organic
- 150 ml tap water
- 1 tbsp coconut oil
- 1 tsp cinnamon, ground
- 1 stalk of mint

INSTRUCTIONS

1. Add raspberries, banana, mint, and water to the blender and puree. • Add soy drink, coconut oil, and cinnamon and mix again.
2. Divide the smoothie into two glasses and garnish with mint and berries as desired.

207. Avocado Salmon Rolls

INGREDIENTS

- 2 avocados
- 4-8 slices of smoked salmon, wild catch
- 1 organic lemon
- 2 tomatoes
- Sea salt
- pink berries
- Balsamic
- 8-10 bars of chives

INSTRUCTIONS

1. Halve the avocados, remove each core and cut crosswise with a knife • Cut the tomatoes • Halve the lemon and cut one half into thin shells.
2. Pour pepper in a mortar and sprinkle it into the avocado halves. • Roll up the salmon and place it in the avocado hollow. • Make lemon zest from the second half of the lemon with the grater and sprinkle over the salmon.
3. Add the tomato and lemon to the salmon and garnish with chives and pink berries. • Sprinkle with balsamic as desired.

208. Spinach, Strawberry & Avocado Salad

INGREDIENTS

- 200 g spinach
- 4 large strawberries
- 100 g avocado
- 2 tsp black sesame
- Sea salt
- pepper
- 2 tbsp balsamic-

INSTRUCTIONS

1. Wash spinach, drain and remove stalks too long • Wash strawberries, remove green stem and quarter.
2. Halve the avocado, peel it off and cut into strips. • Spread the spinach leaves, strawberries, and avocado on two plates and season with salt and pepper. • Sprinkle with sesame and sprinkle with balsamic as desired.

209. Hot Salmon Snacks with Cream Cheese & Cucumber

INGREDIENTS

- 3 slices of low-carb bread
- 100 g smoked salmon in slices, wild catch
- 2 tbsp cream cheese
- 2 tsp horseradish
- 6 cucumber slices
- freshly squeezed lemon juice
- 2 stalks dill
- chili flakes
- Colorful pepper
- Sea salt

INSTRUCTIONS

1. Mix the cream cheese with the horseradish and spread on the low-carb bread. • Place the cucumber slices on the cream cheese.
2. Put salmon on top and sprinkle with salt, pepper and chili flakes. • Dill small, spread on the appetizers and drizzle each with a little lemon.

210. Blueberry Yogurt Cream

INGREDIENTS

- 125 g blueberries
- 400 soya yogurt
- 1 Bourbon vanilla pod
- 1 egg (only the protein)
- 1 tsp Xucker

INSTRUCTIONS

1. Wash and drain the blueberries • Cut the vanilla pod lengthways and scrape out the pith with a knife.
2. Puree the yogurt, vanilla, xucker, and ¾ of the blueberries with the hand blender • Beat the egg whites until stiff and fold under the cream.
3. Fill the blueberry yogurt cream in bowls, garnish with the remaining blueberries and serve.

211. Strawberry Vanilla Shake

INGREDIENTS

- 150 g strawberries
- 25 g Gluten Free & Vegan Vanilla Protein Powder
- 100 g soy yogurt
- 200 ml water

INSTRUCTIONS

1. Wash the strawberries and remove the stem.
2. Put the INGREDIENTS into the blender and finely puree.
3. Divide the shake into two glasses and chill.

212. Pickled Salmon with Avocado

INGREDIENTS

- 300 g pickled salmon
- 1 avocado
- 1 shallot
- 3-4 stalks Dill
- 1 organic lemon
- Sea salt
- White pepper

INSTRUCTIONS

1. Rinse the salmon and dab the salmon into fresh pieces. Season with salt and pepper and lemon juice. • Peel the shallot and finely dice. • Dill the dill and the shallots under the salmon.
2. Halve the avocado, remove the pulp with the tbsp and cut into thin strips • Drizzle the avocado with salt and lemon juice.
3. Place the dressing ring on a plate, first distribute half of the avocado in the ring. • Then distribute half of the salmon over the avocado in the dressing ring. • Repeat for the second serving.

213. Fruit Salad

INGREDIENTS

- 3 tbsp of strawberries
- 3 tbsp blueberries

- 2 tbsp blackberries
- 1 tbsp pineapple, fresh
- 1 tbsp red grapes
- ½ green kiwi

INSTRUCTIONS

1. Wash berries and grapes and drain in the strainer • Remove strawberries from the stalk and cut in half
2. Peel kiwi and cut into pieces • Peel pineapple and cut into pieces
3. Put everything in a bowl or on a large plate and enjoy fresh.

214. Fresh Chanterelle Omelet

INGREDIENTS

For the chanterelles
- 200 g fresh chanterelles
- 1 shallot
- 1/2 bunch chives
- 1 tbsp butter
- 1 clove of garlic
- 1/2 tsp thyme, rubbed
- Sea salt & pepper
- 1 tsp olive oil
- 1 tbsp. fresh cream

For the omelet
- 6 eggs
- 2 tbsp cream
- 1 tsp butter
- Sea salt & pepper
- nutmeg
- 1 tbsp olive oil

INSTRUCTIONS

1. Brush mushrooms • Peel and finely chop the shallot and garlic • Rinse chives and cut into rings • Melt butter in an air fryer and fry the shallot and garlic • Add mushrooms, thyme and olive oil, stir and fry for a short time.
2. Whisk eggs and cream with a hand blender in a tall container and season to taste with salt and pepper. • Heat butter in an air fryer.
3. Add the egg mixture, place the lid on top and let the mixture stand for 8-10 minutes over low heat.
4. Grate the fresh nutmeg on the omelet and coat with fresh cream. • Put the mushrooms on the omelet, sprinkle with chives and serve

215. HAZELNUT MUFFINS

INGREDIENTS

- 500 g low-fat quark
- 50 g hazelnut sauce
- 4 eggs
- 30 g coconut flour
- 75 g vanilla protein powder
- 75 g erythritol
- 2 tsp of tartar baking powder
- 125 g oat bran
- 100 g powder-Xucker

INSTRUCTIONS

1. Put the coconut flour, protein powder, erythritol, baking powder, and bran in a large bowl and mix. • Add the quark, hazelnut, and eggs and mix with a hand mixer to a dough.
2. Lay the muffin dish with paper baking cups and divide the dough evenly • bake muffins in a preheated air fryer at 175° C circulating air for about 30 minutes

3. After about 20 minutes of baking time, stick them in the muffins with a wooden stick and test whether dough remains sticky.
4. Allow muffins to cool after baking.
5. Put powder Xucker in a small colander and sprinkle over the muffins.

216. Vegetable Sticks with Dip

INGREDIENTS

- 50 g organic cucumber
- 1 celery stick
- 1 carrot
- 4 cherry tomatoes
- 2 radishes
- For the dip
- 50 ml soy yogurt
- 50 g quark
- 1 tbsp fresh lemon juice
- dill
- Sea salt
- Colorful pepper
- nutmeg
- chili flakes

INSTRUCTIONS

1. Wash the cucumber, cut in half and cut into long strips. • Clean the celery stick and cut it into long strips.
2. Peel the carrot and cut into thin strips • Clean and quarter the radishes, wash the tomatoes and drain.
3. Mix quark, soy yogurt and lemon juice together in a bowl • Add the dill tips, salt, pepper, nutmeg and some of the chili flakes and mix.
4. Put vegetables on a large plate or in a pourable tin and enjoy together with the dip.

217. Strawberry & Melon Coconut Shake

INGREDIENTS

- 100 g strawberries
- 50 g watermelon
- 100 ml coconut milk
- 1 tbsp coconut oil
- 200 ml water

INSTRUCTIONS

1. Rinse the strawberries and cut the stalk • Cut the melon from the bowl
2. Add both to the blender, add water, coconut milk, and liquid coconut oil and mix until a smooth shake is obtained. If necessary, add a few ice cubes to the shake and serve.

218. Melon Salad with Cucumber

INGREDIENTS

- 200 g watermelon
- 2 small organic cucumbers
- 10 g almonds
- 1 lime
- 4 stalks of fresh mint

INSTRUCTIONS

1. Chop the watermelon into small cubes • Rinse the cucumbers and slice them • Chop the almonds • Rinse mint and pluck the leaves • Quarter the lime.
2. Arrange all the INGREDIENTS on 2 plates, add a little lime juice and serve.

219. Vanilla Cream with Blueberries & Redcurrants

INGREDIENTS

- 200 g quark
- 200 g soy yogurt
- 100 ml cream
- Mark a bourbon vanilla pod
- Powder Xucker
- 50 g blueberries
- 50 g redcurrants
- 25 g pistachios
- 1 organic lime

INSTRUCTIONS

1. Put the cream in a tall beaker and whip with an electric whisk. Halve the vanilla pod lengthways and carefully scrape out the pith with the back of the knife. Chop the pistachios. Wash and rinse the berries. Wash the lime and rub the skin.
2. Put the quark, soy yogurt, powder-sugar and the vanilla in a bowl. • Carefully lift the whipped cream and lime grated underneath and smooth.
3. Divide the vanilla cream into small bowls, add the berries and the chopped pistachios as a topping.

220. Scrambled Eggs with Bacon & Chives

INGREDIENTS

- 4 eggs
- 3 tbsp cream
- 3 tbsp mineral water
- 2 slices of bacon
- 1/2 cucumber
- nutmeg
- Bamboo salt
- White pepper
- 1/2 bunch chives
- 2 tsp butter

INSTRUCTIONS

1. Whisk eggs, cream and mineral water in a tall container with the hand blender • Season with salt and pepper • Wash chives and cut into fine rolls • Wash the cucumber and cut it into slices.
2. Cut the bacon into small pieces. • Put the butter in a coated air fryer and sauté the bacon for a short time, remove it and drain it on a paper towel.
3. Add the remaining butter to the air fryer, add the egg mixture and cook over medium heat. Pull the egg mixture several times from the edge of the air fryer to the center with a spatula. • Just before the scrambled eggs are ready, add the bacon.
4. Rub fresh nutmeg over it and serve.

221. Zucchini Omelet Cake

INGREDIENTS

For the omelets

- 20 eggs
- 100 ml cream

- 100 ml mineral water
- 60 g butter
- 1 tbsp olive oil

For the zucchini filling

- 300 g zucchini
- 300 g cream cheese
- 200 g grated Gouda
- 2 spring onions
- 1 clove of garlic
- 1 bunch of parsley
- sea salt
- White pepper
- nutmeg

INSTRUCTIONS

1. Mix eggs, cream, and mineral water with a hand blender, whisk in a tall jug, season with salt and pepper, if necessary work in multiple layers • In an air fryer some butter and heat oil-egg mixture to give to cover the air fryer and the egg mixture over low heat Let it set for 6-8 minutes. • Repeat this process until you have 5-6 omelets out of it. • Let the finished omelets cool down on a paper towel.
2. Wash zucchini and grate with a grater • Wash spring onion, cut into fine rings and chop finely • Peel and squeeze garlic • Wash the parsley and finely chop.
3. Put the cream cheese in a bowl, add the cheese, zucchini, spring onion, garlic, and parsley and mix well to make nice cream. • Season with salt, pepper, and nutmeg.
4. Take an omelet, coat it with the zucchini cream and layer the next omelet over it. Repeat this process until everything is used up.
5. Cut the zucchini omelet cake into pieces and serve.

222. Cottage Cheese & Radish Stuffed Peppers

INGREDIENTS

- 1 red pepper
- 200 g cottage cheese
- 100 g radish
- 5-6 stems of chives
- Bamboo salt
- White pepper

INSTRUCTIONS

1. Wash the peppers, cut in half and remove the seeds. • Wash the radishes, cut into quarters and cut into thin slices. • Rinse the chives, shake dry and cut into fine rings.
2. Put cream cheese in a bowl, add radishes, chives, salt and pepper, and mix.
3. Spread the cream cheese mixture into the halves of the pepper and serve.

223. Ham & Zucchini Omelet

INGREDIENTS

- 6 eggs
- 2 tbsp cream
- 100 g zucchini
- 100 g cooked ham
- 3 cherry tomatoes
- Salad, of your choice
- Himalayan salt
- White pepper
- 1 tbsp butter
- 1 tsp olive oil

INSTRUCTIONS

1. Wash the zucchini and cut into tiny slices • Cut the ham into thin strips • Halve the cherry tomatoes • Wash and read the salad.
2. Whisk the eggs and the cream with a hand-held blender in a tall container, season with salt and pepper. • Heat the butter in air fryer. • Add the egg mixture, zucchini and ham strips, place the lid on top and let the mixture stand for 8-10 minutes over low heat,
3. Arrange the salad on a plate, add the omelet and serve.

224. Vegetarian Omelet

INGREDIENTS

- 6 eggs
- 4 brown mushrooms
- 2 tomatoes
- 1 spring onion
- 1 clove of garlic
- ½ red onion
- 8 stems of parsley
- 2 tbsp cream
- 2 tbsp butter
- Sea salt
- pepper

INSTRUCTIONS

1. Wash tomatoes and dice • Wash spring onions and cut into pieces • Brush mushrooms and slice • Peel garlic and finely dice • Wash parsley, shake dry and finely chop.
2. Eggs, cream with a hand blender, whisk in a tall jug, season with salt and pepper • Heat butter-egg mixture in the air fryer over low heat for 8-10 minutes.
3. Add the vegetables to half of the omelet 3-4 minutes before the end of cooking and allow to cook for a short time. Fold the omelet and serve on a large plate.

225. Chia Seed Gel with Pomegranate & Nuts

INGREDIENTS

- 120 ml almond milk
- 4 tbsp chia seeds
- 20 g hazelnuts
- 20 g walnuts
- 4 tbsp of pomegranate seeds
- 1 splash of lime juice
- 1 tsp agave syrup

INSTRUCTIONS

1. Finely chop the nuts • Mix the Chia seeds with the almond milk, stir and let them swell for about 10 to 20 minutes
2. Stir Chia seed gel occasionally, stir in just before serving. Agave syrup.
3. When the Chia Seed Gel is thickened, add 2 tbsp chia gel in a dessert glass
4. Layer the chopped nuts on top and cover with a spoonful of chia gel and sprinkle the pomegranate seeds over them.

226. Tomato & Egg Salad

INGREDIENTS

- 4 eggs
- 2 tomatoes
- nutmeg
- Himalayan salt
- Colorful pepper
- 2-3 stems dill

For the dressing
- 60 g yogurt
- 1 lemon
- 1 tsp Xucker
- 1 tbsp light balsamic vinegar

INSTRUCTIONS

1. Boil, peel, and quarter eggs.
2. Wash tomatoes and cut into small boat • Pound pepper and salt in a mortar, mix with nutmeg
3. Mix yogurt with 1 tsp fresh lemon juice, balsamic and Xucker.
4. Arrange the eggs and tomatoes in a bowl.
5. Add the dressing and the spice mixture, garnish with dill tips.

227. Blueberry Milkshake with Mint & Cocoa

INGREDIENTS

- 80 g blueberries
- 30 g raspberries
- 200 ml soy milk
- 200 g soy yogurt
- 4 stalks of fresh mint
- 20 g cocoa nibs
- 1 tsp fresh lime juice
- 1 tsp of coconut oil

INSTRUCTIONS

1. Washing blueberries • Finely chop cocoa nibs with a knife • Remove the leaves from 2 sprigs of mints and chop finely.
2. Put soy milk, soy yogurt, lime juice, cocoa nibs, the chopped mint leaves, and coconut oil in a shaker and mix everything.
3. Arrange in two glasses, sprinkle with cocoa nibs and serve with mint.

228. Mediterranean Tomato Omelet

INGREDIENTS

- 6 eggs
- 2 tbsp cream
- 10 cherry tomatoes
- 60 g feta
- 1 spring onion
- 6 stalks of parsley
- Sea salt & pepper
- 2 tbsp butter
- 1 tbsp olive oil

INSTRUCTIONS

1. Wash tomatoes and quarter • Dice feta • Wash parsley, wedge dry and chop finely • Wash spring onions and cut them into rings.
4. Eggs, cream with a hand blender, whisk in a tall jug, season with salt and pepper • Heat butter-egg mixture in the air fryer over low heat for 8-10 minutes.

2. Add the oil to a second air fryer, heat • Add the cherry tomatoes and then add the spring onion, season with salt and pepper • Remove the heat, add the feta and stir everything.
3. Add the tomato-feta salad to the omelet and fold it up.

229. Zucchini Buffer with Salmon & Poached Egg

INGREDIENTS

- 200 g zucchini
- 3 eggs
- 100 g cream cheese
- 30 g Parmesan
- 30 g young spinach
- 50 g smoked salmon
- Sea salt & pepper
- 5 tbsp organic sunflower oil
- 1 tbsp organic apple cider vinegar

INSTRUCTIONS

1. Preheat air fryer to 120° C (top bottom heat) • Wash zucchini, cut ends and grate coarsely • Extract zucchini with a dishcloth • Mix zucchini, 1 egg yolk, cream cheese, grated parmesan, salt and pepper in a bowl • Wash spinach, pat dry and set aside.
2. Heat the oil in an air fryer. • Form the zucchini mass into two larger buffers by hand and fry in the hot oil until golden brown for 1 to 2 minutes. • Remove the zucchini buffer from the air fryer, pat dry with a kitchen towel and bake in the air fryer.
3. Heat the water in a small air fryer • Add the apple cider vinegar to the hot water and stir with a spoon, remove the pot from the plate • Put an egg in a cup and then carefully put in the hot water, put the pot back on the stove and the egg Simmer for 3 minutes in water • Repeat the process with the second egg.
4. Arrange the zucchini buffer on a plate, cover with spinach, smoked salmon and the poached egg. • Cut the egg shortly before consumption.

230. Chia Power Yogurt with Fresh Fruit

INGREDIENTS

- 200 g soy yogurt
- 100 g cottage cheese
- 50 g blackberries
- 70 g raspberries
- 3 tbsp chia seeds
- 3 tbsp sunflower seeds
- 3 tbsp pumpkin seeds
- 1 tbsp of goji berries
- 1 lime
- 3 tbsp xucker

INSTRUCTIONS

1. Mix yogurt, cottage cheese, Xucker and about half of the raspberries and blackberries with a hand blender puree and season with some fresh lime juice.
2. Fill the yogurt mixture into bowls and add the remaining berries, chia seeds, sunflower seeds, pumpkin seeds, and goji berries to the yogurt.

231. Berry Fruit Drink

INGREDIENTS

- 200 ml soy drink
- 200 ml water

- 70 g berry mix, fresh or frozen
- 1 tsp fresh lemon juice
- 1 tsp agave syrup
- fresh mint

INSTRUCTIONS

1. Soy drink, water, berries, lemon juice in a blender and mix everything until all the fruits are minced.
2. Season with agave syrup and fresh mint.

232. Scrambled Eggs with Tomatoes & Ham

INGREDIENTS

- 4 eggs
- 3 tbsp cream
- 3 tbsp mineral water
- 2 tomatoes
- 4 slices of cooked ham
- 4 stems of parsley
- Sea salt
- pepper
- 1 tsp butter

INSTRUCTIONS

1. Whisk eggs, cream and mineral water with the hand blender in a tall container.
2. Season with salt and pepper.
3. Wash the tomatoes, quarter them, remove the inside and then cut into small pieces • Dice the ham • Wash the parsley, wedge it dry and finely chop it.
4. Pour some butter into an air fryer and heat
5. Put the egg mass in the air fryer and let it heat over medium heat, then use a spatula to pull the egg mixture several times from the edge of the air fryer to the center • Add the tomato pieces and ham.

233. Lavender Blueberry Chia Seed Pudding

INGREDIENTS

- 200 ml almond milk, unsweetened
- 2 tbsp chia seeds
- 100 g blueberries
- 50 g soy yogurt
- 70 g organic cottage cheese
- 2 tsp of agave syrup
- 2 tsp lavender
- 30 g hazelnuts

INSTRUCTIONS

1. Boil almond milk with lavender, then simmer for 10 minutes at low temperature, then allow to cool.
2. Add the blueberries to the cooled milk and puree. • Mix almond-lavender milk with chia seeds and agave syrup • Leave to soak in the fridge for one hour.
3. Mix the yogurt and cottage cheese and add mass to the blueberry chia seeds.
4. Add the lavender blueberry chia seeds to the pudding. • Finely chop the hazelnuts with the knife and add as a topping.

234. Raspberry Buttermilk Smoothie

INGREDIENTS

- 200 ml buttermilk
- 200 ml water
- 60 g raspberries, fresh
- 1/2 tsp fresh lemon juice
- grated ginger
- 2 tsp of agave syrup
- 2 stems of fresh mint

INSTRUCTIONS

1. Wash raspberries • Add the buttermilk, raspberries, lemon juice and agave syrup to the blender and puree to a mush.
2. Peel the ginger and finely grate, then add to the raspberry puree.
3. Fill up with water and mix.
4. Fill with glasses and arrange with fresh mint.

235. Chia Seeds with Mango & Blueberries

INGREDIENTS

- 300 ml coconut milk
- 2 tbsp chia seeds
- 1/2 mango
- 50 g blueberries
- 1 tsp agave syrup
- 1 Bourbon vanilla pod

INSTRUCTIONS

1. Halve the vanilla pod and carefully scrape off the vanilla pulp with a spoon.
2. Warm the coconut milk with vanilla pulp and agave syrup and add the chia seeds.
3. Leave to soak in the fridge for at least 2 hours (preferably overnight).
4. Wash blueberries
5. Peel the mango and cut half into small cubes.
6. Mix the mango and blueberries with the chia pudding. • Divide everything into 4 glasses and serve.

236. BROCCOLI FRITTATA

INGREDIENTS

- 1 head of broccoli
- 8 eggs
- 100 ml milk
- 200 ml whipped cream
- 50 g Parmesan
- nutmeg
- Sea salt
- pepper

INSTRUCTIONS

1. Set the air fryer to 180° C • Wash the broccoli and divide into small florets
2. Peel the stems and cut into thin slices • Whisk the eggs with milk and cream and season with salt, pepper, and nutmeg.
3. Place the broccoli in an air fryer-proof air fryer and pour over the egg-and-cream mixture.
4. Cook in the 180° C air fryer for about 20-30 minutes. After 10 minutes, sprinkle the Parmesan over it.

237. Low-Carb Vanilla Muffins

INGREDIENTS

- 200 g organic almond flour, partially oiled
- 75 g butter
- 4 eggs free range
- 1 vanilla pod
- 1 tsp tartar baking powder
- 1 pinch of salt
- 40-50 g Tucker
- dark chocolate 85%

INSTRUCTIONS

1. Cut the vanilla pod then scrape out the pith with a knife. • Melt the butter in a small air fryer. • Chop the chocolate.
2. Separate eggs • Whisk egg whites and Xucker in a bowl until fluffy • Mix egg yolks and liquid butter • Then add flour, baking powder and vanilla seeds and stir.
3. Add the meringue dough and chocolate to the dough and fold into it.
4. Fill muffin dough into 12 small molds and bake at 160° C in the preheated air fryer for 15-20 minutes.

238. Low-Carb Chocolate Chip Biscuits

INGREDIENTS

- 200 g organic almond flour
- 125 g butter
- 80 g Xucker
- 50 g dark chocolate 85%
- 1 egg
- 1 vanilla pod
- 1/2 packet of tartar baking powder
- 1 pinch of bamboo salt

INSTRUCTIONS

1. Remove butter from the fridge to soften it. • Cut the vanilla pod lengthways and scrape out the pith with a knife. • Place the butter, xucker and vanilla pod in a bowl and beat until fluffy with a hand mixer, then add the egg and stir.
2. Add the flour, baking powder and salt and mix. • Chop the chocolate and add to the dough. • Knead the dough with your hands.
3. Preheat the air fryer to 180° C. • Form the dough into hazelnut-sized balls with your hands and place it on a baking sheet lined with parchment paper. • Press the dough balls lightly flat on the tin.
4. Bake for 10-15 minutes. • When the baking time is over, allow the biscuits to cool.

239. Low-Carb Air Fryer Cakes with Blueberries

INGREDIENTS

- 65 g protein powder
- 1 egg
- ½ tsp tartar baking powder
- 3-4 tbsp water
- 50 g fresh blueberries
- 1 tbsp coconut oil

INSTRUCTIONS

1. Wash blueberries and drain in a colander. • Place blueberries in a bowl and set aside.
2. Mix all remaining INGREDIENTS in a bowl with the hand mixer to a smooth dough.

3. Heat the coconut oil in a non-stick air fryer and bake a small ladle of dough in succession. • The small air fryer cakes are baked quickly, so only fry briefly on both sides.
4. Stack ready-made air fryer cakes and garnish with blueberries • The dough yields about 6 small low-carb air fryer cakes.

240. Strawberry-Orange-Mint Smoothie

INGREDIENTS

- 300 g strawberries
- 200 ml water
- 100 ml orange juice, freshly squeezed
- Ice cream, crushed ice

INSTRUCTIONS

1. Wash strawberries, clean and drain • 4-6 Cut the strawberries into small cubes and set aside • Wash mint, dry and lightly beat against the kitchen worktop, so that the mint leaves all its aroma, then pluck the leaves.
2. Put strawberries, orange juice and water in a shaker and mix everything
3. Fill a few mints leaves together with the ice into 4 glasses and then fill up with the smoothie • Use strawberry cubes and a few mints leaves as a topping and serve immediately.

241. Melon Shake

INGREDIENTS

- 800 g watermelon
- 2 tbsp lime juice
- 500 ml mineral water medium
- ice cubes

INSTRUCTIONS

1. Slice the melon, roughly chop the pulp, add to the blender and puree.
2. Add the lime juice and mineral water and mix everything.
3. Put the ice cubes in the glasses and pour in the melon shake, attach half a slice of lime to each glass and serve.

242. Tomato, Cheese & Basil Omelet

INGREDIENTS

- 6 eggs
- 2 tomatoes
- 30 g Gouda
- 1 bunch of basil
- Mineral water
- 30 g butter
- Sea salt & pepper

INSTRUCTIONS

1. Heat the air fryer to 160° C. • Beat the eggs and whisk them into a large bowl with a little mineral water, salt and pepper. • Wash the tomatoes and cut them into thin slices. • Wash the basil, shake dry and cut into thin strips. • Rub the Gouda.

2. Heat a coated air fryer with a little butter and oil, then add the egg mass and let it set. Spread the slices of tomato on the omelet, add the grated cheese and place in the pre-cooked air fryer for about 10 minutes.
3. Sprinkle with basil and serve.

242. Chocolate Muffins with Strawberries

INGREDIENTS

- 250 g strawberries
- 150 g almond flour, de-oiled
- 3 eggs
- 100 g dark chocolate 70%
- 2 tbsp of curd cheese
- 1 tsp tartar baking powder
- 2 tbsp butter
- 2 tsp organic cocoa, de-oiled
- Xucker to taste

INSTRUCTIONS

1. Preheat the air fryer to 180° C. • Place the chocolate and butter in a bowl and melt over a hot water bath.
2. Separate the eggs and beat the egg whites with a whisk until frothy.
3. Mix the flour, baking powder, xucker and yolks with the chocolate-butter mixture. • Add the egg whites and skimmed curd cheese and mix with an electric mixer.
4. Put the muffin cups in a muffin tin and fill with dough. • Bake the muffins for 25-30 minutes in the preheated air fryer. • Clean and wash the strawberries.
5. Let the muffins cool, then sprinkle with the cocoa powder and serve with the strawberries.

243. Strawberries On Spinach Leaves

INGREDIENTS

- 300 g young spinach leaves
- 250 g strawberries
- 1 tbsp sesame seeds
- Balsamic cream

INSTRUCTIONS

1. Wash spinach, spin dry and divide into 4 small bowls • Wash strawberries, cut in half, place on spinach leaves and garnish with balsamic cream as desired.
2. Place sesame seeds in a non-stick air fryer and lightly roast, then add to the spinach and strawberries.

244. Low-Carb Strawberry Dessert

INGREDIENTS

- 500 g fresh strawberries
- fresh mint leaves
- star anise
- 1 tbsp Xucker
- 1 lemon

INSTRUCTIONS

1. Rinse the strawberries and then drain in a colander. • Remove the green and cut the strawberries into thin slices. • Wash and dry the mint. • Remove the mint leaves from the stalk and add to the strawberries.
2. Rub a little star anise over the strawberries • Add Xucker and a few drops of lemon and stir.

245. Cottage Cheese & Blueberry Cream with Fresh Mint

INGREDIENTS

- 200 g cottage cheese
- 100 g soy yogurt
- 50 g blueberries
- 1 tsp Xucker
- fresh mint
- 1 lime

INSTRUCTIONS

1. Whisk the soy yogurt, Xucker, a few mint leaves and 3/4 of the blueberries.
2. Mix the cottage cheese with the blueberry and yogurt mixture and carefully fold in the remaining blueberries with a spoon. • Season the cream with a little lime juice.
3. Divide everything into 2 small bowls and garnish with fresh mint.

246. Scrambled Eggs with Chives & Nutmeg

INGREDIENTS

- 8 eggs
- 3 tbsp soy milk
- 3 tbsp mineral water
- 1/2 bunch chives
- nutmeg
- Sea salt & pepper (mill)

INSTRUCTIONS

1. Whisk eggs, milk and mineral water in a bowl with a fork. • Season with salt and pepper.
2. Pour the egg mass into a coated air fryer and let it stand at low heat, using a spatula to pull it several times from the edge of the air fryer to the center through the egg mass.
3. Season the eggs with a little nutmeg and serve with the chopped chives.

247. Zucchini Rolls with Cream Cheese & Salmon

INGREDIENTS

- 1 large zucchini
- 200 g cream cheese
- 150 g smoked organic salmon
- ½ bunch of chives
- a little horseradish
- 1 organic lemon
- sea salt
- White pepper

INSTRUCTIONS

1. Slice the zucchini lengthwise into slices approx. 5 mm thick. • Heat oil in air fryer and briefly fry the zucchini slices.
2. Pick some long chives and set aside to add to the zucchini rolls • Finely chop the chives, then mix with cream cheese, horseradish, salt and pepper
3. Coat the fried zucchini slices with fresh cheese mixture, put some salmon on top, roll up and tie together with chives. • Sprinkle with fresh lemon juice and serve.

248. Buttermilk Wild Berry Shake

INGREDIENTS

- 300 ml buttermilk
- 200 ml water
- 50 g blueberries
- 50 g blackberries
- Fresh mint
- 1 tsp Xucker

INSTRUCTIONS

1. Put the buttermilk and washed berries in a blender and mix everything to a shake.
2. Add the Xucker and a few mint leaves and mix everything once more.
3. Put buttermilk and berry shake into glasses and serve.

249. Soy Yogurt with Strawberries, Mango, Mint & Nuts

INGREDIENTS

- 300 g soy yogurt
- 150 g fresh strawberries
- 100 g fresh mango
- 2 stalks of mint
- 5 walnuts
- 5 almonds

INSTRUCTIONS

1. Wash the strawberries, remove the green, cut in half and cut out the stalk • Cut the strawberries into small bite-sized pieces • Peel the mango and cut into small cubes.
2. Chop walnuts and almonds and lightly roast in air fryer.
3. Put a layer of soy yogurt into a glass, then add strawberries, mango and nuts • Add another layer of yogurt and spread the remaining strawberries, mango pieces and nuts • Garnish with some mint and serve.

250. MUFFINS WITH BLUEBERRY ICING

INGREDIENTS

Muffins
- 100 g almond flour
- 100 g butter
- 50 g Xucker
- 2 eggs
- 1/2 tsp tartar baking powder
- a pinch of salt

Blueberry Cream
- 100 g whipped cream
- 50 g butter
- 150 blueberries
- 2 tsp of Xucker
- 1 vanilla pod

INSTRUCTIONS

1. Preheat air fryer to 170° C (circulating air). • Beat the butter until smooth with a pinch of salt until a creamy mixture has formed. • Mix the eggs one at a time. • Sift the almond flour and the tartar powder under the creamy mixture.
2. Fill the muffin cups 2/3 with the dough and bake for 13-15 minutes.
3. Wash the blueberries and set aside 12 of them for the garnish. • Crush the remainder of the blueberries with the blender and pass through a very fine sieve. • Bring the cream with Xucker and the pith of the vanilla pod to a boil, then add the blueberry puree and mix well until a smooth mass is obtained • Add the mass to the butter and homogenize with the blender • Leave the cream at room temperature for 4-5 hours until it has a syrup-like consistency
4. Mix the cream with a fork, fill it into a pastry bag with a star spout of your choice and place it on top of the cooled low-carb muffins. • Add another blueberry as a topping and serve.

251. Blueberry-Yogurt Smoothie with Mint

INGREDIENTS

- 50 g blueberries
- 300 g soy yogurt
- 100 g honeydew melon
- 6 sprigs of fresh mint

INSTRUCTIONS

1. Wash blueberries • Remove the honey melon from the skin and cut into small pieces • Wash the mint, shake dry and lightly beat over a side of the table, the mint unfolds its full aroma.
2. Put everything together in a blender, fill up with yogurt and water and mix.
3. Garnish with a little mint.

252. Fried Egg On Green Asparagus

INGREDIENTS

- 200 g green asparagus
- 2 eggs
- fresh water cress
- 2 tsp butter
- nutmeg
- Salt and pepper (mill)

INSTRUCTIONS

1. Peel the green asparagus if necessary and cut from the end 2-3 cm
2. Tie into two even bundles of kitchen yarn • Bring about 2 liters of water to boil, add salt, a little sugar and butter and cook the asparagus for 8-10 minutes.
3. Brush a coated air fryer with oil and roast two fried eggs in it.
4. Arrange the asparagus on the plates with a skimmer. • Add the fried eggs and season with nutmeg, salt, pepper and freshly cut water cress.

253. Low-Carb Strawberry Cake

INGREDIENTS

- 100 g almonds
- 200 g walnuts
- 200 g strawberries
- 1 tbsp coconut flakes
- 1 vanilla pod
- 1 orange
- 6 dates, pitted

INSTRUCTIONS

1. Chop almonds and walnuts with a mill until they are ground. • Squeeze orange and pour the juice into a measuring cup. • Cut the vanilla pod and scrape out the pith with a knife. • Put the vanilla pod and four pitted dates in the measuring cup and mix with a mixer until one creamy mixture is formed.
2. Pour the juice-date mixture into a bowl, add the ground nuts and coconut flakes, stir and form the dough into a ball. • Place the dough ball on a cake plate and roll out to a 1 cm thick bottom.
3. Wash strawberries, dry, remove green halve and halve • Place 2 dates and half of the strawberries in a measuring cup and finely puree with a blender
4. Spread fruit puree on the cake base • Put the pieces of strawberry on it and the cake is ready.

254. Low-Carb Chocolate Brownies

INGREDIENTS

- 150 g dark chocolate (at least 75%)
- 220 g butter
- 150 g almond flour
- 4 eggs
- 200 g Xucker
- 1 tbsp powdered sugar
- 20 g almonds
- 30 g of walnuts
- 3/4 rack of baking soda
- pinch of salt

INSTRUCTIONS

1. Preheat the air fryer to 175° C (circulating air). • Grease the baking tin. • Chop walnuts and almonds. • Break the chocolate into pieces, dice the butter and melt both together in a hot water bath, then allow to cool.
2. Whisk eggs, add Xucker and salt and beat until fluffy. • Add flour, baking powder and the chocolate butter mixture and mix with a hand mixer.
3. Lifting nuts under the dough • Put everything in the greased baking tin and bake for 15-20 minutes • After 10 minutes, make a chopstick tasting, who likes it very juicy, will bring the cake out of the air fryer at the desired consistency
4. Let it cool down and with sprinkle with sugar.

255. Tuna & Egg Salad

INGREDIENTS

- 2 eggs
- 60 g tuna, in its juice (canned)
- 50 g arugula
- 50 g cucumber

- 8 cherry tomatoes
- 1 spring onion
- 30 g mozzarella, grated
- 2 tbsp olive oil
- sea salt
- pepper

INSTRUCTIONS

1. Boil eggs for 8-10 minutes. • Quench eggs with cold water and peel, then slice.
2. First, open the tuna can one piece at a time and drain the tuna juice. • Open the can and then pluck the tuna into pieces with the fork.
3. Wash the arugula and remove long stalks • Wash and slice the tomatoes • Wash the cucumber and cut into pieces • Clean the spring onions and cut them into thin rings.
4. Arrange everything on a plate and drizzle with oil • Season the salad with tuna and egg with salt and pepper and then sprinkle with mozzarella.

256. Sauerkraut with Pork Belly

INGREDIENTS

- 500 g sauerkraut, from the glass
- 600 g pork belly, in whole
- 4 onions
- 2 tsp Dijon mustard
- Whole Pimento
- cloves
- 1 tsp caraway
- 2 bay leaves
- 500 ml meat Broth
- sea salt
- pepper
- 2 tbsp olive oil

INSTRUCTIONS

1. Rinse the pork belly and pat dry, then slice with a sharp knife. • Season the slices with salt and pepper and sprinkle with mustard. • Heat the oil in the air fryer and fry the slices on both sides.
2. Peel the onions and cut into rings • Fry the onions golden yellow in the air fryer • Put the sauerkraut in an air fryer and distribute half of the onions • Add cumin, bay leaves, cloves and allspice and finally add the pork belly with the remaining onions.
3. Add the meat stock and simmer over low heat until the meat is tender and the bottom is almost overcooked. • Serve the slices of meat on the plates.
4. Season the sauerkraut with salt, sweeten something if necessary and serve with the meat.

257. Tomato Salad with Herbs & Basil

INGREDIENTS

- 200 g tomatoes
- 2 stems of parsley
- 2 stems of basil
- 1 tbsp balsamic vinegar
- date and fig
- sea salt
- pepper

INSTRUCTIONS

1. Wash tomatoes and drain, then quarter
2. Wash parsley and basil and shake dry, then peel off leaves and chop.
3. Season the tomatoes with salt and pepper.
4. Drizzle the balsamic over the tomatoes and sprinkle with parsley and basil.

258. Low-Carb Vegetable Wraps

INGREDIENTS

For the wraps
- 2 eggs
- 50 g butter
- 85 ml soy drink or other milk
- 20 g spelt flour, type 630
- 45 g coconut flour

For the filling
- 50 g broccoli
- ½ red pepper
- 2 tbsp corn (canned)
- 4 salad leaves
- 1 spring onion
- 4 tbsp yogurt, natural
- sea salt
- pepper
- Herbs at will

INSTRUCTIONS

1. Melt the butter in an air fryer and allow it to cool briefly. • Mix the eggs, butter, flour and soy drink in a bowl to a smooth dough.
2. Wash vegetables and lettuce leaves and drain • Cut the broccoli florets from the stem, cut into small florets • Cut the peppers into small pieces • Drain the corn in a sieve • Small pluck the lettuce leaves • Clean the spring onion and cut into fine rings.
3. Heat a small coated air fryer, then add about ¼ of the dough and spread evenly in the air fryer. • As soon as the rim is detached from the air fryer bottom, invert the wrap and bake briefly on the other side. • Prepare the other 3 wraps in the same Procedure • Stack finished wraps and keep them warm and flexible.
4. Spread each wrap in the middle with 1 tbsp yogurt and salt and pepper • Center the wraps with the prepared INGREDIENTS and fold them together.

259. Fried Egg with Asparagus Bacon Rolls

INGREDIENTS

- 1 egg
- 6 stalks of green asparagus
- 100 g bacon
- 2 tbsp olive oil
- sea salt
- pepper

INSTRUCTIONS

1. Peel the green asparagus in the lower third and cut off the dry ends
2. Wrap two asparagus spears in the middle with bacon slices.
3. Heat the oil in the air fryer and roast the asparagus with bacon. • Beat the egg and add to the air fryer. • Fry for several minutes, then season with salt, pepper and serve.

260. Paprika with Vegetables & Meat

INGREDIENTS

- 3 peppers
- 200 g chicken breast fillet
- 4 slices of cheddar cheese or cave cheese
- 100 g zucchini
- 100 g mushrooms
- 2 shallots
- 2 tbsp olive oil
- sea salt
- pepper

INSTRUCTIONS

1. Cut the peppers in half, core them and wash them • Wash the zucchini and cut into small pieces • Clean the mushrooms, remove the dry ends of the stems and cut the mushrooms into pieces
2. Peel the shallots and finely chop.
3. Wash chicken breast and pat dry, then cut into small pieces. • Heat oil in air fryer and sauté shallots and meat. • Add zucchini and mushrooms, fry everything and season with salt and pepper.
4. Fill vegetables and meat mixture in the halves of the pepper and top with cheese.
5. Put the peppers in a refractory dish and gratinate in a preheated air fryer for 10-15 minutes at 175° C. • Serve with herbs as desired.

261. Chicken Breast Fillet with Shallots & Tomatoes In Red Wine Sauce

INGREDIENTS

- 500 g chicken breast fillet, 2 pieces
- 200 g cherry tomatoes
- 200 ml red wine
- 6 shallots
- 3 cloves of garlic
- 2 sprigs of parsley
- 2 sprigs of rosemary
- 2 tsp honey
- 4 tbsp olive oil
- sea salt
- pepper

INSTRUCTIONS

1. Wash chicken breasts and pat dry • Peel garlic and crush with the wide side of the knife • Wash herbs and shake dry • Peel the shallots.
2. Heat 2 tbsp of oil in an air fryer and fry chicken fillets with thyme and two cloves of garlic • Cook the chicken in the air fryer for about 10 minutes in a preheated air fryer at 160° C.
3. In a second air fryer, heat 2 tbsp of oil and fry shallots, remaining garlic and tomatoes. • Deglaze everything with red wine and cook for a few minutes. • Season the sauce with honey, salt and pepper.
4. Slicing the chicken breast • Arrange the shallots, tomatoes, red wine sauce and parsley leaves with the chicken and serve.

262. Colorful Air Fryer Vegetables with Herbs

INGREDIENTS

- 300 g zucchini
- 200 g mushrooms
- 150 g red pepper
- 100 g tomatoes
- 2 shallots
- 4 sprigs of thyme
- 2 sprigs of rosemary
- 1 organic lemon
- 100 ml vegetable stock
- 2 tbsp olive oil
- 1 tbsp tomato paste
- ½ tsp Harissa
- sea salt
- pepper

INSTRUCTIONS

1. Wash vegetables and drain • Quarter the zucchini and cut into pieces • Halve and core the peppers, then cut into strips • Clean the mushrooms and remove the dry ends of the stems, then slice the mushrooms.

2. Peel and chop the shallots • Wash and dry the herbs, pluck the leaves and chop them • Wash and dry the lemon, then zest with the grater • Cut the lemon and squeeze the juice from both halves • Halve the tomatoes.
3. Heat the olive oil in the air fryer and fry the shallots until smooth. • Add the harissa and tomato puree and sauté. • Add the zucchini, mushrooms, peppers and tomatoes and stir fry. • Add the stock and simmer for several minutes.
4. Add herbs to the vegetables and season with lemon juice, salt and pepper. • Finally, add the lemon peel and stir again.

263. Brussels Sprouts & Bacon with Parmesan

INGREDIENTS

- 150 g Brussels sprouts
- 200 g bacon or ham
- Juice of half a lemon
- 1 tbsp olive oil
- 40 g butter
- 1 tsp lemon zest, freshly grated
- 30 g Parmesan
- sea salt
- pepper

INSTRUCTIONS

1. Place Brussels sprouts in a pot with steaming insert. Bring the water to a boil in the air fryer and steam Brussels sprouts for 4-6 minutes.
2. Dice the bacon • Heat butter and olive oil in the air fryer and fry the bacon with Brussels sprouts for a few minutes.
3. Add the lemon juice and zest then season with salt and pepper.
4. Put Brussels sprouts and bacon on a plate and sprinkle with freshly grated Parmesan cheese.

264. Pork Fillet in Bacon Coat

INGREDIENTS

- 500 g pork tenderloin
- 300 g bacon
- For the herb crust
- 1 clove of garlic
- 1 tsp lemon zest
- 2 sprigs of rosemary
- 3 sprigs of thyme
- 2 sprigs of basil
- 1 branch chervil
- 60 ml olive oil
- sea salt
- pepper

INSTRUCTIONS

1. Wash herbs and shake dry, then pluck the leaves • Peel and chop garlic. • Crush the herbs, oil, garlic, salt, pepper and lemon peel into mortar.
2. Using a sharp knife, remove the pork fillet from the silver skin and fat. • Wrap the bacon around the fillet. • Brush it all with the herb paste. • Put the pork fillet in a bacon coat with herbs into a hot air fryer.
3. Cook in preheated air fryer at 180° C for 15-20 minutes. • Place the remainder of the herb paste on the meat.

265. Mozzarella Salad with Citrus Dressing

INGREDIENTS

For the salad

- 150 g endive salad
- 100 g cherry tomatoes
- 20 g red onion
- 2 sprigs of basil
- 125g mozzarella
- 20 g of corn

For the dressing

- 2 tbsp olive oil
- 1 tsp lemon juice, freshly squeezed
- 1 tbsp orange juice, freshly squeezed
- 2 sprigs of rosemary
- 1 clove of garlic
- 1 tsp maple syrup
- sea salt
- pepper

INSTRUCTIONS

1. Wash the lettuce leaves and dry in the salad spinner • Toss the salad into pieces • Wash and drain the tomatoes, then halve • Wash the herbs and shake them dry, then pluck the leaves from the stalk.
2. Peel the onion and cut into rings • Drain the corn in a sieve • Cut the mozzarella into pieces • Divide the lettuce leaves into two plates and spread the tomatoes, onion, corn, basil and mozzarella.
3. For the dressing, mix the oil, maple syrup, lemon and orange juice in a bowl • Peel the garlic, squeeze with the garlic press and add • Rosemary leaves, salt and pepper and mix well • Dress over the salad and serve.

266. Grilled Sweet Potato with Avocado Cream & Egg

INGREDIENTS

- 2 slices of sweet potato, 70 g
- 1 avocado
- 2 eggs
- Juice of a lime
- 4 tbsp olive oil
- 1 tsp Black sesame seeds
- chili flakes
- Sea salt
- pepper

INSTRUCTIONS

1. Boil eggs for 8-10 minutes. Then chill eggs cold, peel and slice.
2. Halve the avocado, remove seed and remove the flesh. • Cut one avocado half into strips and drizzle with lime juice. • Crush the second half with a fork on a plate, drizzle with lime juice and fold in chili flakes, salt and pepper.
3. Put the sweet potato slices in a baking sheet lined with parchment paper and pre-heat for 10 minutes at 160° C. • Brush with oil. • Put the sweet potato slices in the hot air fryer and grill until the roasting strips are visible, then turn.
4. Spread avocado on top of the sweet potato slices and top with eggs and avocado • Sprinkle sesame over the eggs and season with salt and pepper.

267. Vegetable Salad with Dried Tomatoes

INGREDIENTS

- 400 g mixed salad
- 200 g mushrooms
- 2 peppers
- 50 g broccoli
- 100 g carrot
- 50 g dried tomatoes
- 5 tbsp olive oil
- sea salt
- pepper

INSTRUCTIONS

1. Wash lettuce leaves and dry them in the salad spinner. • Cut the salad into pieces. • Clean the mushrooms and cut off the dry ends of the stalk. • Cut the mushrooms into slices.
2. Halve the peppers, core them and wash them thoroughly. • Cut the pepper into strips. • Wash the broccoli and cut the florets from the stem. • Peel and slice the carrots. • Drain the tomatoes and cut them into pieces.
3. Put the salad, mushrooms, peppers, broccoli, carrots and tomatoes in a bowl and season with salt and pepper • Drizzle the salad with oil, mix and place on two plates.

268. Low-Carb Pumpkin Seed Bread

INGREDIENTS

- 200 g almonds, ground
- 150 g flax seed, crushed
- 25 g pumpkin seeds, ground
- 250 g low-fat quark
- 5 eggs
- 2 tbsp pumpkin seeds
- 2 tbsp sunflower seeds
- 1 packet of tartar baking powder
- 1 tsp of cocoa powder
- ½ tsp cumin
- 2 tsp sea salt

INSTRUCTIONS

1. Mix ground almonds and pumpkin seeds, flaxseed, baking powder, cocoa, cumin and salt in a bowl • Add sunflower and 1 tbsp pumpkin seeds and stir.
2. First mix cottage cheese and eggs in a second bowl, then add to the dry INGREDIENTS. • Mix everything into a dough. • Lay out a box tin with parchment paper and fill in the dough.
3. Sprinkle the remaining pumpkin seeds over the bread dough and press lightly • Bake the dough for 50-60 minutes in a preheated air fryer at 160° C (circulating air) • After the baking time, remove the bread from the tin and let it cool completely.

269. Low-Carb Klopse

INGREDIENTS

Knock

- 600 g veal mince
- 2 onions
- 2 tbsp butter
- 1 egg
- 100 ml milk
- 50 g spelt rolls, without crust
- sea salt
- pepper

- nutmeg

Meatballs

- 1.5 l of stock (vegetable or meat)
- 1 tbsp organic apple cider vinegar
- 2 bay leaves
- 3 pimento grains, whole
- 1 tsp black peppercorns

Sauce

- 200 ml cream
- 50 g butter
- 2 tbsp capers
- Juice of half a lemon
- 1 tsp lemon zest
- 1 tsp locust bean gum
- Agave syrup
- nutmeg
- sea salt
- pepper

INSTRUCTIONS

1. Cut spelt buns into small cubes and soak in milk in a bowl. • Peel the onions and dice finely. • Melt the butter in the air fryer and fry the onions.
2. Mix the veal minced meat, onions and egg in a bowl. • Express the rolls and add to the minced meat. • Season everything with salt, pepper and freshly grated nutmeg and mix with the hands into a meat dough.
3. Boil the stock with apple cider vinegar, bay leaves, allspice and peppercorns in air fryer. • Form the meatloaf and make a tenderloin. • Reduce the heat and thicken for 15-20 minutes.
4. Melt the butter in a pot first. • Add about 500 ml of the boiled beef to the boil and bring to a boil. • Mix carob seed flour with a little cold water and add salt, pepper and freshly grated nutmeg. Cook for about 5 minutes. • Add stock until the desired consistency is achieved.
5. Add the cream, lemon juice and grated cheese and stir until smooth. • Season the sauce with agave syrup, salt and pepper. • Add cooking broth to the sauce. • Add the capers and everything for 2-3 minutes, then serve.

270. Egg, Avocado & Chicken Salad with Basil

INGREDIENTS

- 300 g chicken breast fillet
- 1 avocado
- 6 eggs
- 100 g basil, fresh
- 60 g mayonnaise
- Sea salt
- pepper

INSTRUCTIONS

1. Wash chicken breasts and pat dry, then cut into bite-sized pieces. Bring water to a boil with salt. • Add chicken breast fillet, then reduce heat and cook for 10-15 minutes. • Drain meat into a sieve and strain well. Cool it down.
2. Boil eggs for 8-10 minutes. Then chill eggs, peel and cut into small pieces. Halve avocado, remove and flesh. Cut avocado into small cubes.
3. Wash basil and shake it dry Peel off leaves and chop.
4. Put the eggs, avocado, mayonnaise, basil and pieces of meat in a bowl and season with salt and pepper • Stir everything carefully and place on two plates.

271. Walnut Basil Pesto

INGREDIENTS

- 100 g basil, fresh
- 120 ml olive oil
- 60 g walnut kernels
- 60 g Parmesan
- 1 clove of garlic
- sea salt
- pepper

INSTRUCTIONS

1. Wash the basil and shake dry. • Pick leaves from the stalk and chop them roughly. • Roast walnuts in an air fryer over low heat for about 5 minutes, turning the nuts occasionally. • Remove walnuts from the air fryer and allow them to cool.
2. Grate Parmesan coarsely or cut into small pieces. Peel and slice garlic. Place basil, walnuts, Parmesan cheese, garlic and oil in a mixing bowl and puree to a fine paste with the hand blender.
3. Add salt and pepper and mix again briefly. • Pour walnut-basil pesto into a clean glass, making sure that the pesto is covered with oil, then close the glass and leave to cool.

272. Fried Fish Fillet with Vegetables

INGREDIENTS

- 2 zander fillets with skin, 200 g
- 1 red pepper
- 1 yellow pepper
- 100 g broccoli
- 1 shallot
- 1 organic lemon
- ½ bunch dill
- 2 tbsp olive oil
- 2 tbsp butter
- sea salt
- pepper

INSTRUCTIONS

1. Wash zander fillets and pat dry • Scrape fillets with a sharp knife on the skin side several times • Wash and drain vegetables • Peel and finely dice the shallot.
2. Cut the peppers and remove the cores and partitions, rinse again if necessary. • Cut the peppers into short strips • Cut the broccoli florets from the stalk • Wash the dill and shake dry, then finely chop • Wash the lemon, dry and slice.
3. Heat 1 tbsp butter and 1 tbsp oil in the air fryer and roast the zander on the skin side for 5 minutes. • Remove the fillets and place them in a fireproof dish with the skin side up. • Continue cooking Zander for about 10 minutes in a preheated air fryer at 160° C.
4. Add the rest of the oil to the hot air fryer • Sauté the shallot, then add the rest of the vegetables • Finally add the remaining butter and season the air fryer with salt and pepper

273. Beef Steak with Colorful Salad

INGREDIENTS

- 1 beef steak, 150 g
- 150 g salad (lamb's lettuce, Swiss chard, arugula salad)
- 2 cloves of garlic
- 1 sprig rosemary
- 60 ml olive oil
- 2 tbsp butter
- 1 tbsp barbecue sauce
- 1 tsp pink berries
- sea salt

INSTRUCTIONS

1. Wash beef steak and dab dry • Wash lettuce leaves and dry in salad spout • Remove long stalks of arugula and chard, then place the leaves on a plate • Wash rosemary sprigs and shake dry • Peel garlic and chop.
2. Heat the butter and 1 tbsp of oil in the air fryer and fry the steak with rosemary and garlic. • Fry the steak on each side for about 2-3 minutes. • Place the steak on a warm plate, cover with a second plate and let it sit briefly.
3. Warm up the barbecue sauce in the hot air fryer • Cut the steak into strips, then spread the barbecue sauce over it • Put the steak to the salad on the plate • Crush the pink berries in the mortar, mix with the remaining oil and the meat and salad.

274. Chicken Breast Fillet with Brussels Sprouts

INGREDIENTS

- 400 g chicken breast fillet
- 400 g Brussels sprouts
- 40 g corn, canned
- 1 tbsp olive oil
- 1 tsp thyme, rubbed
- sea salt
- pepper

INSTRUCTIONS

1. Wash chicken breast and dab it dry. • Rub meat with thyme and salt all around.
2. Heat the olive oil in the air fryer and fry the fillet until golden brown on both sides.
3. Brush the Brussels sprouts with oil and steam in an air fryer with a little water for 8-10 minutes. •
4. Drain the corn into a sieve and add.

275. Fish Patties

INGREDIENTS

- 600 g fish fillet without skin (salmon, perch)
- 1 egg
- 2 shallots
- 1 clove of garlic
- 6 stems of coriander
- 4 stalks dill
- 1 tbsp of lemon juice, freshly squeezed
- 1 tsp ginger, grated
- 2 tbsp butter
- 1 tbsp olive oil
- Himalayan salt
- pepper

INSTRUCTIONS

1. Wash fish fillets and pat dry • Place fillets on a platter and chop with a knife • Peel the shallots and finely chop them • Wash the herbs and shake dry, then finely chop.
2. Mix the fish, shallots, herbs, ginger and the egg in a bowl • Peel the garlic and squeeze over the fish with the garlic press. • Season the fish mixture with lemon juice, salt and pepper and knead.
3. Forming meatballs from the fish mix with your hands • Heat the oil in the air fryer and fry the meatballs for 2 to 3 minutes on each side. • Add butter to the air fryer and roast the fish cakes again on each side for about 2 minutes.

276. Zucchini Rolls with Ricotta & Parmesan Filling

INGREDIENTS

- 1 zucchini, 300 g
- 150 g ricotta
- 100 g Parmesan
- Juice of half a lemon
- 4 stems of parsley
- 1 tsp olive oil
- nutmeg
- sea salt
- pepper

INSTRUCTIONS

1. Wash the zucchini, dry and cut the ends. • Cut lengthways into thin strips.
2. Wash the parsley and shake dry, peel off the leaves and chop.
3. Grate the parmesan and mix with ricotta, parsley and lemon juice in a bowl • Season the ricotta mixture with freshly grated nutmeg, salt and pepper.
4. Heat the air fryer and brush with oil.
5. Grate the zucchini strips in the air fryer on both sides until you can detect the roasting strips.
6. Place the zucchini strips on a platter and spread with the ricotta mixture • Roll up the strips, fix with toothpicks as needed and arrange on a plate.

277. Colorful Salad with Chicken Breast & Walnuts

INGREDIENTS

- 300 g chicken breast fillet
- 200 g salad (iceberg, endives)
- 100 g tomatoes
- ½ red onion
- 50 g radish
- 50 g walnut kernels
- 3 tbsp olive oil
- sea salt
- pepper

INSTRUCTIONS

1. Wash the lettuce and dry it in the salad spinner • Toss lettuce leaves • Wash tomatoes and cut into pieces • Peel onions and cut into thin rings • Clean radishes and slice • Put everything in the salad bowl.
2. Wash the chicken breast and pat dry with a kitchen crepe. • Cut the meat into pieces. • Heat 1 tbsp of olive oil in the air fryer and roast the chicken pieces all around golden brown. • Season the meat with salt and pepper.
3. Season the salad with salt and pepper and mix. • Put the salad on two plates and drizzle with olive oil. • Spread walnuts and hot chicken breast pieces on the salad and serve.

278. Baked Cod with Spicy Crust

INGREDIENTS

- 2 cod fillets, 150 g
- 300 g broccoli
- 50 g coconut flakes
- 50 g Parmesan
- 50 g almonds, ground
- 2 cloves of garlic
- 1 egg yolk
- Juice of a lime
- 5 sprigs of thyme
- 2 tbsp of coconut oil

- sea salt
- pepper

INSTRUCTIONS

1. Wash the cod fillets and pat dry • Mix the grated coconut and almonds with the egg yolk in a bowl • Peel the garlic, squeeze with the garlic press and add to the coconut-almond mixture.
2. Finely grate the Parmesan • Wash the thyme and shake it dry, then remove the leaves and chop finely • Add the Parmesan and thyme to the coconut-almond mixture and season with salt and pepper • Stir well.
3. Heat the coconut oil in the air fryer and sauté the cod fillets on each side for 1-2 minutes. • Remove the fish from the air fryer and place it in a casserole dish. • Sprinkle lime juice over the fillets. Add the coconut-almond mixture to the fillets and place in the preheated air fryer at 160° C. Bake for 15 minutes.
4. Meanwhile, cut broccoli florets and stalk • Place the broccoli in a pot with stew and cover for 5-8 minutes. • Bake cod with spicy crust and broccoli on two plates and serve.

279. ARUGULA SALAD WITH CHARD, BEETROOT AND ORANGE FILLETS

INGREDIENTS

- 200 g beetroot, cooked or raw
- 100 g arugula
- 50 g chard
- 1 orange
- 2 tbsp olive oil
- sea salt
- pepper

INSTRUCTIONS

1. Wash the rucola and chard leaves and dry them in the salad spinner.
2. Remove long stalks from the arugula. • Peel the orange and cut into pieces.
3. Cook beetroot and peel.
4. Cut beetroot in thin slices.
5. Mix the arugula, Swiss chard, beetroot and orange in a salad bowl. • Season the salad with salt and pepper, mix and arrange on a plate. • Sprinkle the olive oil over the salad

280. Air Fryer Mushroom & Fennel

INGREDIENTS

- 400 g mushrooms, brown
- 150 g fennel
- 1 lemon
- 1 sprig rosemary
- 2 cloves of garlic
- 1 tsp ginger, grated
- 2 tbsp olive oil
- 1 tbsp butter
- 1 bay leaf
- nutmeg
- sea salt
- pepper

INSTRUCTIONS

1. Clean the mushrooms and remove the dry ends of the stems • Slice the mushrooms • Clean the fennel and cut into thin slices • Peel the garlic and cut into thin slices.
2. Wash the rosemary and shake it dry, peel the leaves and chop finely • Heat the butter and oil in the air fryer and fry the garlic until golden brown. • Add the mushrooms and fennel and fry them. • Halve the lemon and squeeze out the juice.

3. Add ginger and lemon juice to the mushrooms and stir • Add the rosemary and bay leaf and fry for several minutes. • Season the mushroom and fennel air fryer with freshly grated nutmeg, salt and pepper.

281. Zucchini Soup

INGREDIENTS

- 400 g zucchini
- 1 onion
- 1 clove of garlic
- 50 g potatoes
- 2 sprigs of thyme
- 1 sprig rosemary
- 500 ml vegetable stock
- 100 ml cream
- 4 tbsp olive oil
- 1 tbsp butter
- nutmeg
- sea salt
- pepper

INSTRUCTIONS

1. Rinse and dry the zucchini, then cut into quarters and cut into pieces of about 1 cm. • Peel the onion, garlic and finely dice. • Peel and grate the potatoes.
2. Wash the thyme and rosemary, shake dry and pluck the leaves from the stem. • Finely chop the herbs. • Heat the butter and 2 ml of oil in an air fryer and sauté the onion and garlic. • Add the potato and steam briefly.
3. Deglaze with the stock and simmer the vegetables for about 10 minutes with the pot closed. • Add the zucchini and cook for another 5 minutes. • Remove the air fryer and add the cream.
4. Puree everything with a hand blender • Season the soup with freshly grated nutmeg, salt and pepper • Arrange the soup in small bowls, drizzle with a spoonful of oil and garnish with fresh herbs.

282. Veal Schnitzel with Tomatoes & Cheese

INGREDIENTS

- 2 veal cutlets of 150 g each
- 200 g tomatoes
- 200 g cheese (Gouda or Cheddar)
- 1 tbsp olive oil
- paprika
- nutmeg
- sea salt
- pepper

INSTRUCTIONS

1. Wash schnitzel and dry with a kitchen towel. • Beat schnitzel evenly with a meat tenderizer. • Mix the paprika, freshly grated nutmeg, salt and pepper on a plate and fold into the schnitzel.
2. Wash and slice the tomatoes • Slice the cheese or grate it roughly • Heat the oil in the air fryer and fry the schnitzel for about 2 minutes • Turn the meat and cover with tomatoes and cheese.
3. Cook schnitzel in the air fryer on the top rack in a preheated air fryer at 200° C with the grill function. • Put the schnitzel on two plates and serve hot.

283. Sweet Salad with Quail Eggs

INGREDIENTS

- 100 g corn salad
- 5 cherry tomatoes
- 4 black olives, pitted
- 3 quail eggs

- 30 g pomegranate seeds
- 1 tbsp olive oil
- 1 tsp sesame
- sea salt
- pepper

INSTRUCTIONS

1. Wash corn salad and spin dry in a salad spinner • Cook the quail eggs in a small air fryer covered with water for 4 minutes. • Drain the olives and cut lengthways.
2. Wash the tomatoes, drain and then cut in half. • Mix lamb's lettuce, olives, tomatoes and pomegranate seeds in a bowl. • Sprinkle olive oil over the salad and season with salt and pepper.
3. Remix the salad, fill in a bowl and sprinkle with sesame seeds • Chill the eggs, peel and cut in half • Add the eggs to the salad and serve.

284. Fruit Salad with Arugula, Avocado & Walnut

INGREDIENTS

- 100 g arugula
- 1 avocado
- 1 apple
- 50 g grapes
- 50 g walnut kernels
- 1 tbsp olive oil
- pepper
- Sea salt

INSTRUCTIONS

1. Wash the arugula, drain and remove long stalks. • Wash and drain the grapes and apples. • Quarter the apple, remove the core casing and cut into bite-size pieces. • Chop walnuts roughly.
2. Halve the avocado, remove the peel and core and cut the flesh into pieces
3. Mix the arugula, avocado, grapes, apple, walnuts and olive oil in a salad bowl
4. Season the salad with salt and pepper and place it on two plates.

285. Zucchini, Tomato & Spinach Frittata

INGREDIENTS

- 8 eggs
- 150 ml cream
- 150 g Parmesan
- 100 g cherry tomatoes
- 1 tomato
- 50 g baby spinach
- 50 g zucchini
- 2 sprigs of thyme
- 4 stems of coriander
- 1 tbsp olive oil
- nutmeg
- sea salt
- pepper

INSTRUCTIONS

1. Whisk eggs with cream in a bowl and season with salt and pepper. • Wash herbs and shake dry. • Remove coriander leaves from the stalk. • Wash baby spinach and drain well.
2. Wash and drain the tomatoes, then halve the cherry tomatoes, slice the large tomato • Wash and slice the zucchini.
3. Boil the olive oil in the air fryer and add the egg mass. • Leave the egg mixture on medium heat, then add the zucchini, tomatoes and herbs. • Sprinkle the grated Parmesan over the vegetables.

4. Cook frittata for 15-20 minutes in a preheated air fryer at 180° C • Add the baby spinach to the frittata shortly before the end of the cooking time • Season the frittata with freshly grated nutmeg, salt and pepper and serve.

286. Tomato Salad with Cucumber & Apple

INGREDIENTS

- 300 g small tomatoes
- 300 g organic cucumber
- 200 g organic apple
- ½ red onion
- 4 stems of parsley
- Juice of half a lemon
- Sea salt
- pepper

INSTRUCTIONS

1. Wash the tomatoes, cucumber and apple and drain. • Cut the tomatoes and cucumber into pieces. • Quarter the apple, remove the core casing and cut into pieces. • Peel the onion and dice.
2. Wash and shake the parsley dry, pluck the leaves from the stalk and chop finely.
3. Mix the tomatoes, cucumber, apple, onion and parsley with lemon juice in a bowl.
4. Season the salad with salt, pepper and place in two bowls.

287. Grilled Cod with Tomato Salad & Herbs

INGREDIENTS

- 2 cod fillets, 250 g, ready to cook
- 200 g cherry tomatoes
- 2 tbsp butter
- 2 tbsp olive oil
- 2-3 stems of basil
- Juice of half a lemon
- sea salt
- pepper

INSTRUCTIONS

1. Wash the cod and pat dry. • Wash and drain the tomatoes, then cut in half. • Wash the basil and shake it dry, peel off the leaves and cut into strips.
2. Heat butter and oil in the air fryer and roast cod fillets on one side for 3-4 minutes • Turn the fillets, season with salt and pepper and fry for another 3-4 minutes on the other side.
3. Put the tomatoes and basil to the air fryer for the last few minutes and let it heat up. • Pour lemon juice over the fish. • Put cod fillets on a plate and serve with tomato salad.

288. Tuna with Spicy Herb Crust & Lemon

INGREDIENTS

- 2 tuna steaks, 200 g
- 1 organic lemon
- 2 tbsp of sesame oil
- For the herb crust
- 2 stalks of rosemary
- 2 stems of thyme
- 1 chili pepper
- 1 clove of garlic
- 2 tbsp of sesame oil
- 1 tbsp of pink berries
- 1 tsp lemon zest
- sea salt

INSTRUCTIONS

1. Wash the tuna and dab it dry with a kitchen towel. • Wash the lemon hot, dry and slice. • Halve the chili pepper lengthwise, core and then chop finely. • Peel and finely chop the garlic.
2. Wash rosemary and thyme and shake dry, peel off the leaves and place in a mortar. • Add lemon zest, garlic, chili, pink berries, salt and sesame oil and pound well.
3. Heat the sesame oil in the air fryer and fry the tuna steaks on both sides. Then add the herb mixture to the steaks and cook with the lemon slices in the preheated air fryer for 5 to 10 minutes at 120° C.

289. Roasted Pumpkin & Brussels Sprout Salad with Pecans

INGREDIENTS

- 200 g squash, Hokkaido or butternut
- 150 g Brussels sprouts
- 60 g pecans
- 20 g cranberries
- 2 tbsp of orange juice
- 1 tbsp olive oil
- Sea salt
- pepper

INSTRUCTIONS

1. The Hokkaido pumpkin is a little faster; it only needs to be thoroughly washed and dried. • The butternut squash must be peeled.
2. Cut the pumpkin into small cubes.
3. Clean Brussels sprouts, remove the withered leaves and cut in half.
4. Heat the olive oil in the air fryer and sauté the squash and Brussels sprouts • Add the orange juice, pecans and cranberries and fry for a short time • Season with salt and pepper and stir.

290. Paleo Hamburger with Avocado & Beans

INGREDIENTS

- 400 g ground beef
- 200 g green beans, fresh
- 1 egg
- 4-6 slices of bacon
- a few salad leaves
- 1 tomato
- 1 red onion
- 1 shallot
- 1 avocado
- 1 clove of garlic
- 10 almonds
- 2 tbsp olive oil
- sea salt
- pepper

INSTRUCTIONS

1. Peel the shallot and garlic and finely dice • Heat the olive oil in the air fryer and brown the shallot and garlic until golden brown. • Mix the minced meat with the shallot, garlic, and egg in a bowl and season with salt and pepper.
2. Form two patties from the minced meat mixture and fry them hot on both sides in the hot air fryer. • Cook patties in the air fryer for 10 to 15 minutes at 175° C in the air fryer.
3. Meanwhile, clean the beans and cook in an air fryer with water for 8-10 minutes • Beans then drain in a sieve • Fry the bacon in an air fryer until crispy, turn in between.

4. Wash lettuce leaves and shake dry. • Wash tomato and slice. • Halve the avocado, remove seed, and peel flesh. • Slice avocado. • Chop almonds. • Peel onions and cut them into rings.
5. Roast the beans and almonds briefly in the air fryer and season with salt and pepper • Arrange the beans with almonds on two plates • Add the salad, tomato, bacon and one patty each • Add the avocado and onion rings and serve.

291. Scrambled Eggs with Bacon & Chard

INGREDIENTS

- 6 eggs
- 3 tbsp cream
- 100 g bacon
- 20 g chard
- 2 cherry tomatoes
- 2 tbsp olive oil
- sea salt
- pepper

INSTRUCTIONS

1. Whisk eggs and cream in a bowl and season with salt and pepper. • Put the bacon in a hot air fryer and fry until crispy. • Wash tomatoes and chard and drain well. • Halve tomatoes.
2. Heat the oil in a second air fryer and pour in the eggs. • Once the egg mass has stopped, pull through the air fryer several times with the spatula and cook the scrambled eggs on all sides over medium heat.
3. Place the scrambled eggs on two plates and serve with bacon, tomatoes, and salad.

292. Cauliflower Rice with Eggs

INGREDIENTS

Cauliflower rice

- 400 g cauliflower
- 2 tbsp butter
- Juice of half a lemon
- sea salt
- 2-3 sprigs of mint

Eggs

- 4 eggs
- 1 tbsp cream
- 1 tsp butter
- sea salt
- pepper

INSTRUCTIONS

1. Wash the cauliflower and drain well • Grate the cauliflower so that it has a rice-like consistency • Place the cauliflower rice in a cheesecloth or tea towel and press out the liquid with your hands.
2. Melt the butter in the warm air fryer. • Mix the cauliflower rice, melted butter and lemon juice in a bowl and season with salt • Wash the mint and shake dry, cut into strips and add to the cauliflower.
3. Whisk the eggs and cream in a bowl and season with salt and pepper. • Heat the butter in the air fryer and pour in the egg mass. • Once the egg mass has set, turn over and bake. • Then cut the omelet into bite-sized strips and add to the salad.

293. Salmon Fillet with Vegetables

INGREDIENTS

- 2 salmon fillets, 250 g
- 200 g zucchini
- 200 g paprika
- 200 g carrots
- 150 g leek
- 150 g broccoli
- 100 g green beans, fresh or frozen
- 100 g cherry tomatoes
- 2 shallots
- 2 tbsp olive oil
- 2 stems of parsley
- sea salt
- pepper

INSTRUCTIONS

1. Wash vegetables and drain well • Peel the carrot and slice • Clean and chop beans • Place carrots and beans in a steaming bowl and steam in the pot with little water for 6-10 minutes until firm.
2. Core the paprika and cut into bite-sized pieces • Peel the shallots and finely dice • Halve tomatoes • Slice the zucchini and leeks • Cut the broccoli florets from the stalk • Wash the parsley and shake it dry, pluck the leaves.
3. Wash the salmon and pat dry • Heat 1 tbsp of olive oil in the air fryer and sear the fish fillets on the top, then turn over and sauté on the skin side over medium heat • Season the fillets with salt and pepper.
4. In the second air fryer, heat 1 tbsp of oil and sauté the shallots • Add leek, zucchini, broccoli, and paprika and sauté • Add beans and carrots and fry for a short time • Finally add the tomatoes and let them warm.
5. Season the vegetables with salt and pepper and stir again. • Add the parsley to the vegetables and serve with the fried salmon fillets.

294. Grilled Chicken in Herb Marinade

INGREDIENTS

Chicken

- 4 chicken thighs, ready to cook
- 1 small garlic bulb
- 2-3 chili peppers

Marinade

- 3-4 sprigs of thyme
- 1 sprig rosemary
- 3 tbsp olive oil
- Juice of half a lemon, organic
- ½ tsp fennel seeds
- 1 clove of garlic
- Pinch of sea salt
- 1 tsp. pepper

INSTRUCTIONS

1. Wash chicken drumsticks and dab them dry. • Cut the garlic bulb in half. • Wash chili peppers and drain.
2. Wash for the marinade herbs and shake dry • Pluck thyme and rosemary leaves from the stems • Peel garlic • Crush thyme, rosemary, olive oil, lemon juice, fennel, salt and pepper in the mortar • Add garlic with a garlic press.

3. Rub chicken thighs with marinade • Place meat and remaining marinade and garlic bulb in a preheated air fryer at 175° C for about 30-45 minutes.

295. Raw Salad with Orange Dressing
INGREDIENTS

- 200 g salad (iceberg, endives, Chinese cabbage)
- 100 g red cabbage
- 1 carrot
- 5-6 stems of coriander orange dressing
- 2 tbsp olive oil
- Juice of an orange
- Juice of half a lemon
- 1 tsp agave syrup
- 1 pinch of sea salt

INSTRUCTIONS

1. Wash lettuce leaves and dry them in salad lettuce • Cut lettuce into bite-sized strips • Peel the carrot and cut into thin strips • Remove the dry leaves from red cabbage, then cut off red cabbage and cut into thin strips • Wash cilantro and shake dry, then Pluck leaves.
2. For the dressing, mix the orange, lemon and agave syrup in a bowl with olive oil and sea salt. • Put all prepared salad INGREDIENTS in a salad bowl and add the dressing. • Mix the salad and serve.

296. Grilled Lamb with Vegetables
INGREDIENTS

- 600 g lamb fillet, ready to cook
- 200 g mushrooms
- 200 g broccoli
- 100 g dried tomatoes
- 1 pepper
- 4 cloves of garlic
- 2 sprigs of rosemary
- 2-4 sprigs of thyme
- 3 tbsp olive oil
- sea salt
- pepper

INSTRUCTIONS

1. Wash the lamb fillet and pat dry with a kitchen towel. • Rub the fillet with salt. • Wash and dry the herbs. Heat the oil in a large frying air fryer and fry the lamb fillet all around brown. • Put the fillet and herbs in a fireproof mold and meat in a preheated air fryer at 180° C. Cook for 20 minutes.
2. Meanwhile, clean the mushrooms, remove the dry ends of the stems, and cut mushrooms in half. • Cut the broccoli florets from the stalk, wash and drain. Cut the peppers in half, remove the seeds and partitions, wash and drain. • Cut the peppers into strips • Peel the garlic and chop finely.
3. Fry the garlic in the hot air fryer, then add mushrooms, broccoli and paprika, and roast. • Finally, add the dried tomatoes and season with salt and pepper. • Remove the fillet from the air fryer and slice.

297. Tuna Salad with Avocado, Tomato, & Mayonnaise
INGREDIENTS

- 200 g tuna, canned
- ½ red onion, finely diced
- 4-5 cherry tomatoes
- ½ avocado
- 1 lime
- 2 tbsp mayonnaise

- 1 tsp capers, finely chopped
- sea salt
- pepper

INSTRUCTIONS

1. Pull the tuna apart with a fork, strain into a sieve and drain • Halve the lime and squeeze out the juice • Remove the avocado flesh from the skin and cut into pieces • Drizzle the avocado with lime juice.
2. Wash tomatoes and quarter
3. Mix avocado, tuna, onions, tomatoes and capers with mayonnaise in a bowl • Season tuna salad with lime juice, salt, and pepper.

298. Avocado Chicken Paprika Omelet

INGREDIENTS

- 6 eggs
- 2 tbsp cream
- ½ red pepper
- ½ green pepper
- 100 g chicken breast fillet, cooked
- ½ avocado
- 2 stems of parsley
- 1 tbsp olive oil
- 1 tbsp butter
- sea salt
- pepper

INSTRUCTIONS

1. Whisk the eggs and cream in a bowl with the whisk • Season the eggs with salt and pepper • Halve the peppers, core and wash them, then cut into small cubes • Remove avocado flesh from the peel and cut into strips.
2. Wash the parsley, shake dry and peel the leaves. • Heat the butter and oil in the air fryer and add half of the egg mass. • Cook omelet over medium heat, then turn over. • Put a few slices of chicken breast and avocado on the omelet and add to the air fryer. Keep warm at 50° C.
3. Make the second omelet in the same way. • Then fold the omelet and spread the diced peppers on it. • Sprinkle each omelet with parsley and serve hot.

299. Eggplant, Tomato & Basil Pizzas

INGREDIENTS

- 2 eggplants, approx. 250 g each
- 300 g tomatoes
- 125g mozzarella
- 1 bunch of basil
- 1 clove of garlic
- 4 tbsp olive oil
- Oregano
- sea salt
- pepper

INSTRUCTIONS

1. Wash the eggplant, dry them and remove the ends • Slice the eggplant and salt them • Wash and drain the tomatoes, then cut into small pieces, remove the stem.
2. Wash the basil, shake dry and chop, put a few leaves aside to garnish. • Peel the garlic. • Mix some oregano with olive oil in a bowl. • Slice the mozzarella.

3. Add tomatoes and basil to the oil mixture. • Add the garlic with the garlic press, season with pepper and salt and mix everything. • Put the eggplant slices on a baking sheet lined with parchment paper and spread the tomato mixture on top.
4. Put the mozzarella over the tomatoes and bake the eggplant pizzas in a preheated air fryer at 175° C for 10-15 minutes. • Remove eggplant pizzas from the air fryer and serve with basil leaves.

300. Coleslaw with Mint & Lime Juice

INGREDIENTS

- 400 g Chinese cabbage
- 250 g carrots
- Juice of a lime
- 3-4 stalks of mint
- 1-2 tsp of agave syrup

INSTRUCTIONS

1. Remove the outer leaves of Chinese cabbage • Cut Chinese cabbage into thin strips with a large knife • Peel carrots and slice finely
2. Wash mint, shake dry and peel off the leaves • Cut mint into strips • Mix cabbage, carrots, and mint in a bowl with lime juice and season with agave syrup.

301. Zucchini Salad with Cheese & Herbs

INGREDIENTS

- 400 g zucchini, yellow and green
- 100 g feta
- 5-6 stems of parsley
- 4 tbsp olive oil
- 1 tsp sesame
- sea salt
- pepper

INSTRUCTIONS

1. Wash and dry the zucchini, then slice • Place the zucchini slices on a plate, season with salt and pepper and drizzle with olive oil.
2. Cut the feta into small cubes • Wash the parsley and shake dry, then chop. • Pour the feta, parsley and sesame seeds over the zucchini slices and serve.

302. Roasted Broccoli with Garlic

INGREDIENTS

- 250 g broccoli
- 2 tbsp olive oil
- 2 cloves of garlic
- Sea salt

INSTRUCTIONS

1. Wash the broccoli and cut the florets from the stalk • Drain the florets on a kitchen towel • Peel and slice the garlic.
2. Heat the olive oil in the air fryer and sauté the broccoli with garlic on all sides. • Put the broccoli on a plate and sprinkle with salt and herbs of your choice.

303. Vegetable & Ham Frittata

INGREDIENTS

- 10 eggs
- 400 g cooked ham, organic
- 200 ml cream
- 150 g Parmesan
- 1 tomato
- 1 pepper
- 2 sprigs of thyme
- 1 tbsp olive oil
- sea salt
- pepper

INSTRUCTIONS

1. Wash and drain vegetables, and herbs • Slice tomato • Cut paprika into halves, remove seeds and partitions and dice • Pick thyme leaves from stalk • Cut ham into cubes.
2. Beat the eggs in a bowl and whisk with cream and thyme. • Season the eggs with salt and pepper. • Heat the oil in the air fryer and sauté the ham with pepper. • Add the eggs and allow to stand. • Lay the tomato slices on the eggs and sprinkle with Parmesan cheese.
3. Place in the preheated air fryer on the middle rack and bake the frittata for 30-40 minutes at 180° C • If necessary, use the grill function for the last 5 minutes to get a crisp, golden surface.

304. Roast Pork with Herbs

INGREDIENTS

- 1.6 kg pork loin (boneless, chop roast)
- 100 g pine nuts
- 50 ml olive oil
- 10 sprigs of rosemary
- 10 sprigs of thyme
- 4-5 stems of sage
- 1 bunch of basil
- 2 cloves of garlic
- 1 tbsp mustard
- sea salt
- pepper

INSTRUCTIONS

1. Wash herbs and shake dry • Pluck leaves from stalks and chop finely • Put pine nuts and herbs in a mortar and chop everything • Peel garlic and squeeze with garlic press • Mix the herb mixture with garlic, mustard, olive oil, salt and pepper in a bowl.
2. Wash the meat and pat dry with a kitchen towel. • Then cut the pork loin in the middle to ¾ with a sharp knife. • Carefully fold the meat apart and spread the herb mixture on it. • Fold the meat back together and tie tightly with kitchen string
3. Place the meat on the air fryer grill and cook in a preheated air fryer on a medium rack with top/bottom heat for about 30 minutes at 180° C. • Place a tray under the grill to catch the escaping gravy • Turn the roast and cook for another 60 minutes, in between turn again.
4. Remove roast pork from the air fryer and let it rest briefly • Remove the string and slice the roast with a sharp knife.

305. Beetroot Spinach & Feta Salad

INGREDIENTS

- 400 g beetroot
- 200 g baby spinach
- 100 g feta
- 2 tbsp avocado oil

- Juice of a lime
- nutmeg
- sea salt
- pepper

INSTRUCTIONS

1. Wash beetroot, put in an air fryer and cover with water until soft for 30-40 minutes. • Let beets cool slightly, then peel and slice.
2. Wash and drain the spinach • Put the spinach leaves on a plate and place the beetroot slices on top • Crumble the feta with your fingers and pour over the salad.
3. Drizzle lime juice and avocado oil over the salad. • Finally, season the beetroot salad with freshly grated nutmeg, salt, and pepper and serve.

306. Meatloaf with Cheese Filling

INGREDIENTS

- 800 g veal minced meat, organic
- 1 onion
- 2 cloves of garlic
- 1 spelled roll or a slice of bread from the previous day
- 100 g Gouda, small diced
- 100 ml milk
- ½ bunch of parsley
- 2 tbsp yogurt
- 1 tbsp Dijon mustard
- nutmeg
- sea salt
- pepper

INSTRUCTIONS

1. Put the veal mince into a bowl • Cut the rolls into pieces and soak in milk in a small bowl • Peel the onion and garlic and finely dice • Wash the parsley, shake dry and chop.
2. Add onions and garlic to the minced meat. • Take the bread rolls out of the milk and squeeze them out, then add the minced meat with yogurt and mustard. • Add some freshly grated nutmeg, salt, and pepper and knead everything with your hands. • Finally, mix in the small gouda cubes and parsley.
3. Put the minced meat mixture in a tin air fryer and bake in a preheated air fryer at 220° C for 50-60 minutes. • Remove the meatloaf from the air fryer and allow it to cool for a few minutes. • Then remove the meatloaf from the mold and slice.

307. Tomato Soup with Cream Cheese & Parsley

INGREDIENTS

- 1 kg ripe tomatoes
- 200 ml vegetable broth
- 1 pepper
- 3 cloves of garlic
- 2 onions
- 1 chili pepper
- Juice of a lemon, organic
- 5-6 stems of basil
- 4 tbsp olive oil
- 1 tsp honey
- 100 g cream cheese
- ½ bunch of thyme
- ½ bunch of parsley
- sea salt
- pepper

INSTRUCTIONS

1. Wash and drain the tomatoes, and herbs • Halve the chili pepper, remove the kernels and chop finely • Pick the basil leaves off the stalk • Peel and finely chop the onions and garlic • Wash the peppers, cut in half, remove the seeds and partitions and cut into pieces.
2. Heat 1 tbsp of olive oil in a large air fryer and roast the onions, garlic, and basil leaves • Add the tomatoes to a large casserole dish and add onions, garlic, and basil.
3. Put the thyme sprigs, and a little oil over the tomatoes • Bake the tomatoes in the casserole dish in a preheated air fryer at 170° C for about 30 minutes. • Remove the thyme sprigs after baking. • Remove the skin on fresh tomatoes after the baking time.
4. Heat 2 tbsp of olive oil in the large pot and sauté paprika, chili, tomatoes, onions, garlic, and basil. • Remove the pot from the heat and finely puree with the hand blender.
5. Put the pot with the tomato puree back on the hotplate and top up with the stock. • Cover everything for about 20 minutes. • If necessary, add a little water.
6. Add the lemon juice and honey to the tomato soup and stir • Season the soup with salt and pepper • Chop the parsley • Put the tomato soup in deep plates or bowls and stir in a little cream cheese • Sprinkle with parsley and serve.

308. Salmon Fillet with Dill Dip

INGREDIENTS

- 1 salmon fillet, approx. 200 g
- 2 tbsp olive oil
- For the dill dip
- 2 El Quark
- 1 tbsp yogurt
- 2 tbsp chopped dill tips
- 2 tbsp of lemon
- 1 tsp agave syrup
- sea salt
- pepper

INSTRUCTIONS

1. Wash the salmon fillet and pat dry with the kitchen cheesecloth • Heat the olive oil in the air fryer and sauté the salmon fillet on both sides.
2. Place the salmon in the air fryer for 5-10 minutes in the preheated air fryer at 175° C and continue cooking.
3. Meanwhile mix all INGREDIENTS for the dip in a bowl
4. Remove salmon from the air fryer, season with salt and pepper and serve together with the dip.

309. Green Salad with Beans, Cheddar & Lime Dressing

INGREDIENTS

Salad

- 100 g corn
- 50 g peas
- 50 g thick beans
- 30 g of cheddar cheese
- 100 g zucchini
- 2 spring onions

Lime dressing

- 1 organic lime
- 3-4 stems of coriander
- 50 ml olive oil
- 1 tsp chervil, chopped

- 1 tsp honey
- sea salt
- pepper

INSTRUCTIONS

1. Wash corn lettuce and drain • Pluck lettuce leaves from the root and place in a bowl • Remove fresh peas and beans from the pods.
2. Wash the zucchini, dry and slice with the grater into thin pins • Clean the spring onions and cut into rings • Cut the cheese into small cubes • Put everything in the salad bowl and stir.
3. For the dressing, zest and halve lime and squeeze juice from both halves • Wash coriander, shake dry and chop • Liquefy solid honey in a warm water bath with a temperature up to 40° C.
4. Mix lime zest and juice in a small bowl with honey, chervil, coriander and olive oil and season with salt and pepper. • Add the dressing to the salad and stir.

310. Roasted Butternut Squash with Cranberries & Walnut

INGREDIENTS

- 400 g butternut squash
- 100 g salad (lamb's lettuce, arugula, endive salad)
- 30 g cranberries
- 50 g of walnuts
- 2 cloves of garlic
- 5 tbsp olive oil
- sea salt
- pepper

INSTRUCTIONS

1. Peel the butternut squash with the peeler • Cut the pumpkin in half and then remove the seeds with a spoon • Cut the butternut squash into bite-sized pieces • Peel the garlic and finely dice it.
2. Wash lettuce leaves and dry in a salad spinner
3. Toss lettuce into pieces
4. Chop walnuts roughly with a large knife • Place lettuce leaves on two plates and sprinkle with nuts and cranberries.
5. Mix the oil with garlic in a bowl
6. Brush the air fryer with the garlic oil and roast the butternut squash on all sides
7. Season the squash with salt and pepper and place on the salad plates
8. Drizzle the remaining warm oil over the salad.

311. Fish In Mediterranean Tomato Sauce

INGREDIENTS

- 1 kg fish (cod, perch, salmon)
- 500 g tomatoes
- 250 ml Passata
- 200 g black olives, pitted
- 2 shallots
- 3-4 cloves of garlic
- 1 organic lemon
- 3-4 rosemary branches
- 3 tbsp olive oil
- nutmeg
- sea salt
- pepper

INSTRUCTIONS

1. Wash the fish and drain on a kitchen towel • Cut the fish into pieces • Wash the tomatoes, dry and cut into pieces • Peel and slice the garlic.
2. Wash and drain the rosemary • Zest lemon. • Halve the lemon, juice one half, and slice the other half • Peel the shallots and finely dice.
3. Heat the oil in the air fryer and fry the fish with the shallots. • Add the garlic and tomatoes and roast. • Add the Passata, add the sprigs of rosemary and lemon slices and simmer for 10-15 minutes.
4. Add olives, lemon peel, and juice to the air fryer and stir. • Season fish with freshly grated nutmeg, salt, and pepper.

312. Meatball, Herb & Chili Frittata

INGREDIENTS

Meatballs
- 400 g ground beef
- 1 shallot
- 5-6 stems of parsley

Frittata
- 8 eggs
- 200 g cream

- 100 g Parmesan
- 1 chili pepper

Additional
- 2 tbsp olive oil
- sea salt
- pepper

INSTRUCTIONS

1. For the meatballs, peel the shallot and finely dice • Wash parsley, shake dry and chop • Mix ground beef with shallot and parsley in a bowl, then season with salt and pepper.
2. From the ground beef mixture into balls • Heat oil in the air fryer and meatballs on all sides • Remove meatballs and set aside.
3. For the frittata, first stir eggs and cream in a bowl • Wash the chili pepper, dry and cut into rings • Rub the parmesan, then add to the egg mixture and stir.
4. Pour the egg mixture into the casserole dish and put the meatballs into it. • Sprinkle the chili pepper over it. • Bake the frittata in a preheated air fryer at 180° C for 30-45 minutes. • Sprinkle the frittata with herbs and serve as desired.

313. Tomato Salad with Onions & Parmesan

INGREDIENTS

- 600 g colorful tomatoes
- 1 red onion
- 50 g Parmesan
- 5-6 stems of basil

- 4 tbsp olive oil
- sea salt
- pepper

INSTRUCTIONS

1. Wash tomatoes and drain • Halve tomatoes and remove stem stems • Slice tomatoes.
2. Peel the onion and cut into rings • Wash the basil and shake it dry, then pluck the leaves from the stalk.
3. Serve tomato slices on a large plate • Add onion and freshly grated Parmesan.

4. Drizzle tomato salad with olive oil and season with salt and pepper. • Place basil leaves over the salad and serve.

314. Pumpkin Soup with Roasted Cashews

INGREDIENTS

- ½ Hokkaido pumpkin
- 2 carrots
- 1 shallot
- 3 cm ginger
- ½ chili pepper
- 40 g butter
- 750 ml vegetable broth
- 100 ml orange juice, juice
- 1 tbsp of lemon juice, freshly squeezed
- 4 tbsp pumpkin seed oil
- 4 tbsp of cashew nuts
- 3-4 stems of parsley
- 4 flowers nasturtium
- sea salt
- White pepper

INSTRUCTIONS

1. Thoroughly wash the pumpkin with warm water, then dry. • Cut the pumpkin in half with a large knife and remove the seeds with a spoon. • Cut a pumpkin half into small pieces.
2. Peel and slice the carrots • Peel the shallot and finely dice it • Peel the ginger and chop it into small pieces • Halve the chili, core it and cut it into pieces.
3. Melt the butter in an air fryer and sauté the shallot • Add the carrots and the pumpkin and sauté everything • Deglaze with the stock and pour in • Add the chili pepper and simmer for 15 minutes over medium heat.
4. Meanwhile, wash the parsley, shake dry and chop • Roast cashews in an air fryer without fat on all sides • Then place cashews on a kitchen board and chop with a large knife.
5. Stir in the ginger, lemon and orange juice and then remove the pot from the hot plate. • Puree the soup with the hand blender. • Add some warm water to the soup if necessary and mix again until it has the desired consistency.
6. Season the pumpkin soup with salt and pepper • Fill the soup with small bowls and drizzle with pumpkin seed oil • Add the parsley and cashews to the soup and garnish with the edible flower.

315. Zoodles with Feta & Tomatoes

INGREDIENTS

- 500 g zucchini
- 250 g cherry tomatoes
- 200 g feta
- 3 cloves of garlic
- 4 tbsp olive oil
- Basil shredded
- sea salt
- White pepper

INSTRUCTIONS

1. Wash the zucchini and drain.
2. Cut the zucchini into long thin noodles with the spiral cutter. • Wash, dry and quarter the tomatoes.
3. Dice the feta.
4. Peel the garlic and squeeze it out with the garlic press.
5. Heat the oil in the air fryer and sauté garlic.
6. Add the zucchini noodles to the air fryer and fry for several minutes until they are firm.
7. Add the tomatoes, feta and basil and stir. • Season the zucchini noodles with salt and pepper.

316. Chinese Vegetables with Beef Strips

INGREDIENTS

- 200 g beef fillet
- 200 g broccoli
- 200 g mushrooms
- 2 carrots
- 2 cloves of garlic
- 1 chili pepper
- 4 tbsp organic soy sauce
- 2 tbsp of sesame oil
- sea salt
- pepper

INSTRUCTIONS

1. Wash the beef fillet and dry with a kitchen cloth, then cut into strips. • Clean the mushrooms, cut off the dry ends of the stems and slice the mushrooms • Peel the carrots and cut them into thin strips with the peeler.
2. Wash the broccoli, drain and cut the florets from the stalk • Peel the garlic and chop finely • Wash the chili pepper, cut in half and remove the seeds and partitions • Finely chop the chili pepper.
3. Heat the sesame oil in the wok and sauté the beef fillet. • Add the garlic and chili and sauté. • Add carrots, broccoli and mushrooms and roast. • Add the soy sauce to the air fryer with beef strips and season with salt and pepper.

317. Fig, Kiwi & Pomegranate Salad

INGREDIENTS

- 50 g lettuce
- 1 fig
- 1 kiwi
- 20 g grapes, about 5-6 pcs.
- 25 g pomegranate seeds
- 1 tsp agave syrup

INSTRUCTIONS

1. Wash lettuce leaves and dry them in a salad spinner • Small pluck or cut lettuce leaves
2. Wash the figs and drain, then cut into pieces • Peel and slice the kiwi.
3. Wash and drain the grapes.
4. Carefully remove the pomegranate seeds.
5. Mix the salad, fig, kiwi, grapes and pomegranate seeds with a little agave syrup in a bowl. • Refine the salad with other spices and serve.

318. Mushroom & Boiled Ham Omelet

INGREDIENTS

- 4 eggs
- 3-4 mushrooms
- 100 g cooked ham from the butcher
- 20 ml mineral water, medium
- 2 tbsp cream
- 1 tsp olive oil
- ½ bunch of parsley
- sea salt
- pepper

INSTRUCTIONS

1. Whisk eggs in a bowl with mineral water and cream • Wash the parsley, shake dry and chop • Add the parsley to the eggs • Season the egg mixture with salt and pepper and mix.

2. Clean and slice the mushrooms • Cut the ham into strips • Heat the olive oil in the air fryer and sauté the mushrooms • Remove the mushrooms and pour the egg mixture into the hot air fryer.
3. Cook the omelet over medium heat until the underside has stabilized
4. Turn the omelet and cover with mushrooms and ham.
5. Remove the omelet from the air fryer and fold it up.

319. Tuna Salad with Eggs & Tomatoes

INGREDIENTS

- 1 can of tuna
- 100 g salad
- 2 eggs
- 10 green olives, pitted
- 5-6 cherry tomatoes
- 2 tbsp olive oil
- nutmeg
- sea salt
- pepper

INSTRUCTIONS

1. Cover the eggs in an air fryer with water. Cook for 8-10 minutes. • Wash the lettuce leaves and dry in the salad spinner. • Then cut the salad leaves into pieces.
2. Wash the tomatoes, drain and cut in half. • Halve the olives. • Place the salad on a plate, drizzle the olive oil over it and spread the tomatoes and olives over the salad.
3. Drain the tuna and pour in portions over the salad • Peel and quarter the eggs • Add the eggs to the salad and season with freshly grated nutmeg, salt, and pepper.

320. Cherry Tomato Frittata with Cucumber Salad

INGREDIENTS

Frittata

- 8 eggs
- 200 ml cream
- 100 g Parmesan
- 200 g cherry tomatoes
- 1 spring onion
- 1 tbsp olive oil

Salad

- 300 g cucumber
- 1 carrot
- 1 spring onion
- 4 tbsp olive oil
- Juice of a lemon
- 1 tsp dill tips
- 1 tsp sesame
- sea salt
- pepper

INSTRUCTIONS

1. Beat the eggs in a bowl and whisk with cream • Season the egg and cream mixture with salt and pepper • Wash and halve the tomatoes • Clean the spring onion and cut into fine rings
2. Rub the parmesan.
3. Heat the olive oil in the air fryer and then add the egg-cream mixture.
4. Add the tomatoes and spring onion and sprinkle with Parmesan. • Put in the preheated air fryer and bake the frittata for 30-45 minutes at 180° C.

5. For the cucumber salad, wash and drain the vegetables • Slice the cucumber
6. Peel the carrot and grate it in strips • Clean the spring onion and cut into rings • Pluck the dill tips from the stalk.
7. Mix the salad INGREDIENTS in a bowl with oil and lemon juice.
8. Season the cucumber salad with salt and pepper and add the sesame seeds.
9. Remove the frittata from the air fryer and serve with the cucumber salad.

321. Grilled Salmon Steaks with Soy & Honey Marinade

INGREDIENTS

- 4 salmon steaks, 230 g
- 4 tbsp organic soy sauce
- 1 tbsp olive oil
- 1 tbsp. Sesame oil
- 1 tbsp honey
- Juice a lime
- sea salt
- pepper

INSTRUCTIONS

1. Wash salmon steaks and pat dry with a kitchen towel
2. Mix soy sauce, oils, honey and lime juice in a bowl to a marinade and season with salt and pepper.
3. Brush salmon steaks with the marinade and cook in the hot grill air fryer or on the grill
4. Grill the fish on each side for a few minutes over high heat, then reduce the temperature or remove it from the grill zone and let the steaks soak for a few minutes.

322. Broccoli Salad with Peppers, Feta & Walnuts

INGREDIENTS

- 200 g broccoli
- ½ red pepper
- 70 g feta
- 5 walnuts
- 2 tbsp yogurt, natural
- Juice of half a lime
- sea salt
- pepper

INSTRUCTIONS

1. Wash broccoli and drain • Add enough water to a pot with a steamer insert so that the steamer does not touch the water • Cut broccoli florets from the stalk and place them on the steamer • Cook the broccoli for 5-7 minutes until firm.
2. Core the peppers, wash them and cut into small cubes • roughly chop walnuts • mix yogurt and lime juice • place the broccoli and paprika on a plate and spread the yogurt mixture over it.
3. Crumble the feta in your hand and sprinkle with the nuts over the salad • Season the salad with salt and pepper.

323. Air Fryer Pepper Chicken

INGREDIENTS

- 500 g chicken breast fillet
- 200 g green beans, fresh
- 2 spring onions
- 1 red pepper
- 1 yellow pepper
- 1 onion

- 1 red chili pepper
- 1 clove of garlic
- 4 tbsp sesame oil
- 3 tbsp organic soy sauce
- 2 tsp honey
- 1 tsp lime juice
- 1 tsp cumin
- ½ tsp carob seed flour
- sea salt
- pepper

INSTRUCTIONS

1. Wash the chicken, dry with a kitchen towel and cut into strips. • Wash fresh beans, drain and clean. • Place the beans in an air fryer and cover with water. • Bake beans for 8-10 minutes, then drain in the strainer.
2. Halve the peppers, remove the seeds and partitions and rinse the halves under running water • Cut the peppers into strips • Clean the spring onions and cut into strips at an angle • Peel the onion and garlic and finely chop.
3. Cut the chili pepper in half, core it and cut it into pieces. • Heat the sesame oil in the air fryer and fry the chicken. • Add the onion, garlic, and chili and sauté. • Add the peppers and beans and fry for several minutes over medium heat.
4. Put the soy sauce, honey, lime juice, cumin, and carob bean flour in a small bowl and stir. • Add the sauce mixture to the air fryer. • Season the chicken and pepper air fryer with salt and pepper. • Simmer for a few minutes over low heat.
5. Add the spring onion to the air fryer • If necessary, add some more water to the air fryer and stir once more and season to taste • Finally, sprinkle the dish with sesame seeds.

324. Zucchini with Tomato & Vegetable Sauce

INGREDIENTS

- 2 large zucchini
- 10 mushrooms
- 1 red pepper
- ½ chili pepper
- 400 g tomatoes, lumpy
- 2 cloves of garlic
- ½ bunch of basil
- 200 g mozzarella
- 1 tbsp olive oil
- sea salt
- pepper

INSTRUCTIONS

1. Wash the zucchini, dry and cut in half lengthwise. • Scrape the kernels out of the halves of the zucchini with a spoon to create even pits. • Clean the mushrooms and cut off the dry ends of the stalk. • Cut the mushrooms into pieces.
2. Cut the peppers in half, then remove the seeds and partitions • Wash the halves of the paprika, drain and cut into small cubes • Halve the chili, remove the seeds and chop them into small pieces • Peel the garlic and chop finely.
3. Wash the basil, shake it dry and pluck the leaves from the stem. • Finely chop the basil leaves. • Heat the oil in the air fryer and sauté the mushrooms, paprika, chili and garlic. • Add the tomatoes and stir.
4. Add the basil to the sauce and season with salt and pepper. • Add the tomato-vegetable sauce to the halves of the zucchini and sprinkle with mozzarella.
5. Put the zucchini in a casserole dish and cook for about 20 minutes at 180° C in a preheated air fryer.

325. Eggs Benedict

INGREDIENTS

HOLLANDAISE SAUCE

- 2 eggs
- 1 1/2 tsp fresh lemon juice
- 55 g butter, melted
- 1/4 tsp salt

EGGS

- 4 slices of bacon
- 1 tsp of vinegar
- 4 eggs

INSTRUCTIONS

1. In a large bowl, mix two eggs and lemon juice vigorously.
2. Fill a large air fryer with 2.5 cm of water and heat until the water is simmering. Reduce the heat to medium.
3. Wear an air fryer mitt and hold the bowl with the eggs above the water and make sure that it does not touch the water. Beat 3 minutes and make sure that the eggs are not mixed.
4. Slowly add butter to egg mixture and beat for about 2 minutes.
5. Cool the sauce.
6. Add bacon to the air fryer and fry 3 minutes per side. Place the bacon on paper towels.
7. Add vinegar and place over low heat in an air fryer that is half full of water.
8. The eggs gently break in the water and make sure that the yolk does not break. Set the heat on Low to medium and cook 3 to 4 minutes.
9. Remove the eggs. Drain and set aside.
10. Break bacon in half. Place two halves on a plate and garnish with an egg. Repeat with 2 more halves and another egg. Cover with Hollandaise sauce

326. Scottish Eggs

INGREDIENTS

- 100 g of breakfast sausage
- 1/2 tsp garlic powder
- 1/4 tsp salt
- 1/8 tsp freshly ground black pepper
- 2 hard boiled eggs, peeled

INSTRUCTIONS

1. Preheat the air fryer to 200° C.
2. Mix the sausage, garlic powder, salt and pepper in a medium bowl.
3. Form two balls, pressing each ball on a piece of parchment paper to a 0.8 cm patty.
4. Place a hard-boiled egg in the center of each cake and gently mold the sausage around the egg.
5. Place the covered with sausage eggs on a non-greased baking sheet and place in the preheated air fryer.
6. Bake for 25 minutes. Let cool 5 minutes and then serve.

327. Biscuits In Sausage Sauce

INGREDIENTS

Biscuits

- 60 g of coconut flour
- 60 gram almond flour
- 2 tsp baking powder
- 1 tsp garlic
- powder
- 1/2 tsp onion powder
- 1/2 tsp salt
- 100 g of grated cheddar cheese
- 50 g butter, melted
- 4 eggs
- 1 sour cream

Sauce

- 450 g of milled breakfast sausage
- 1 tsp finely chopped garlic
- 1 tbsp almond flour
- 350 ml unsweetened almond milk
- 110 ml whipped cream
- 1 1/2 tsp freshly ground black pepper
- 1/2 tsp salt

INSTRUCTIONS

1. Preheat the air fryer to 180° C.
2. Cover a baking sheet with parchment paper.
3. Mix coconut flour, almond flour, baking powder, garlic powder, onion powder and salt in a large bowl and stir in the cheddar slowly.
4. Make a pit in the center of the dry INGREDIENTS before adding the wet ingredients.
5. Add the melted butter, eggs and sour cream in this pit. Fold until a dough forms.
6. Drop biscuits on the prepared baking sheet. Bake until they are firm and light brown.
7. Heat a large skillet over medium heat. Add the minced meat, open it with a spoon and bake them brown on all sides.
8. Add the chopped garlic when the meat is brown. Cook for 1 minute.
9. When the garlic smells, sprinkle the almond flour over. Turn the heat to low to medium-low. The almond flour with the fat mix to develop a light roux, stirring for about 5 minutes.
10. Add the almond milk, stirring constantly.
11. Add the whipped cream. Increase the temperature to medium high, stir and reduce the mixture for 3 minutes.
12. Turn the heat to low to medium-low. Add pepper and salt. Stir for 1 minute.
13. Reduce the heat under the sausage sauce to a minimum.
14. Serve 1 biscuit per person and garnish it with a ⅓ cup of the sauce.

328. Portobello, Sausage & Cheese Breakfast Burger

INGREDIENTS

- 1 tbsp olive oil
- 2 Portobello mushrooms, stem removed
- 60 g breakfast sausage
- 2 (50 g) slices cheddar cheese

INSTRUCTIONS

1. Heat the olive oil in the air fryer for 1 minute over medium heat.
2. Add the mushrooms in the hot oil, with the convex side up.
3. Bake 5 minutes per side, or until browned.
4. Heat another medium skillet over medium heat.
5. Cut breakfast sausage to a 1 cm thick pasty form. Put it in the middle of the hot air fryer. Bake for 5 minutes, then turn and cook for another 2 to 3 minutes.
6. When the sausage is almost ready, turn down the heat. garnish the burger with cheddar cheese. Bake until the cheese is melted.
7. Cover with the remaining mushrooms and serve.

329. Butter Glazed Muffins

INGREDIENTS

MUFFINS

- 200 g of almonds
- Flour 60 g of coconut flour
- 2 tsp baking powder
- 55 g of erythritol and other sugar substitutes such as stevia
- 6 eggs
- 55 g butter, melted
- 120 ml mineral water
- 1 tsp of pure vanilla extract
- 1 1 1 12 spoonful of cinnamon

GLAZE

- 1 package of cream cheese, at room temperature
- 1 tbsp of sour cream
- 1/2 tsp pure vanilla extract

INSTRUCTIONS

1. Preheat the air fryer to 180° C.
2. Mix the almond flour, coconut flour, baking powder, and erythritol.
3. Break the eggs into a large bowl whisk together. Add the melted butter, the mineral water and the vanilla. Stir to mix.
4. Add the INGREDIENTS to the wet ingredients. Mix well.
5. Pour the mixture evenly into a mold. garnish each muffin with an equal amount of cinnamon.
6. Stir in the cinnamon with a toothpick through the dough.
7. Place the dish in the preheated air fryer and bake 20 to 25 minutes or until golden brown.
8. Remove the mold from the air fryer and let the muffins cool for 5 to 10 minutes.
9. Mix cream cheese, sour cream and vanilla in a medium bowl. Spread evenly over the muffins before serving.

330. Raspberry Scones

INGREDIENTS

- 120 g almond flour
- 2 eggs beaten
- 75 g Splenda, stevia or other sugar substitute
- 1 1/2 tsp pure vanilla extract
- 1 1/2 tsp baking powder
- 115 g raspberries

INSTRUCTIONS

1. Preheat the air fryer to 180° C.
2. Cover a baking sheet with parchment paper.
3. Mix almond flour, eggs, Splenda, vanilla and baking powder in a large bowl.
4. Place the raspberries in the bowl and fold in gently.
5. Place 2 to 3 tbsp of dough per scone draw on the lined baking tray.
6. Place in the preheated air fryer-bake 15 minutes or until light brown.
7. Remove the baking sheet from the air fryer and place the scones on a grid to cool for 10 minutes.

331. Waffles with Whipped Cream

INGREDIENTS

WAFFLES

- Cooking spray for the waffle iron
- 30 g coconut flour
- 30 g almond flour
- 30 g canvas flour
- 1 tsp baking powder
- 1 tsp Stevia or other sugar substitutes
- 1/4 tsp cinnamon
- 170 g protein
- 4 eggs
- 1 tsp of pure vanilla extract

WHIPPED CREAM

- 118 ml whipped cream
- 1 tsp Stevia or other sugar substitutes

INSTRUCTIONS

1. Heat the waffle iron to medium heat and spray with cooking spray.
2. In a large bowl, combine the coconut flour, almond flour, the linen flour, baking powder, stevia and cinnamon.
3. Beat the egg white in another medium bowl until it is stiff.
4. Add the whole eggs and the vanilla to the dry ingredients. Mix well.
5. Pull the beaten egg whites gently through the dry INGREDIENTS until it is completely absorbed.
6. Pour the batter onto the preheated waffle iron. Bake according to the instructions of the waffle iron.
7. Prepare the whipped cream.
8. Beat the whipped cream in a medium bowl for 3 to 4 minutes, until it is thick.
9. Add the stevia. Continue beating until it is stiff, about 1 minute.
10. The waffles with the same amount of whipped cream garnish and serve.

332. Cream Cheese Air Fryer Cakes

INGREDIENTS

- 55 g cream cheese, room temperature
- 2 eggs
- 1/2 tsp Stevia
- 1/4 tsp nutmeg

INSTRUCTIONS

1. Place the cream cheese in a blender. Add the eggs, stevia and nutmeg. Mix until the dough is smooth.

2. Slowly pour a small amount of batter onto the preheated griddle, about an eighth of a cup per air fryer cake. The dough will be very thin and easy to spread.
3. Bake the air fryer cakes a little longer than a minute and then flip and bake for another minute.
4. Repeat with the remaining dough.

333. Butter Coffee
INGREDIENTS

- 350 ml hot coffee
- 2 tbsp unsalted butter
- 1 1/2 ml MCT oil or coconut oil
- Sugar-free sweetener

INSTRUCTIONS

1. Prepare fresh coffee in your favorite style.
2. Mix coffee, butter and oil in a blender until frothy, about 1 minute.

334. Fried Eggs In Hambakjes
INGREDIENTS

- Cooking spray for a cupcake form
- 4 slices of Black Forest ham
- 4 eggs
- 1 tsp dried parsley

INSTRUCTIONS

1. Preheat the air fryer to 200° C.
2. Spray the cupcake form.
3. Place a slice of ham into each of the cups. The ham is hanging over the sides.
4. Add 1 egg into each cup and garnish with parsley.
5. Place the cupcake in the preheated air fryer. Bake for 15 minutes until the egg is cooked, but the yolk is still soft.

335. Bacon, Egg & Cheese Plates
INGREDIENTS

- 6 slices of bacon
- 4 eggs beaten
- 118 ml whipped cream
- 1/4 tsp salt
- 1/8 tsp freshly ground black pepper
- 1/2 cup grated Monterey Jack cheese

INSTRUCTIONS

1. Preheat the air fryer to 180° C.
2. Wrap a slice of bacon in a cupcake-shape around the edges, so that it covers the sides of the mold. Repeat with three more discs in three other shells.
3. Cut the remaining two slices of bacon into 5 cm pieces. Insert 2 to 3 bacon on the bottom of each wrapped with bacon cupcake-shape so that each is completely covered.
4. Mix the eggs, cream, salt and pepper in a medium bowl.
5. Pour egg mass evenly into the container. Spoon 2 tbsp cheese on top.
6. Bake 35 minutes or until golden brown.

336. Crustless Quiche Lorraine

INGREDIENTS

- Cooking spray
- 1 pound thick sliced bacon
- 1 tbsp garlic, minced
- 55 g chopped onion
- 4 eggs, beaten
- 350 ml whipped cream
- 225 g grated Swiss cheese
- 115 g grated Gruyere cheese
- 3/4 tsp salt
- 1/4 tsp freshly ground black pepper

INSTRUCTIONS

1. Preheat the air fryer to 180° C.
2. Air fry bacon until crispy, 6 to 8 minutes. Remove the bacon from the air fryer and let it sit on paper towels. After cooling, cut the bacon into small pieces and set aside.
3. Add chopped garlic and onion to the remaining fat in the skillet over medium heat. Cook for 3 to 4 minutes. Remove air fryer from heat. Pour the onion-garlic mixture in a small bowl. Set aside to cool.
4. The eggs and the cream mix in a large bowl for 2 minutes with a whisk.
5. Add Swiss and Gruyere cheese, pickled bacon, onions, garlic, salt and pepper to the eggs. Stir to mix.
6. Pour the egg mixture slowly into the air fryer. Bake for 20 to 25 minutes, until the center has solidified.
7. Remove from the air fryer. Let cool 5 minutes and serve.

337. Chia Yogurt Parfait

INGREDIENTS

- 225 g yogurt
- 60 ml unsweetened almond milk
- 2 tbsp chia seeds
- 6 tsp chopped almonds
- 1/4 tsp cinnamon

INSTRUCTIONS

1. Mix yogurt, almond milk and chia seeds in a medium bowl.
2. Place a third of the yogurt mix in a tall glass. Sprinkle 2 tsp almonds and a hint of cinnamon. Repeat to form three layers.
3. Thicken for 10 minutes in the refrigerator.

338. Naughty Avocado Fried Eggs

INGREDIENTS

- 1 avocado, halved lengthwise, seeded
- 2 eggs
- 4 tbsp grated Colby cheese
- 1/8 tsp salt
- 1/8 tsp freshly ground black pepper

INSTRUCTIONS

1. Preheat the air fryer to 250° C.
2. From each half avocado, remove enough meat to fit an egg.
3. Place each avocado half in a bowl, cut side up.

4. Break an egg carefully into each one. Do not break the yolk.
5. Sprinkle 2 tbsp of Colby cheese on each avocado half. Season with salt and pepper.
6. Bake 15 to 20 minutes.

339. Broccoli & Cheese Quiche

INGREDIENTS

- Cooking spray
- 1/2 tsp salt
- 340 g broccoli florets
- 5 eggs
- 180 ml whipped cream
- 1/4 tsp freshly ground black pepper
- 1/2 tsp garlic ground
- 170g grated sharp cheddar cheese

INSTRUCTIONS

1. Preheat the air fryer to 180° C.
2. Four Aries models with cooking spray inject and place on a baking sheet.
3. Bring a medium pot of salted water to a boil. Add the broccoli. cook 1 minute, take the broccoli from the pot and drain.
4. Cut the drained broccoli. Put aside.
5. Mix eggs, cream, salt and pepper in a large bowl. Add broccoli, garlic and cheese.
6. Spread the egg mixture evenly on the prepared ramequins. Place the baking sheet in the preheated air fryer.
7. Bake until the egg broccoli mixture has risen and is light brown, about 35 minutes.

340. Hot Dog Rolls

INGREDIENTS

- 340 g grated mozzarella cheese
- 2 tbsp cream cheese at room temp
- 180 ml almond flour
- 1 egg
- 1 tsp garlic
- 1 tsp Italian herbs
- 4 hot dogs

INSTRUCTIONS

1. Preheat the air fryer to 220° C.
2. Mix the cream cheese and the mozzarella in a large microwaveable bowl. Heat a minute in the microwave. Stir and heat for 30 more seconds.
3. Mix almond flour, egg, garlic and Italian herbs with the cheese mass.
4. Divide the dough into four equal pieces. Wrap a piece of dough around each hot dog.
5. Place the dough-covered hot dogs on a lined baking tray. Make holes with a fork in each piece of dough to prevent it from bubbling during baking.
6. Place the baking sheet in the preheated air fryer and bake 7 to 8 minutes.
7. Remove the baking sheet from the air fryer. Check for air bubbles (possibly with a fork to pierce). Flip the hot dogs and bake for an additional 6 to 7 minutes.
8. Remove the baking sheet from the air fryer. Let cool for 5 minutes.

341. Garlic Pepperoni Chips

INGREDIENTS

- 180 g of pepperoni
- 1/2 tsp garlic powder

INSTRUCTIONS

1. Preheat the air fryer to 220° C.
2. Place the pepperoni slices on a lined baking tray.
3. Sprinkle the slices with garlic powder.
4. Place the baking sheet in the preheated air fryer. Bake 7 to 8 minutes. Remove the plate from the air fryer and turn the slices.
5. Bake an additional 2 to 3 minutes or until the pepperoni slices are golden brown and crispy. Take a baking sheet from the air fryer and place the pepperoni slices to dry on paper towels.

342. Caprese Salad Snacks

INGREDIENTS

- 12 cherry tomatoes, halved
- 12 Bocconcini (small mozzarella balls) or 30g mozzarella, diced
- 12 fresh basil leaves
- 2 tbsp olive oil
- 1 tbsp balsamic vinegar
- 1/4 tsp salt
- 1/8 tsp freshly ground black pepper

INSTRUCTIONS

1. Impale a tomato half and a bocconcini on a toothpick.
2. Cover the cheese with a basil leaf and add the second half of the tomato. Put aside.
3. Repeat with the remaining ingredients.
4. Place the skewers on a plate. Drizzle with olive oil and balsamic vinegar-season with salt and pepper.

343. Bacon-Wrapped Mozzarella Sticks

INGREDIENTS

- Oil for frying
- 2 mozzarella cheese rolls
- 4 slices of bacon

INSTRUCTIONS

1. Heat 5 cm oil in a large air fryer to 180° C.
2. Cut each cheese stick in half.
3. Wrap in a slice of bacon. Secure with a toothpick.
4. Once the oil is hot, let the coated cheese with bacon pieces fall into the oil. Bake for 2 to 3 minutes or until the bacon is well browned. Transfer to paper towels to drain fat.

344. French Onion Dip

INGREDIENTS

- 2 tbsp butter
- 115 g chopped onion,
- 3/4 tsp salt
- 240 ml sour cream
- 1/2 cup mayonnaise
- 1 tsp garlic, chopped
- 1 tsp sauce
- 1/2 tsp freshly ground black pepper

INSTRUCTIONS

1. Dissolve the butter in a large skillet over medium heat. Add the onions and ¼ tsp salt. Cook for 1 to 2 minutes. Reduce the heat to medium-low. Caramelize, occasionally stirring the onion for 35 to 40 minutes.
2. Remove the onions from the heat. Allow to cool while you make the rest of the ingredients.
3. Mix sour cream, mayonnaise, garlic, Worcestershire sauce, pepper and remaining ½ tsp salt in a bowl.
4. Add the cooled onions in the mixture. Mix well.

345. Goat Cheese Stuffed Peppers

INGREDIENTS

- 170 g goat cheese at room temperature
- 1 tsp chopped garlic
- 2 tsp chopped fresh basil
- 1/4 tsp salt
- 1/8 tsp freshly ground black pepper
- 12 sweet cherry peppers without seeds and stem
- 1 tbsp olive oil

INSTRUCTIONS

1. Heat the air fryer to 220° C.
2. Mix goat cheese, garlic, basil, salt and pepper in a small bowl.
3. Fill the peppers with goat cheese mixture with a spoon.
4. Place the peppers on a lined baking tray. The peppers with olive oil, sprinkle. Place the baking sheet in the air fryer.
5. Bake for 15 minutes or until the peppers are brown and the cheese bubbles.

346. Spinach Artichoke Dip

INGREDIENTS

- 2 tbsp butter
- 2 tbsp minced garlic
- 225 g spinach, chopped
- 400 g cup artichoke hearts cut,
- 220-230 g (1 pack) cream cheese
- 225g parmesan
- 115g grated mozzarella cheese
- 1/2 cup grated Gruyere cheese
- 3 tbsp sour cream
- 1 tbsp mayonnaise
- 1/2 tsp salt
- 1/2 tsp freshly ground black pepper
- 1/2 tsp paprika

INSTRUCTIONS

1. Preheat the air fryer to 190° C.

2. Dissolve the butter in a large skillet over medium heat. Add the garlic. Cook for 1 minute, add the finely chopped spinach and cook for another 1 to 2 minutes. Add artichokes cook for another minute. Place the artichokes and the spinach mixture in a bowl.
3. Reduce the heat of the air fryer. Add the cream cheese to the air fryer. Let it melt.
4. Add ½ cup Parmesan cheese, mozzarella and Gruyere. Stir until the cheese is melted, about 2 minutes.
5. Pour the melted cheese over the spinach and artichoke mixture. Stir to mix.
6. Add sour cream, mayonnaise, salt, pepper and paprika. Mix well.
7. Place the spinach and artichoke mixture into a 9-inch air fryer. Sprinkle the remaining ½ cup of parmesan cheese on top.
8. Bake 20 to 25 minutes or until the top is brown and bubbling.

347. Zucchini Mini Pizzas

INGREDIENTS

- 1 medium zucchini, cut diagonally (approximately 8 bars)
- 1 tsp of olive oil
- 2 tbsp sugar-free pizza sauce
- 55 g grated mozzarella cheese
- 55 g goat cheese crumbles
- 16 pepperoni slices (optional)
- 1/8 tsp salt
- 1/8 tsp freshly ground black pepper
- 1 tsp Italian herbs

INSTRUCTIONS

1. Set the air fryer to Roast.
2. Place the zucchini slices on a baking sheet and drizzle with olive oil.
3. Fry the zucchini for 2 minutes per side. Remove the baking sheet from the air fryer.
4. Cover each zucchini with pizza sauce, mozzarella and goat cheese garnish.
5. Garnish each with two pepperoni slices (if desired).
6. Season with salt, pepper and Italian herbs.
7. Return the baking sheet to the air fryer and fry 2 minutes or until cheese is brown.

348. Prosciutto & Cream Stuffed Mushrooms

INGREDIENTS

- 170 g cream cheese, room temperature
- 60 ml sour cream
- 4 slices Prosciutto, in pieces
- 1 tsp fresh parsley
- 1/4 tsp salt
- 1/8 tsp freshly ground black pepper
- 16 small mushrooms, without handle
- 1 tbsp olive oil

INSTRUCTIONS

1. Preheat the air fryer to 200° C.
2. Mix the cream cheese and the sour cream in a large bowl. Add prosciutto, parsley, salt and pepper. Stir to mix.
3. Add the cream cheese and prosciutto mixture equally into the mushrooms.
4. Place the mushrooms on a lined baking sheet with cream cheese side up. Drizzle with olive oil and bake 20 minutes.

349. Bleu Cheese Cauliflower

INGREDIENTS

CAULIFLOWER

- 450 g cauliflower florets
- 1 tbsp olive oil
- 1 tsp garlic
- 1 tsp onion powder
- 1/4 tsp salt
- 1/8 tsp freshly ground black pepper

Sauce

- 55g butter
- 80 ml hot sauce
- 1 tbsp white vinegar
- 1/4 tsp Worcestershire sauce

FOR BLEU CHEESE SAUCE

- 2 tbsp blue cheese dressing
- 2 tbsp sour cream
- 30 g blue cheese crumbles

INSTRUCTIONS

1. Preheat the air fryer to 220° C.
2. Mix the cauliflower florets, olive oil, garlic powder, onion powder, salt and pepper in a large bowl. Mix well to spice evenly.
3. Divide the cauliflower into an even layer on a lined with parchment paper baking sheet. Bake for 20 minutes or until the edges of cauliflower brown.
4. Melt butter in a large skillet over medium heat.
5. Add the hot sauce, vinegar and Worcestershire sauce. Mix on medium heat until the mixture swells. Remove air fryer from heat.
6. Mix the bleu cheese dressing and sour cream in a small bowl. Stir in the crumbled cheese. Cover and refrigerate until ready to serve.
7. In a large bowl, combine the cooked cauliflower with the buffalo sauce to cover.

350. Crispy Kale Chips

INGREDIENTS

- 450 g kale leaves, rinsed and dried
- 1 tbsp olive oil
- 1/2 tsp salt
- 1/2 tsp freshly ground black pepper
- 1/2 tsp onion powder
- 1/2 tsp garlic powder

INSTRUCTIONS

1. Preheat the air fryer to 150° C.
2. Mix the leaves evenly with the oil.
3. Add salt, pepper, onion powder and garlic powder into the bowl.
4. Mix again to evenly cover the leaves.
5. Place the kale on a lined baking tray in an even layer. Place the baking sheet in the air fryer.
6. Bake for 10 minutes, turn the baking sheet and bake for another 15 minutes.

7. Remove the baking sheet from the air fryer.

351. Fried Avocado

INGREDIENTS

- oil
- 1 egg
- 1 tbsp whipped cream
- 1 avocado, peeled and pitted
- 1/4 tsp salt
- 1/4 tsp freshly ground black pepper
- 55 g grated Parmesan cheese
- 55 g rind ground
- 1/4 tsp onion powder
- 1/4 tsp garlic powder

INSTRUCTIONS

1. Fill a large air fryer with about 3.5 cm oil. Preheat to 190° C.
2. Mix the egg and cream in a small bowl.
3. Cut the avocado into 2.5 cm thick slices and season with salt and pepper.
4. Mix Parmesan cheese, bark, onion powder and garlic powder.
5. Each avocado slice dive into the egg mixture, drain the excess and then fully immersed in the shell.
6. Once the oil is hot, place the avocado slices one at a time.
7. Fry 1 to 2 minutes or until golden brown. Remove the slices and put them to drain on paper towels. Repeat with remaining slices.

352. Buffalo Dip

INGREDIENTS

- 115g butter
- 1 tsp garlic, chopped
- 4 chicken thighs, boneless
- 60 ml sour cream
- 1/4 tsp salt
- 1/4 tsp ground black pepper
- 1/4 tsp cayenne pepper
- 1/4 tsp pepper
- 110 g cream cheese, softened
- 120 ml hot sauce, according to taste
- 120 ml Ranch Dressing
- 225 g mozzarella cheese, grated
- 115 g cheddar cheese, grated

INSTRUCTIONS

1. Preheat the air fryer to 230° C.
2. Heat a large skillet over medium heat. Melt the butter.
3. Put the garlic and chicken in the air fryer. Bake for 3 minutes, and reduce heat to medium. Turn the chicken so that it bakes on all sides, a total of about 12 to 15 minutes.
4. Place the chicken in a large bowl. Set aside to cool.
5. Cut the cooled chicken into bite-size pieces.
6. Mix sour cream, salt, black pepper, cayenne pepper and pepper and add to the chicken pieces.
7. Spread the cream cheese in a 23 cm air fryer on the bottom and sides evenly and cover. Pour the chicken mixture over the cream cheese layer.
8. Sprinkle the hot sauce and ranch dressing over the chicken mixture and spread evenly.
9. Garnish with mozzarella and cheddar cheese.
10. Mix the INGREDIENTS in the air fryer with a butter knife.
11. Place in preheated air fryer. Bake for 15 minutes or until the top layer is brown.

353. Black Forest Ham, Cheese & Chive Roll-Ups

INGREDIENTS

- 6 slices of Black Forest ham (about 5 oz total)
- 85 g cream cheese at room temp
- 1 tbsp fresh chives
- 55 g Monterey Jack cheese grated
- 1/2 tsp garlic powder
- 1/2 tsp onion powder
- 1/8 tsp salt
- 1/8 tsp freshly ground black pepper

INSTRUCTIONS

1. Place the six slices of ham on a cutting board. Distributed ½ oz of cream cheese evenly on each slice.
2. Distribute chives evenly over each piece of ham.
3. Evenly sprinkle each piece with Monterey Jack cheese, garlic powder, onion powder, salt and pepper.
4. Roll up and enjoy.

354. Rosemary Roasted Almonds

INGREDIENTS

- 340 g almonds
- 1 tbsp olive oil
- 1 tbsp fresh rosemary, finely chopped
- 1/2 tsp salt
- 1/2 tsp freshly ground black pepper
- 1/4 tsp ground ginger

INSTRUCTIONS

1. Preheat the air fryer to 160° C.
2. Mix the almonds and the olive oil in a medium bowl. Blend until the almonds are evenly covered.
3. Mix rosemary, salt, pepper and ginger.
4. Place almonds evenly on a baking sheet with aluminum foil in the preheated air fryer.
5. Bake for 15 minutes.

355. Bacon Guacamole

INGREDIENTS

- 4 slices of bacon
- 2 avocados, diced
- 115 g yellow onion
- 75 g tomato
- 2 tsp garlic, chopped
- 1 jalapeño pepper, chopped
- 1 serrano pepper, chopped
- 1 tbsp fresh coriander
- 1 tsp fresh lemon juice
- 1/4 tsp salt
- 1/8 tsp freshly ground black pepper
- 1/4 tsp cayenne pepper

INSTRUCTIONS

1. Heat a large skillet over medium heat. Add the bacon and fry for 3 minutes. Place the bacon to cool on paper towels. After cooling, cut the bacon and set aside.
2. Mix avocado, onion and tomato in a large bowl.
3. Add garlic, jalapeño peppers and serrano peppers. Mix the INGREDIENTS carefully.
4. Mix cilantro, chopped bacon, lime juice, salt, black pepper and cayenne pepper in a bowl.

356. Bacon Deviled Eggs

INGREDIENTS

- 6 eggs
- 3 to 4 slices of bacon
- 1 1/2 tbsp mayonnaise
- 1 tbsp mustard
- 1/2 tsp paprika
- 1/8 tsp salt
- 1/8 tsp freshly ground black pepper

INSTRUCTIONS

1. Bring water to a boil in a large air fryer (half filled). Place the eggs gently into the water and make sure that you do not break the shell. Cook for 10 minutes. Then set aside to cool.
2. Add bacon to the air fryer. Bake for 3 minutes per side. Place the bacon on a paper towel to drain.
3. Once the eggs have cooled, peel them and cut lengthwise.
4. Place the egg yolks in a medium bowl. Add mayonnaise, mustard, ¼ tsp pepper, salt and pepper. Mix well.
5. Cut the bacon into small pieces. Add a ¼ cup bacon to the yolks. Mix well.
6. Place the egg whites with the cut side up on a plate. Scoop an equal amount of egg yolk mixture into each half.
7. Use the remaining ¼ cup bacon and ¼ tsp pepper to garnish the eggs.

357. Asparagus & Eggs in Bacon Envelopes

INGREDIENTS

- 4 slices of bacon
- 12 asparagus
- 1 tsp chopped garlic
- 1 tsp Knoflook
- 2 tsp onion powder
- 1/2 tsp salt
- 1/4 tsp freshly ground black pepper
- 1 tbsp butter
- 4 eggs

INSTRUCTIONS

1. Preheat the air fryer to 200° C.
2. Wrap a slice of bacon around each bundle of three asparagus stalks. Place each bundle on a lined baking tray.
3. Sprinkle garlic, onion powder, ¼ tsp salt and a pinch of pepper over the bundles.
4. Place the baking sheet in the preheated air fryer for 12 minutes or until the bacon is crispy.
5. Melt the butter over medium heat. Place the eggs into an air fryer in pairs. Try to keep the yolks intact.
6. Boil the eggs for about 5 minutes and season with the remaining salt and pepper.
7. Remove the asparagus from the air fryer.
8. Remove the eggs from the air fryer. Place two eggs in two bundles of asparagus per serving.

358. Strawberry Spinach Smoothie

INGREDIENTS

- 225 g ice, crushed
- 120 ml unsweetened almond milk
- 2 cups fresh spinach
- 115 g Strawberries
- 1 tbsp coconut oil

INSTRUCTIONS

1. Put the ice in a blender. Add almond milk, spinach, strawberries and coconut oil. Mix well.

359. Strawberry Milkshake

INGREDIENTS

- 225 g ice, crushed
- 60 ml unsweetened almond milk
- 120 ml whipped cream
- 1 tbsp coconut oil
- 115 g Strawberries
- 1 tsp of pure vanilla extract

INSTRUCTIONS

1. Place ice in a blender. Add almond milk, whipped cream and coconut oil.
2. Add the strawberries, vanilla and blend.

360. Avocado Coconut Smoothie

INGREDIENTS

- 225 g ice, finely ground
- 1 avocado, shelled
- 240 ml full-fat coconut milk
- 1 tbsp coconut oil
- 1 tbsp unsweetened coconut

INSTRUCTIONS

1. Mix ice, avocado, coconut milk and coconut oil and grated coconut in blender.

361. Fried Spaghetti

INGREDIENTS

- 1 large spaghetti squash (5 cups)
- 115g butter
- 250 g lean ground beef
- 250 g Italian sausage
- 250 g of chicken sausage
- red wine
- 1 large onion, chopped
- 5 garlic cloves, finely chopped
- 250 g of mushrooms
- 1 (170 g) can tomato paste
- 1 (510 g) can of tomato dice
- 1 tbsp Italian herbs
- 110 g of ricotta cheese
- 110 g of mozzarella cheese
- 230 g of grated Parmesan cheese
- 1/2 tsp salt
- 1/2 tsp freshly ground black pepper

INSTRUCTIONS

1. Preheat the air fryer to 175° C.
2. Place the spaghetti squash in a large bowl in the microwave and pierce with the tip of a sharp knife. Heat 15 to 20 minutes in the microwave, depending on the size of the pumpkin. Remove from the microwave and let cool.

3. Melt the butter over medium heat.
4. Place Italian sausage and chicken sausage in the air fryer. Approximately Sauté 10 minutes.
5. Add the red wine and reduce heat to medium. where the wine with the meat stand 3 to 5 minutes is allowed.
6. Add the onion and garlic. Cook for about 4 minutes until soft. Add the mushrooms and cook for 8 to 9 minutes, stirring.
7. Add tomato paste, diced tomatoes with juice and Italian herbs. Stir well to mix. Cook 10 to 15 minutes, until reduced by half.
8. Go back to the spaghetti squash. Cut it lengthwise. Remove the seeds and scoop the flesh out with a fork.
9. Place half of the spaghetti squash in a large baking dish with a lid. Garnish with half of the ricotta, mozzarella and parmesan cheese. Cover with the tomato sauce. Cover with the remaining half of the spaghetti squash.
10. Garnish with remaining ricotta, mozzarella and parmesan cheese.

362. Classic Mozzarella Sticks

INGREDIENTS

- 50 g of Parmesan cheese powder
- 1 tsp Italian herbs
- 1 egg
- 5 mozzarella cheese sticks
- Cooking oil for baking
- Pizza sauce or ranch dressing for serving

INSTRUCTIONS

1. Mix the powdered Parmesan cheese and Italian herbs in a large bowl.
2. Whisk the egg in a separate bowl for 1 minute.
3. Cut crosswise on a cutting board each mozzarella stick in a total of 15 parts.
4. Submerge a piece of mozzarella in the egg and roll in the parmesan cheese.
5. Repeat step 4.
6. Roll the covered piece of mozzarella between the hands so that the coating adheres.
7. Repeat with remaining mozzarella pieces.
8. Freeze the cheese sticks for at least 1 hour.
9. When finished, heat 2-3 cm oil in a large skillet to 180° C.
10. Place 2 to 3 cheese sticks simultaneously in the air fryer. Bake 4 to 6 minutes, turning the halfway.
11. Place on paper towels to drain.
12. Serve with pizza sauce or ranch dressing.

363. Grilled Onion & Goat Cheese Flatbread

INGREDIENTS

FLATBREAD

- 2 tbsp coconut flour
- 1/8 tsp baking soda
- 4 proteins
- 1/4 tsp onion powder
- 1/4 tsp garlic powder
- 60 ml coconut milk

SAUCE

- 2 tbsp sugar-free barbecue sauce
- 170 goat cheese, crumbled

- 1/2 cup yellow onion, sliced
- 1/2 tsp garlic, minced
- 1/8 tsp freshly ground black pepper

INSTRUCTIONS

1. In a medium bowl, combine the coconut flour, baking powder, egg white, onion powder, garlic powder and coconut milk, beating until smooth.
2. Heat a large skillet over medium heat. Pour the Kokosnussteig into the air fryer and rotate the air fryer so that the batter covers the entire bottom. Bake 2 minutes or until the edges are brown. Turn around. Cook for 1 to 2 minutes.
3. Remove flat bread from the air fryer.
4. Preheat the air fryer to 425° F.
5. Spread barbecue sauce, goat cheese, onion, garlic and pepper evenly on flatbread.
6. Bake in the preheated air fryer for 5 to 7 minutes or until the cheese melts.

364. Pumpkin Spaghetti with Meatballs

INGREDIENTS

PUMPKIN SPAGHETTI

- 1 large spaghetti squash
- 3 tbsp of water
- 2 tbsp olive oil
- 115 g fresh, chopped parsley

MEATBALLS

- 250 g ground beef
- 250 g of minced pork
- 115 g Parmesan cheese
- 2 tbsp fresh, chopped basil
- 2 tbsp fresh, chopped Oregano
- 1/2 tsp onion powder
- 1/2 tsp finely chopped garlic
- 1/4 tsp salt
- 1/4 tsp freshly ground black pepper
- 240 g sugar-free pasta sauce

INSTRUCTIONS

1. Place the spaghetti squash in a large bowl in the microwave and pierce with the tip of a sharp knife. Heat 15 to 20 minutes in the microwave, depending on the size of the pumpkin. Remove from the microwave and let cool.
2. Use a fork to scoop the pumpkin flesh from the skin.
3. Heat a tbsp of olive oil in a large skillet over medium-high heat for about 1 minute. Add pumpkin to the air fryer and mix so the moisture will evaporate. Cook for 7 minutes, until the squash is brown.
4. Remove from heat. Put the pumpkin in a large bowl. Add ¼ cup parsley on the tray and put them aside.
5. Mix Parmesan cheese, basil, oregano, onion powder, garlic, salt and pepper in a medium bowl. Add the remaining ¼ cup parsley, beef and pork.
6. Form 12 meatballs.
7. Heat the remaining tbsp of olive oil for about 1 minute in the air fryer over medium heat. Add the meatballs. Broil until golden brown on each side for 1 to 2 minutes.
8. Add the pasta sauce to the air fryer. Stir the meatballs thoroughly.
9. Turn down the heat. Cover air fryer. Cook until the meatballs are done.
10. Sprinkle the remaining ¼ cup Parmesan cheese evenly over the meatballs.

365. Pepperoni Pizza

INGREDIENTS

- 1 1/2 cup grated Mozzarella cheese, cut into strips
- 115g cheddar cheese
- 1 egg
- 1/2 tsp garlic powder
- 1/4 tsp salt
- 1/8 tsp ground black pepper
- 60 ml sugar-free pizza sauce
- 20 slices of pepperoni

INSTRUCTIONS

1. Preheat the air fryer to 220° C.
2. Mix in a large bowl 1 cup mozzarella cheese, cheddar cheese, egg, garlic powder, salt and pepper.
3. Spread the cheese paste evenly on a 40-cm baking sheet lined with parchment paper. The crust must be thin, but there are no holes.
4. Place the baking sheet in the air fryer. The crust is baked until it is brown. Check the air fryer after 10 minutes to ensure that the crust does not burn.
5. Remove the crust from the air fryer.
6. Remove excess grease with paper towels from the crust.
7. Spread the sauce on the crust. Garnish with the remaining ½ cup mozzarella and pepperoni.
8. Baking sheet in the air fryer back-Bake 3 to 4 minutes or until the cheese melts and swells.

366. Cauliflower Pizza

INGREDIENTS

CRUST

- 3/4 tsp salt
- 2 cups cauliflower florets
- 1 egg
- 2 1/2 cup grated mozzarella cheese
- 1/2 tsp garlic powder
- 1/8 tsp freshly ground black pepper

PIZZA

- 60 ml sugar-free pizza sauce
- 10 pepperoni slices

INSTRUCTIONS

1. Preheat the air fryer to 230° C.
2. Bring a large pot of water to a boil -with a ½ tsp seasoning salt. Place the cauliflower carefully into the boiling water. Cook for 8 minutes and drain thoroughly with paper towels to absorb excess moisture.
3. Place the drained cauliflower in a food processor. mix 1 minute, until the cauliflower looks like rice.
4. Place the cauliflower in a large bowl. Mix with the egg, 225 g mozzarella cheese, garlic powder, remaining ¼ tsp salt and add pepper. Stir until the cheese is completely melted.
5. Divide the Blumenkohlteig into two equal balls.
6. Distribute each ball in a 20 cm long crust on a designed with baking tray. The coating must be very thin.
7. Place the crust in the preheated air fryer-bake 15 to 20 minutes or brown can. The edges of the crust should look almost dark brown.
8. Remove the crusts from the air fryer.
9. Spread a cup ⅛ pizza sauce on each crust.

10. Garnish each crust with a cup mozzarella ¾ and half the peppers.
11. Return the baking sheet to the air fryer. The pizzas bake until the cheese is melted and bubbling.
12. Remove the baking sheet from the air fryer and let cool 3 to 5 minutes the pizzas before they are cut and served.

367. Cauliflower Puree

INGREDIENTS

- 3 cups cauliflower florets
- 6 tbsp butter
- 4 tbsp of Parmesan cheese
- 2 tbsp sour cream
- 2 tbsp cream cheese
- 2 tbsp whipped cream
- 1 tsp chopped garlic
- 1 tsp salt
- 1/2 tsp freshly ground black pepper

INSTRUCTIONS

1. Boil the water in a large pot. Add the cauliflower florets. Cook for 4 minutes. Drain the cooked cauliflower and run excess moisture.
2. Puree the cauliflower, butter, Parmesan cheese, sour cream, cream cheese, whipped cream, garlic, salt and pepper in a food processor.

368. Tofu Fries

INGREDIENTS

- Oil for frying
- 1 package (350 g) extra-firm tofu, sliced
- 1 tsp salt
- 1 tsp freshly ground black pepper
- 1 tsp ground cumin
- 1 tsp dried parsley
- 1 tsp garlic powder 1/2 tsp onion powder
- 1/4 tsp paprika
- 1/4 tsp of cayenne pepper

INSTRUCTIONS

1. Heat 10 cm oil in a large air fryer to 175° C.
2. Dry each slice of tofu thoroughly between paper towels or a dish towel.
3. Mix salt, black pepper, cumin, parsley, garlic powder, onion powder, paprika and cayenne pepper in a medium bowl.
4. Place the tofu fries in the spice mixture and set aside.
5. Bake for about 4 minutes each. Place on paper towels to dry out.
6. Repeat the process with the remaining tofu strips.

369. Almond Butter Bread

INGREDIENTS

- 1/2 cup unflavored, unsweetened whey protein powder
- 1/8 tsp salt
- 2 tsp baking powder
- 115 g unsweetened almond butter
- 4 eggs
- 1 tbsp butter

INSTRUCTIONS

1. Heat the air fryer to 150° C.
2. In a small bowl mix the whey, salt and baking powder.
3. with an electric mixer, beat the butter until creamy almond. Add one egg at a time and stir well after each addition.
4. The whey paste under the almond lift. Mix gently until they are smooth.
5. Cover the inside of an air fryer with a tbsp of butter, rubbing on the walls and at each corner.
6. Pour mixture into the preheated air fryer. Bake until the medium is finished.
7. Remove from air fryer. 5 Allow the bread to cool to 10 minutes. Run a knife through the inside edges to loosen the bread shape, and tilt the mold down to remove it.

370. Zucchini Lasagna

INGREDIENTS

- 2 tbsp olive oil
- 225 g chopped onion
- 1 tsp chopped garlic
- 500 g lean ground beef
- 2 cups unsweetened pasta sauce
- 1 tbsp fresh oregano
- 1/4 tsp salt
- 1 tbsp chopped fresh basil
- 2 medium zucchini, sliced about 3mm thick (about 24 slices)
- 225 g ricotta cheese
- 8 tbsp grated mozzarella cheese
- 115 g grated Parmesan cheese
- 1/4 tsp freshly ground black pepper

INSTRUCTIONS

1. Preheat the air fryer to 190° C.
2. Pour olive oil in a large air fryer for one minute over medium heat. Add onion and garlic. Bake until tender, about 6 minutes.
3. Add the minced meat and bake for 5 minutes.
4. Add the pasta sauce. Bring the mixture to a boil. Turn down the heat. Mix oregano, salt and basil.
5. Place 6 zucchini slices on a 20 cm square baking dish. Pour a quarter of the meat sauce over the zucchini. Add a layer of ¼ cup ricotta and 2 tbsp mozzarella.
6. Repeat the process three times with remaining zucchini, sauce and cheese, and change the direction of the zucchini slices.
7. Garnish with Parmesan cheese and pepper.
8. Place in preheated air fryer. Bake it until the top is brown and bubbling.
9. Remove from the air fryer. Allow to cool before serving for 15 minutes.

371. Coconut Almond Flour Bread

INGREDIENTS

- 10 tsp butter, melted, plus 1 tbsp
- 1 tbsp honey
- 1 1/2 tbsp apple cider vinegar
- 8 eggs
- 85 g almond flour
- 3/4 tsp baking soda
- 3/4 tsp salt
- 75 g coconut flour

INSTRUCTIONS

1. Preheat the air fryer to 150° C.
2. Butter, honey and apple cider vinegar mix in a small bowl. Let the mixture cool.
3. Whisk the eggs in a medium bowl.
4. Add almond flour, butter mixture, baking powder and salt to the eggs. Mix thoroughly.
5. Pour the coconut flour slowly into the bowl. Mix well.
6. Coat the inside of a loaf pan with a tbsp of butter by rubbing on the sides and in every corner.
7. Pour the mixture into the bread form. Put in the preheated air fryer and bake 50 to 60 minutes.

372. Cauliflower Tortillas

INGREDIENTS

- 3/4 fresh cauliflower
- 2 eggs
- 1/2 tsp salt
- 1/4 tsp freshly ground black pepper

INSTRUCTIONS

1. Preheat the air fryer to 190° C.
2. Place the cauliflower in a food processor and blend into very fine pieces.
3. Cook the cauliflower in a large microwave-safe bowl in the microwave on high for about 5 minutes.
4. Remove excess water from the cauliflower with a tea towel or cheesecloth.
5. Add the cauliflower back into the bowl. Add eggs, salt and pepper. Mix well.
6. Form 6 or 7 patties on a lined baking tray and gently flatten.
7. Place the baking sheet in the preheated air fryer and bake for 10 minutes.
8. Remove the baking sheet from the air fryer. Gently flip the cauliflower tortillas and bake another 6 to 7 minutes.

373. Cauliflower Macaroni & Cheese

INGREDIENTS

- 1 tsp salt
- 1 fresh cauliflower, cut into small florets
- 240 ml whipped cream
- 75 g cream cheese, diced
- 225 g grated cheddar cheese
- 115 g grated mozzarella
- 1/2 tsp finely chopped garlic
- 1/4 tsp freshly ground black pepper
- Cooking spray for air fryer
- 1/2 cup shredded Parmesan cheese

INSTRUCTIONS

1. Preheat the air fryer to 200° C.
2. Boil the cauliflower for 5 minutes. Drain well and place the florets on paper towels to absorb the remaining moisture. Place the cauliflower in a large bowl and set aside.
3. Add the whipped cream in a large skillet over medium heat and simmer. Stir in the cream cheese until smooth. Add cheddar, mozzarella and garlic. Whisk until the cheese is melted, about 2 minutes.
4. Remove the cheese sauce from the heat and pour over the cauliflower. Sprinkle with the remaining ½ tsp salt and pepper.
5. Spray a 20 cm square baking AIR fryer with cooking spray. Add cauliflower mixture to the air fryer. Garnish with Parmesan cheese.

374. Keto Zucchini

INGREDIENTS

- 900 G of zucchini
- 1 Lemon (juiced)
- 1 pinch salt
- 4 eggs
- 3 ml almond flour
- 120 G Cheese (grated)
- 2 stk onion
- 2 shots Oil

INSTRUCTIONS

1. Wash the zucchini and grate. Soak in a bowl of salt and lemon juice for about 30 minutes. Then express well with your hands.
2. Peel the onion and finely chop. Now mix the zucchini, onion, cheese, eggs and flour well in a bowl. Season the finished mixture with salt again.
3. From the mass into patties and bake in an air fryer with oil on both sides until golden brown.

375. Zucchini Curry

INGREDIENTS

- 1 shot oil
- 1 stk onion
- 3 stk Garlic cloves
- 3 stk Chili peppers (green, fresh)
- 2 cm ginger
- 1 tbsp chili powder
- 2 stk zucchini
- 2 stk tomatoes
- 2 tbsp Fenugreek seeds

INSTRUCTIONS

1. Peel and finely chop onion, ginger, garlic and chili peppers.
2. The zucchini and the tomatoes are washed and sliced.
3. In an air fryer, heat oil and add onion, ginger, garlic, chili and chili powder and sauté. Then add the tomato and zucchini slices and sauté for 6 more minutes, stirring constantly.
4. Now add the coriander leaves and seeds and sauté for another 5 minutes until the vegetables are cooked.

376. Zucchini Brunch Spaghetti

INGREDIENTS

- 2 stg zucchini
- 1 Pk Brunch nature or brunch balance herbs
- 1 pinch salt
- 2 ml oil
- 1 pinch freshly ground pepper
- 50G feta cheese
- 2 ml grated Grana or Parmesan
- 1 stk clove of garlic

INSTRUCTIONS

1. Cut the zucchini into fine "spaghetti" with a spiralizer. Start from the shell, process the pulp and leave the inside with the seeds. Fry in an air fryer with a little oil over medium heat, stirring occasionally.
2. For the sauce: coarsely chop the inside of the zucchini and sauté in a second air fryer with the finely chopped garlic clove. Brunch Nature or Brunch Balance Add herbs and heat. Chop feta and stir. Season with salt and pepper.

3. Arrange the zucchini noodles on plates, add the sauce and sprinkle with freshly grated Grana or Parmesan cheese.

377. Zucchini Puffs

INGREDIENTS

- 1 kg zucchini
- 1 stk lemon
- 1 pinch salt
- 4 eggs
- 100 g gray cheese
- 2 stk onion
- 2 ml almond flour

INSTRUCTIONS

1. Halve the lemon and juice it. Wash the zucchini, grate and mix with lemon juice and salt for 30 min.
2. Peel the onions and cut them into fine pieces. Express the vegetables well. Then drain off the water. Finely grate the gray cheese.
3. Add eggs, cheese, chopped onions and almond flour. Mix well. Heat oil in an air fryer and fry small portions of the zucchini mixture until golden brown on both sides.

378. Air Fryer Zucchini & Mushroom

INGREDIENTS

- 300 G mushrooms
- 1 stk Zucchini (large)
- 3 ml olive oil
- 1 pinch salt and pepper
- 1 shot Balsamic vinegar
- 0.5 Pack Italian herbs

INSTRUCTIONS

1. Wash zucchini and mushrooms and slice.
2. Heat oil in an air fryer and fry zucchini and mushrooms.
3. Season with salt and pepper and deglaze with a little vinegar. Season with the herbs.

379. Zucchini Melanzane Spread with Hazelnuts

INGREDIENTS

- 200 G Melanzani
- 100 G zucchini
- 4 ml olive oil
- 2 ml lemon juice
- 150 ml vegetable soup
- 100 ml whipped cream
- 2 stk Garlic cloves
- 20 G hazelnuts
- 0.5 tbsp coriander
- 0.5 tbsp sea salt
- 0.5 tbsp White pepper

INSTRUCTIONS

1. First dice the melanzani and zucchini and mince the garlic; then roast vegetables in oil in the air **fryer**.
2. Now pour in vegetable soup and then add garlic and lemon juice and fry for about 15 minutes.
3. Add whipped cream, bring to the boil and season with salt and pepper. Finally, puree the mixture and mix with chopped hazelnuts for 3-4 hours.

380. Spinach & Vegetables

INGREDIENTS

- 500 G   spinach
- 1 stk   paprika
- 1 pinch salt and pepper
- 1 stk onion
- 3 stk Garlic cloves
- 2 ml olive oil
- 3 ml tomato paste

INSTRUCTIONS

1. Clean and wash the peppers and spinach and cut into small pieces.
2. Simmer in a pot with a little water for 10 minutes.
3. Peel onion and garlic and finely chop. Fry in an air fryer with oil and stir in the tomato paste.
4. Strain the cooked vegetables and place them in the air fryer. Mix well with salt and pepper.

381. Fried Egg on Green Salad

INGREDIENTS

- 1 kpf salad
- 1 pinch salt
- 1 pinch turmeric
- 1 ml Pumpkin seed oil
- 1 ml Balsamic vinegar
- 4 eggs
- 1 tbsp coconut oil

INSTRUCTIONS

1. First divide the salad into bite-sized pieces, wash and place in a salad bowl. Heat the coconut oil in the air fryer for the fried eggs. Beat the eggs little by little and slide gently in the air fryer. When the egg white is white, the fried eggs are ready.
2. Season the salad with salt and turmeric, marinate pumpkin seed oil and balsamic vinegar and mix well. Then serve on plates, carefully cut the fried eggs into 4 pieces and place 2 fried eggs on the salad.

382. Sautéed Mushrooms

INGREDIENTS

- 200 G   mushrooms
- 2 ml butter
- 1 pinch salt and pepper
- 0.5 Federation parsley

INSTRUCTIONS

1. Wash parsley, drain and finely chop.
2. Clean and slice mushrooms. Sauté in an air **fryer** with butter.
3. Season with salt, pepper and parsley.

383. Scrambled Eggs with Ham & Mushrooms

INGREDIENTS

- 100 G mushrooms
- 70 G ham
- 1 stk onion
- 1 tbsp butter
- 4 eggs
- 1 pinch salt and pepper

preparation

1. Clean the mushrooms and slice them. Peel onions and cut them into fine pieces. Cut ham into strips.
2. Heat butter in an air **fryer** and sauté the onion. Add mushrooms and ham and simmer briefly.
3. Mix the eggs with salt and pepper and empty over the mass. Stir and tear with a fork.

384. Roast Beef

INGREDIENTS

- 1 kg roast beef
- 1 stk Oil (for the sheet metal)
- 1 pinch salt and pepper

for the remoulade sauce

- 120 G Pickles (small)
- 1 ml capers
- 2 stk Sardine fillets
- 0.5 Federation chives
- 0.5 Federation parsley
- 150 G mayonnaise
- 1 tbsp mustard
- 50 ml Pickles water
- 1 pinch salt and pepper

INSTRUCTIONS

1. Dry off the piece of roast beef, remove it from the bone with the knife and rub with salt and pepper.
2. Coat fryer tray with oil (or butter) and place the roast beef with the fat side up on the plate.
3. Roast the meat in a preheated fryer (about 220 C) for 15 minutes. Then reduce the temperature to 200 C and fry for another 30 minutes. The meat is still pink inside.
4. For the remoulade sauce, the gherkins are diced small, the capers and anchovies finely chopped, the herbs rinsed, the chives and the parsley finely chopped.
5. Mixed well with the mustard, mayonnaise, cucumber water and seasoned with salt and pepper again.

385. Turkey Steak with Vegetables

INGREDIENTS

- 4 stk turkey steak
- 2 ml oil
- 2 stk zucchini
- 1 stk carrots
- 1 stk onion
- 1 shot water
- 1 pinch salt and pepper
- 1 stk paprika

INSTRUCTIONS

1. Lightly beat the turkey meat with the meat mallet. Season with salt and pepper on both sides. Sauté the meat in hot oil on both sides.
2. Peel the vegetables and cut them into 1 cm cubes. Mix the vegetables in a bowl, season with salt and pepper and let simmer.
3. Put the meat in a greased casserole dish, add the vegetables and pour over a dash of water.
4. Bake for 10 minutes in a preheated fryer.

386. Turkey Sliced with Karfiolpüree

INGREDIENTS

- 500 G Turkey cutlets
- 1 stk onion
- 250 G   mushrooms
- 250 G oyster mushrooms
- 1 kg Carrot (frozen)
- 1 pinch salt
- 1 pinch pepper
- 1 ml oil
- 250 G Cooking cream (15% fat)
- 100 G cream cheese
- 1 pinch grated nutmeg
- 2 ml chopped parsley

INSTRUCTIONS

1. Wash the turkey breasts, pat dry and cut into thin strips. The onion is peeled and cut into fine cubes. Clean the mushrooms and cut them in half or in quarters, depending on their size. Divide the carrot into florets and cook gently in boiling water for about 6 to 8 minutes.
2. Heat oil in an air fryer and fry the turkey strips in it on both sides, season with salt and pepper and remove. Then fry the mushrooms in the fat while turning for about 5 minutes. After about 3 minutes, add the onion and season with salt. Now you can put the meat back in and pour on the cream, bring everything to a boil and simmer for about 5 minutes.
3. Strain the carrot and puree with the cream cheese with a hand blender. The puree is seasoned with salt and nutmeg.
4. Finally, season the sliced with salt and pepper, sprinkle with chopped parsley and serve with the puree.

387. Omelet Roll with Cream Cheese & Salad

INGREDIENTS

- 6 eggs
- 50 G cream cheese
- 10 stk Cherry tomatoes
- 00:25   stk Red pepper
- 00:25   stk yellow paprika
- 00:25   stk green pepper
- 00:25   stk cucumber
- 0.5 stk onion
- 3 branch parsley
- 1 tbsp olive oil
- 1 pinch salt
- 1 pinch pepper

INSTRUCTIONS

1. The vegetables are washed. From the peppers, the cores are removed. Then they are cut into small cubes. Halve the cherry tomatoes. Peel the cucumber and cut into thin slices. The onion is also peeled and finely diced. Now you can mix the vegetables in a bowl and add the parsley leaves.
2. Four of the eggs are separated and only the egg whites are placed in a bowl. The last two eggs are given completely. Now another shot of mineral water comes in and everything is whisked with the whisk.

3. Heat oil in an air fryer. Add egg mixture to the air fryer and season with salt and pepper. Stir the egg over medium heat until it is only slightly liquid on the surface. Then flip it over.
4. Finally, the finished omelet is spread with cream cheese, the vegetables are distributed in the middle and the omelet rolled up.

388. Marinated Zucchini

INGREDIENTS

- 250 G   zucchini
- 1 stk onion
- 3 ml olive oil
- 2 ml lemon juice

INSTRUCTIONS

1. Wash the zucchini and cut into finger-thick pens. Peel onion and dice.
2. Fry in an air fryer with hot oil over high heat, turning and browning.
3. Mix the lemon juice with olive oil and salt. Drizzle spilled zucchini with it.

389. Salmon Fillet with Rice & Beans

INGREDIENTS

- 250 G   salmon fillet
- 1 shot   Oil
- 0.5 stk   Lemon, juice
- 1 pinch   salt
- 1 pinch   Pepper, fresh

for the rice

- 200 G   Basmati rice
- 1 pinch   salt
- 400 ml water
- 1 ml oil

for the breading

- 1 stk egg
- 1 ml Flour
- 0.5 Federation chives

for the beans

- 250 G   green beans
- 1 pinch   salt
- 0.5 ml   butter

INSTRUCTIONS

1. For the salmon fillet with rice and fish, sauté the rice in oil, pour in water, season with salt and cover, and bring to a boil. Then place in the preheated fryer at 180° for 20 minutes.
2. Put the fish and sauce in the air fryer, cover with water and cook for 10 minutes. Then drain off the hot water. Heat the butter in the air fryer and fry the fish in it.
3. Wash the salmon and pat dry with kitchen paper, season with salt and pepper. Cut the chives into fine rolls, whisk the egg. Add the chives to the flour and mix.
4. Squeeze out the lemon and refine the salmon. Turn the salmon pieces first in the chives-flour mixture, then pull through the whisked egg.

5. Heat oil in an air fryer. Fry the salmon until crispy for 5 minutes.

390. Honey Glazed Salmon

INGREDIENTS

- 4 stk salmon fillets
- 3 ml butter
- 1 pinch salt and pepper
- 4 ml honey

INSTRUCTIONS

1. Salt and pepper the salmon fillet first.
2. Heat the butter in the air fryer. Add salmon fillets and fry on both sides over medium heat. After turning, sprinkle with honey and turn at the end again for about 15 seconds and fry on the honey side.

391. Herbed Scrambled Eggs

INGREDIENTS

- 4 eggs
- 120 G ham
- 2 ml olive oil
- 1 pinch salt and pepper
- 0.5 Pack Herbs (TK)

INSTRUCTIONS

1. Whisk the eggs with the herbs and spices.
2. Cut the ham into thin strips and sauté briefly in the air **fryer,** then add the egg and herb mixture. Let it rest briefly.

392. Chicken & Potato Cubes

INGREDIENTS

- 4 stk chicken thighs
- 500 G potato
- 4 ml chicken stock
- 2 stk Garlic cloves
- 00:25 tbsp salt

for the spice mixture

- 1 pinch salt
- 1 ml Spice mixture (oriental)
- 1 ml grapeseed oil

INSTRUCTIONS

1. For the chicken leg on potato cubes, wash the potatoes, peel and cut into cubes.
2. Then peel the garlic cloves, halve and remove the inner shoot, then crush fine.
3. Mix the potato cubes with chicken stock, salt and garlic and pour into the air fryer.
4. The Oriental spice mix with oil and salt mix. Wash the chicken thighs and dry well, place on the potato cubes with the bottom side facing upwards and spread with half the spice mixture. At 180° C, add hot air to the fryer for about 20 minutes.
5. Then turn the clubs and coat with the other half of the spice mixture. Cook for another 20 minutes at 180° top / bottom heat.

393. Hokkaido Sticks

INGREDIENTS

- 1 Hokkaido pumpkin
- 1 pinch salt
- 1 pinch turmeric
- 100 ml olive oil
- 1 pinch pepper

INSTRUCTIONS

1. Wash the pumpkin, pat dry and cut in half. Then use a tbsp to remove the seeds and possibly slightly fibrous pumpkin meat. Then cut into columns.
2. Place the slices on a tray lined with parchment paper, sprinkle with olive oil. Salt, pepper and refine with turmeric spice.
3. At 180 degrees for about 40 minutes, bake at top and bottom heat. The pumpkin slices do not have to be turned over.

394. Gurktaler Bacon Chips

INGREDIENTS

- 100 G air-cured bacon
- 0.5 ml barbecue seasoning

INSTRUCTIONS

1. Cut the bacon into thin slices.
2. Preheat the fryer to 200° C convection and line a baking sheet with parchment paper. Put the bacon on it. Season with the spices and cook in the fryer for about 10-12 minutes.
3. Then remove from the fryer, drain the excess fat on paper towels, and serve.

395. Stuffed Sage Bacon Roulade

INGREDIENTS

- 8th stk pork loin
- 10 G sage leaves
- 8th SchB bacon
- 1 pinch salt
- 1 pinch pepper
- 100 ml Sunflower oil

INSTRUCTIONS

1. For the stuffed sage bacon roulade, pound the pork a bit, and season with salt and pepper.
2. Wash the sage leaves. Put on a cloth and pat dry.
3. Then put the sage leaves and the bacon on the meat and make it into a roulade.
4. Heat oil in an air fryer and fry roulades.
5. Roast the roulades for another 20 minutes over medium heat.

396. Fried Fish with Garlic

INGREDIENTS

- 4 stk Zander fillets
- 0.5 Lemon, juiced

- 2 ml butter
- 2 pinch salt
- 3 Garlic cloves
- 1 pinch pepper

INSTRUCTIONS

1. For the fried zander with garlic, first season the fish fillet with salt, pepper and lemon juice.
2. Chop garlic into fine pieces and simmer a portion in air fryer in hot butter. Fry the zander fillets in garlic butter on both sides.
3. Add the remaining garlic to the fish shortly before the end of the cooking time and let the fillets simmer for a few minutes.

397. Baked Zucchini

INGREDIENTS

- 3 st zucchini
- 1 pinch salt and pepper
- 90 G Flour
- 1 Cup olive oil

INSTRUCTIONS

1. Wash, clean and slice the zucchini.
2. Salt and pepper the flour. Heat plenty of oil in an air fryer.
3. Briefly dip the vegetable slices in cold water, dip into the flour and bake on both sides in the boiling oil until they are completely crispy.
4. Drain and serve.

398. Vegetables with Turmeric & Fennel

INGREDIENTS

- 1 stk Onion (red)
- 1 stk fennel
- 0.5 cups broccoli
- 0.5 kpf cauliflower
- 2 stk Pointed pepper (red)
- 50 ml grapeseed oil
- 1 tsp turmeric
- 1 pinch salt
- 1 ml Lovage (dried)
- 1 pinch pepper

INSTRUCTIONS

1. Wash and roughly cut the vegetables; peel the onion and cut into small pieces.
2. Heat canola oil in an air fryer and fry the vegetables for 30 minutes.
3. Salt and pepper, sprinkle with turmeric, stir and finally sprinkle lovage over the finished dish.

399. Fine Roast Beef with Porcini Mushrooms

INGREDIENTS

- 4 roast beef
- 600 G ceps
- 2 stk onion
- 1 clove of garlic
- 5 ml cooking oil
- 0.5 tbsp salt
- 1 pinch Pepper, White

INSTRUCTIONS

1. First, clean the mushrooms and finely chop them. Dice the onion and finely chop garlic.
2. Season the meat with salt and pepper; sauté in a coated air fryer for 2 minutes on each side in 2 tbsp of oil, turning it several times. Then cook on a foil covered with aluminum foil for about 6 minutes at 180° C in a preheated fryer. Finally, let the roast beef rest in the fryer for about 5 minutes.
3. In the remaining gravy, add another 1 tbsp of oil, fry the bacon and warm in the fryer.
4. Then add 2 tbsp of oil to the air fryer and sauté the onion and garlic. Add the porcini mushrooms and roast them until the porcini's own juice has evaporated. Stir more often.
5. Put the mushrooms on the plate, put the meat on it and cover with the bacon.

400. Minced Roast with Egg

INGREDIENTS

- 500 G Faschiertes (mixed)
- 1 pinch salt
- 1 ml Herbs (mixed, fresh)
- 1 pinch pepper
- 200 G bread crumbs
- 1 egg
- 2 eggs (to fill)
- 1 stk Onion (medium)
- 1 stk garlic
- 100 ml Oil
- 1 pinch Chili flakes (spicy)

INSTRUCTIONS

1. Cook eggs in salted water for about 10 minutes with boiling water. Then chill and peel.
2. Put the minions in a bowl. Peel and chop the onion and garlic, add to the minced meat. Add salt, pepper, chili, bread crumbs, egg and herbs. Mix the mixture well with a wooden spoon.
3. Shape the minion on a board into a rectangle. Place the eggs in the center of the rectangle and wrap around with the mixture.
4. In the air fryer, heat oil, and fry the minced meat. Then place in a suitable and oiled form (with lid) and fry in the fryer for approx. 30 minutes at 180° C.

401. Asian Salmon Cubes with Broccoli

INGREDIENTS

- 250 G Salmon fillet (without skin)
- 1 tbsp sesame oil
- 1 Garlic clove (finely chopped)
- 1 ml soy sauce
- 2 ml sake

INSTRUCTIONS

1. Stew the garlic in a little olive oil until it turns glassy. Now add the salmon and the sesame oil and sauté. Then add 3 tbsp of water and sake and soy sauce and simmer.

2. Divide the broccoli into small florets and simmer in bubbly water. Then place in the air fryer with 1 tbsp butter and roasted almonds.

402. Basic Vegetables

INGREDIENTS

- 250 G   Sunflower seeds
- 2 stk carrots
- 1 stg celery
- 4 stk spring onion
- 1 pinch paprika
- 1 Federation   Herbs
- 0.5 tbsp sea salt
- 3 ml olive oil

INSTRUCTIONS

1. Put the sunflower seeds in water the day before.
2. Wash carrots, celery, peppers and onions, clean and cut very small. Wash herbs, drain and finely chop.
3. Now chop everything in the blender until everything is well mixed.
4. Season with sea salt and form a loaf with your hand and fry on both sides with olive oil in the **air fryer.**

403. Filled Melanzani

INGREDIENTS

- 8 thstk Melanzani
- 2 ml vegetable oil
- 4 stk onion
- 2 stk Garlic cloves
- 2 stk chili
- 1 stk zucchini
- 120 G   coconut cream
- 2 stk Thai basil
- 1 Federation   coriander
- 4 ml Soy sauce

INSTRUCTIONS

1. Peel the garlic and chop it into small pieces. Peel the onion and cut into cubes. Wash the chili pepper and cut into small pieces with a sharp knife. Wash the zucchini and cut into small pieces. Wash the basil, shake it off and chop finely. Heat the fryer to 180 degrees. Bake the melanzani for 10 minutes. Take out, cut in half and hollow out.
2. Heat oil in an air fryer. Stew onions, garlic and chili for 3 minutes. Add zucchini and melanzani pulp. Mix soy sauce, coconut cream and basil and simmer for 3 minutes.
3. Add the mixture to the Melanzani. Bake for another 5 minutes in the fryer.

404. Salmon Fillet on Zucchini

INGREDIENTS

- 1 Prize pepper
- 2 stk salmon fillet
- 300 G   zucchini

pesto

- 90 G basil
- 2 ml pine nuts
- 1 stk clove of garlic
- 1 pinch salt
- 1 pinch pepper

- 40 G Parmesan (grated)
- 90 ml   olive oil
- 1 pinch   salt

INSTRUCTIONS

1. For the pesto, mix the olive oil, pine nuts, peeled and chopped clove of garlic, parmesan and basil and mash well with the hand blender. Season with salt and pepper.
2. The salmon fillets are seasoned with salt and pepper and then fried in an air fryer with a dash of oil on both sides.
3. Meanwhile, cut the washed zucchini lengthwise into strips.
4. The sliced vegetables are sautéed in a second air fryer with oil and seasoned with salt.
5. Finally, the zucchini strips are served on a plate, the salmon fillet is placed on top and everything is covered with pesto.

405. Salmon Fillet with Zucchini Gratin

INGREDIENTS

- 4 stk salmon fillets
- 2 ml olive oil
- 2 pinch sea salt

for the gratin

- 4 eggs
- 2 stk zucchini
- 200 ml whipped cream
- 2 pinch Pepper, freshly ground
- 2 ml olive oil
- 140 G butter
- 100 ml milk

INSTRUCTIONS

1. First preheat the fryer to 180° C convection. Separate the zucchini into thin slices with a vegetable slicer, whisk eggs with whipped cream, salt and pepper.
2. Now grease 4 small casserole dishes with half a tbsp of oil and cut in zucchini, then spread the egg-topping on it and gratinate everything for 25-30 minutes.
3. Heat the olive oil in the air fryer and fry fish on both sides. Whole the fish for 2 to 3 minutes, then it remains glassy inside.

406. Marinated Fish In Wok

INGREDIENTS

- 600 G fish fillets
- 1.5 Cup rice
- 1 Glass morels
- 4 ml sesame oil
- 2 ml soy sauce
- 1 ml honey
- 200 G okra
- 100 G Paprika, yellow
- 100 G Red pepper
- 150 G bean sprouts
- 3 stk carrots
- 2 stk Garlic cloves
- 1 stk Chili pepper, red

INSTRUCTIONS

1. Cut the fish into pieces and marinate with oil, garlic, chili, honey and soy sauce for about 1 hour.
2. In the meantime, prepare rice: measure water according to the package instructions and bring to a boil. Add the jasmine rice, turn off the heat and let the rice swell for about 20 minutes (or according to the instructions on the package). Alternatively, prepare the rice using a rice cooker.

3. Now peeled carrots into slices or cut paprika into strips, cut okra into bite-size pieces.
4. Sear the fish in sesame oil in the wok and remove it. Roast vegetables and add fish. Season with soy sauce and serve with rice.

407. Vegetable Soup

INGREDIENTS

- 2 ml olive oil
- 1 stk onion
- 3 tbsp chili powder
- 1 stk carrot
- 2 stk potatoes
- 300 G tomatoes
- 1 l vegetable soup
- 1 can Kidney beans
- 130 G peas
- 1 can Corn
- 70 G fresh cream Cheese
- 1 pinch salt
- 1 pinch pepper
- 1 shot Salsa

Instructions

1. Heat oil in an air fryer and sauté the chopped onions. Then add the chili powder and mix well.
2. Then fry the chopped carrot, the diced potatoes and the sliced tomatoes for 2-3 minutes. Add the vegetables to the soup and cook on medium with a lid for 20 minutes.
3. Finally add the corn, peas and beans and cook the soup for another 10 minutes. To thicken the soup, add the fresh cream and season with salt, pepper and salsa.

408. Roast Beef Salad

INGREDIENTS

- 500 G beef
- 1 pinch salt
- 1 pinch pepper
- 450 G Fusilli
- 2 ml lime juice
- 2 ml fish sauce
- 2 tbsp honey
- 4 stk spring onion
- 1 stk cucumber
- 3 stk tomato
- 1 Federation mint

INSTRUCTIONS

1. Wash the spring onion and cut into small pieces. Wash, peel and dice the cucumber. Wash the tomatoes and quarter them evenly. Wash the mint, shake it off and finely chop it.
2. Heat up the grill to 230 C. Wash the meat, dab, salt and pepper. Put on a hot grill and fry for 3-4 minutes on each side. Allow to rest for about 5 minutes and cut into very thin slices across the fiber with a sharp knife.
3. Boil a large pot of water and cook the noodles according to the manufacturer. Drain through a sieve, return to the air fryer and mix with a little olive oil. Provide a small pot and mix lime juice, fish sauce and honey. Simmer over low heat for 2 minutes. Add the sliced vegetables and mix well with the sauce. Add the meat and mix again. Season with a little salt and pepper.

410. Char with Mushroom Polenta

INGREDIENTS

- 4 stk char fillets
- 0.75 l vegetable soup
- 150 G ceps
- 100 G corn grits
- 3 ml butter
- 2 ml oil
- 4 tbsp Flour
- 0.5 tbsp salt
- 2 pinch pepper

INSTRUCTIONS

1. First, clean the porcini mushrooms and cut them into pieces. Melt butter and bring to a boil with soup, polenta and porcini mushrooms; swell for a few minutes on low heat.
2. Now remove polenta from the heat and let it rest for about 10 minutes. Season with salt, pepper, rosemary and thyme.
3. In the meantime, wash the fish fillets, pat dry and salt. Dust the fish with flour on the skin side and fry with oil in the air fryer. Now turn it over and let it sit on this side without heat.

411. Sesame Salmon with Asian Broccoli

INGREDIENTS

- 4 stk Salmon fillets with skin (about 170 g)
- 1 pinch salt
- 1 ml Wasabi
- 80 G Sesame seeds
- 2 ml oil

for the broccoli

- 1 kg frozen broccoli
- 1 pinch salt
- 2 stk Garlic cloves
- 1 stk Ginger (walnut size)
- 2 stk red chili peppers
- 1 ml oil
- 3 ml soy sauce
- 1 spritz lime juice

INSTRUCTIONS

1. Bring salted water to a boil in the air fryer and boil broccoli for 4 to 5 minutes.
2. Meanwhile, you can wash the salmon fillets and pat dry with paper towels. Then they are salted on the meat side and coated with wasabi. Then place the sesame seeds on a flat plate and press in the salmon with the coated side. Heat oil in an air fryer and fry the salmon on the skin side for about 5 minutes. Then turn and fry on the sesame side for about 2 to 3 minutes.
3. Meanwhile, strain the broccoli. Garlic and ginger are peeled and finely chopped. The chili peppers are halved lengthwise and the kernels are removed. The pods are washed and cut into thin strips.
4. Saute garlic, ginger and chili for about 2 minutes. Then the broccoli florets are gently stirred. Add soy sauce to taste and cover for about 2 minutes to stew. Finally, the broccoli is drizzled with lime juice and served with the sesame salmon.

412. Zoodles with Paprika & Almond Sauce

INGREDIENTS

- 2 stk onions
- 2 stk Garlic cloves
- 1 stk chili
- 1 stk Red pepper
- 1 stk yellow pepper
- 2 ml olive oil
- 50 G Almond butter
- 150 ml Almond milk
- 2 stk large zucchini
- 1 pinch salt
- 1 pinch pepper

INSTRUCTIONS

1. Peel onions and garlic and cut into small cubes, wash the chilis and peppers well and then chop them into small pieces.
2. Then add 2 tbsp of olive oil to air fryer and cook the vegetables for about 5 minutes.
3. Puree the almond paste and the almond milk in a blender until a creamy sauce is produced.
4. Cut the zucchini into long, thin and add to the other vegetables in the air fryer and simmer for another 3 minutes.
5. Now add a pinch of salt and pepper and serve the Zoodles with the almond sauce.

413. Tandoori Cauliflower

INGREDIENTS

- 2 cinnamon sticks
- 1 tbsp cardamom capsules
- 4 tsp cumin
- 2 tbsp coriander seeds
- 1 tsp cloves
- 1 tbsp grated nutmeg
- 2 tsp cayenne pepper
- 2 tbsp of ground turmeric
- 2 tbsp sweet pepper
- 1 head cauliflower (about 1 kg)
- 4 cloves of garlic
- 1 hazelnut-sized piece of ginger
- Juice of 1 lemon
- 1-2 tsp salt
- 600 g whole milk yogurt
- 1/2 bunch of mint
- 3 tbsp oil
- Lemon slices to serve
- parchment paper

INSTRUCTIONS

1. Cut the cinnamon sticks for the tandoori spice mixture. Crush cardamom, cumin, coriander seeds, cloves and cinnamon in a spice mill or mortar. Put the crushed spices with nutmeg, cayenne pepper, turmeric and paprika in a screw-top jar and shake until everything is mixed.
2. Clean cauliflower, wash and remove outer leaves. Peel garlic and ginger, cut into pieces. Finely grate or crush ginger and garlic. Mix in a bowl with 1 heaped ml Tandoori spice mixture, lemon juice and 1 tsp salt. Stir in 150 g yogurt. Cover the cauliflower in a bowl with marinade all around, cover and allow to marinate for about 1 1/2 hours.
3. Place the cauliflower on a baking tray lined with parchment paper. Cook in a preheated oven (electric cooker: 200° C / circulating air: 175° C / gas: see manufacturer) for approx. 45 minutes. Then reduce the oven temperature (electric cooker: 175° C / circulating air: 150° C / gas: see manufacturer) and cook for approx. 30 minutes.

4. Meanwhile, wash mint, shake dry, peel off leaves and chop. Mix 3/4 of the mint, oil and other yogurt, season to taste with a little salt and pepper. Remove the cauliflower, arrange on a plate, sprinkle with the remaining mint and serve with lemon wedges.

414. Eggplant Yogurt Casserole with Meatballs

INGREDIENTS

- 600 g eggplant
- 800 g tomatoes
- salt
- 10 stems of thyme
- 2 cloves of garlic
- 250 g skimmed yogurt
- 4 eggs
- 1 small onion
- 250 g lamb mince
- 3 stalks of mint
- 1 tbsp Harissa
- 1 tbsp mustard
- Oil for the mold

INSTRUCTIONS

1. Wash eggplants and tomatoes, clean and slice. Lightly season the eggplant slices with salt. Wash thyme, shake dry and strip leaves from stalks. Peel 1 garlic clove and finely chop. Whisk yogurt, eggs and thyme, except for sprinkling.
2. Dab eggplant dry. Eggplant and tomato slices alternately in an oiled ovenproof form layers. Cover with egg milk. In the preheated oven (electric cooker: 200° C / circulating air: 175° C / gas: see manufacturer) bake for about 50 minutes.
3. Peel the onion and remaining garlic and finely dice. Wash the mint, shake dry, fold the leaves from the stems and finely chop. Knead the hack, mint, onion and garlic cubes, harissa and mustard to a smooth dough. Season with salt. Form to 20 small meatballs and distribute after about 20 minutes on the casserole.
4. Remove the prepared casserole from the oven, allow to rest covered for about 10 minutes, cut into portions, serve and sprinkle with thyme.

415. ARTICHOKE OMELET

INGREDIENTS

- 2 shallots
- 1 can of artichoke bottoms
- 20 g butter
- 4 stalks tarragon
- 50 g Parmesan cheese
- 8 eggs
- salt
- pepper

INSTRUCTIONS

1. Peel the shallots and dice them. Drain artichoke bottoms and cut into strips. Heat oil in an air fryer. Braise artichokes in it for about 6-7 minutes. Fry the shallots for the last 2-3 minutes, stirring several times.
2. Wash tarragon, shake dry and peel off leaves. Plane parmesan. Whisk eggs in a bowl. Season with salt and pepper and stir in tarragon leaves.
3. Put the egg mass in the air fryer for 1-2 minutes. Sprinkle the parmesan shavings on the omelet and bake for 15-20 minutes in a preheated oven (electric cooker: 175° C / circulating air: 150° C / gas: see manufacturer). Serve hot or cold with a green salad.

416. Honey Chicken with Fennel & Mushrooms

INGREDIENTS

- 2 fennel tubers
- 500 g mushrooms
- 4 stems of thyme
- 1 tbsp lemon juice
- 1-2 tsp of liquid honey
- salt
- pepper
- 4 chicken fillets (175 g)
- 6 tbsp oil

INSTRUCTIONS

1. Wash the fennel, clean it, put the green aside. Cut tubers in half. Cut out the stalk so that the leaves still stick together. Cut halves into thin slices. Clean mushrooms, clean them and halve or quarter them according to size. Wash thyme, shake dry and finely chop. Mix lemon juice, 1 liter water, honey and thyme, season with salt and pepper. Wash the chicken, pat dry and brush with the honey and thyme marinade.
2. Heat 2 tbsp of oil in the air fryer. Fry chicken fillets over medium heat while inverting for 10-12 minutes. In another air fryer, heat 4 tbsp of oil. Fry mushrooms in an air fryer for about 5 minutes. Add fennel slices to the mushrooms and fry for about 5 minutes. Season with salt and pepper. Arrange chicken fillets and vegetables on plates and garnish with fennel greens.

417. Braised Young Vegetables with Stir-Fried Ham

INGREDIENTS

- 4 young carrots
- 8 spring onions
- 4 small turnips
- 30 g butter
- 150 g (young) peas
- 2 tsp of cane sugar
- 150 ml vegetable broth
- 3 thick slices of cooked ham
- salt
- freshly ground pepper

INSTRUCTIONS

1. Clean carrots and turnips and cut them into pieces. Clean the onions, remove the stalk, and chop into 2 cm pieces.
2. Melt 20 g butter in a casserole dish. Add vegetables (including peas) and sugar and fry for 8-10 minutes while stirring. Add broth and simmer. (Broth should be evaporated and vegetables soft)
3. Cut ham into strips and sauté with remaining butter in air fryer for about 5 minutes on each side. Season with pepper and set aside.
4. After about 20 minutes, remove the lid from the casserole and let it reduce for about 5 minutes.
5. If necessary, reheat the ham just before serving and add to the vegetables.

418. Paprika Turkey Schnitzel with Peas

INGREDIENTS

- 500 g turkey schnitzel
- 150 g sugar peas
- 4 spring onions
- 200 g frozen peas
- Salt, 6 stalks of parsley
- 1 tbsp oil
- 1 tsp paprika powder
- 200 g cream

- 1-2 tsp mustard
- salt
- pepper

INSTRUCTIONS

1. Cut the schnitzel into strips. Wash the peas. Wash the spring onions, clean them and cut them into slices at an angle. Blanch the peas and everything for about 3 minutes in boiling salted water. Drain and cool briefly under cold water. Wash the parsley, shake it dry and cut the leaves into small pieces.
2. Heat oil in an air fryer. Roast the turkey strips for about 3 minutes until golden brown. Remove meat and add vegetables to the air fryer.
3. Sauté vegetables for 1-2 minutes, then dust with paprika powder and cook briefly. Add cream and mustard and simmer for about 2 minutes. Add meat and parsley. Boil and season with salt, pepper and paprika.

420. Chicken Schnitzel with Olive Fig Salsa & Whole Meal Pasta

INGREDIENTS

- 1 small shallot
- 1/2 fig
- 8 black olives without stone
- 1 tsp oil
- 1 tsp white wine vinegar
- salt
- pepper
- 1 chicken fillet (about 150 g)
- 20 g whole meal pasta
- 2 stems of basil
- 50 g tomato sauce

INSTRUCTIONS

1. Peel the shallot and finely dice. Wash the fig and dice. Slice olives. Heat 1/2 tsp of oil in the air fryer. Add shallots and fry until glassy. Deglaze with vinegar. Remove the pot from the heat. Add fig cubes and olives. Season with salt and pepper.
2. Wash meat, pat dry. Season with salt and pepper. Heat 1 tsp of oil in the air fryer. Fry the meat for about 10 minutes while turning over medium heat.
3. Meanwhile, prepare noodles in boiling salted water according to the instructions on the package. Wash basil, shake dry. Leaves, except a few for garnishing, finely chop. Heat the tomato sauce, add the chopped basil. Season with salt and pepper.
4. Serve chicken fillet with salsa, pasta and sauce on a plate. Garnish with basil.

421. Tarragon Turkey with Sugar Peas

INGREDIENTS

- salt
- 40 g sugar peas
- 1 turkey schnitzel (about 150 g)
- 1 small clove of garlic
- 4 stalks tarragon
- 1 tbsp lemon juice
- pepper
- 1 tbsp oil
- pink berries for garnish

INSTRUCTIONS

1. Wash and dry the sugar peas. Wash meat and pat dry. Peel garlic and chop finely. Wash tarragon, shake dry and finely chop. Stir garlic and tarragon with lemon juice. Season with salt and pepper.
2. Turn meat in the marinade. Heat oil in an air fryer. Fry meat on each side for about 2 minutes over medium heat, keep warm. Turn the sugar peas into fat. Deglaze with 75 ml water. Approximately Simmer for 5 minutes, season with salt and pepper.
3. Garnish with pink pepper.

422. KETO SCHLEMMERLÄDCHEN

INGREDIENTS

- 2 bars of leek
- 200 g mushrooms
- 200 ml vegetable broth
- 1 heaped ml cornstarch
- 1 tsp dried marjoram
- 150 g cream for cooking
- salt
- pepper
- 600 g pork tenderloin
- 2 tbsp oil

INSTRUCTIONS

1. Clean the leek, cut into rings, wash thoroughly and drain. Clean mushrooms, clean and cut in half. Stir broth, starch, marjoram and cream, season with salt and pepper.
2. Wash meat, pat dry and cut into medallions. Heat 1 tbsp oil in the air fryer. Roast meat for 5-6 minutes, season with salt and pepper, remove. Add 1 tbsp of oil, fry the leeks and mushrooms in it for 4-5 minutes, deglaze with the cream mixture, bring to the boil and simmer for 2-3 minutes.
3. Put the leek mixture into a casserole dish, add the meat. Grate the cheese, pour over it and bake in the preheated oven (cooker: 200° C / circulating air: 175° C / gas: stage 3) for approx. 10 minutes.

423. Cucumber Salad with Pomegranate Seeds, Cottage Cheese & Radicchio

INGREDIENTS

- 1 cucumber
- salt
- pepper
- 1/2 head radicchio
- 2-3 pieces of spring onions
- 4 figs
- 1/2 pomegranate
- 4 tbsp apple cider vinegar
- 1-2 tsp honey
- 4-5 tbsp olive oil
- 200 g cottage cheese

INSTRUCTIONS

1. Wash the cucumber, clean it and peel thick strips from the shell. Slice the cucumber, season with salt and pepper, mix and let stand for about 10 minutes.
2. Wash radicchio, clean and cut into strips. Clean and wash the spring onions and cut diagonally into thin rings. Clean, wash and ditch the figs. Remove the pomegranate seeds from the peel. Stir the vinegar and honey, add oil.
3. Mix the cucumber, lettuce, spring onions, pomegranate seeds, figs and vinaigrette and season the salad with pepper, honey and possibly a little salt. Arrange salad. Serve with cottage cheese.

424. Sliced Turkey with Spring Vegetables

INGREDIENTS

- 1 onion
- 600 g turkey schnitzel
- 500 g green asparagus
- 150 g sugar peas
- 150 g cherry tomatoes
- 1 lemon
- 2-3 tbsp oil
- salt
- pepper
- 25 g flour
- 600 ml chicken broth

INSTRUCTIONS

1. Peel onion and chop finely. Wash meat, pat dry and cut into strips. Wash asparagus, cut off woody ends. Cut asparagus into pieces. Clean and wash the sugar peas. Clean and wash tomatoes. Wash the lemon thoroughly, rub the skin finely. Halve the lemon, squeeze out 1 half.
2. Heat oil in an air fryer and fry the meat while turning. Add the onion and sauté briefly. Season with salt and pepper. Add tomatoes, sauté briefly. Add lemon zest. Dust with flour, sauté and deglaze with careful stirring with chicken stock. Boil and season with salt, pepper and 2-3 tbsp of lemon juice.
3. Put asparagus in boiling salted water and cook for 3-4 minutes. Add the sugar peas and cook for another 1 minute. Pour into a sieve and drain well.
4. Add the vegetables to the sliced meat, heat, season again with salt and pepper. Place in an air fryer, and sprinkle with pepper.

425. Chicken Fillets with Spinach & Date Filling

INGREDIENTS

- 800 g red beets
- 2 sprigs of rosemary
- 3 tbsp olive oil
- salt
- pepper
- 500 g spinach
- 50 dried dates
- 1 onion
- Cumin
- 4 chicken fillets (approx. 150 g each)
- 200 g cherry tomatoes
- Oil for the baking sheet

INSTRUCTIONS

1. Clean beetroot, peel and cut into slices. Wash the rosemary, shake dry, brush the needles from the branches and chop. Mix beetroot and 2 tbsp oil and season with salt, pepper and rosemary.
2. Clean spinach, wash and shake dry. Finely chop dates. Peel onion and dice. Heat 1 tbsp of oil in an air fryer and sauté the onions and dates for about 4 minutes. Add the spinach and let it collapse in a closed pot. Season with salt and cumin.
3. Wash the meat, pat dry and cut in horizontally a bag. Season with salt and pepper and fill with spinach. Spread beetroot and meat pies on a baking sheet coated with oil. Cook in a preheated oven (electric cooker: 200° C / circulating air: 175° C / gas: see manufacturer) for approx. 30 minutes.
4. Meanwhile, wash and halve tomatoes. Place on the baking tray 10 minutes before the end of the cooking time. Serve meat and vegetables on plates.

426. Keto Cauliflower Tacos

INGREDIENTS

- 1 head cauliflower
- 1 egg
- salt
- pepper
- paprika
- 200 g grated Emmentaler

- 4 tbsp olive oil
- 1 onion
- 1 clove of garlic
- 400 g ground beef
- 8 tomatoes
- 1 avocado
- 200 g fresh cream with herbs

INSTRUCTIONS

1. Clean and wash cauliflower. Cut the florets from the stalk and roll the stalk roughly. Add half of the florets and cubes together with the egg and cheese to the blender, season with salt and paprika and mix to form a homogeneous mass.
2. Lay out two baking sheets with parchment paper and place approx. 3 tbsp of cauliflower for each taco on the parchment paper and shape into a circle. Mix remaining cauliflower florets in a bowl with half of the oil, salt and pepper and add florets to the tacos on the plate. Trays in the hot oven (electric cooker: 200° C / circulating air: 175° C / gas: see manufacturer) bake for 15-20 minutes until golden brown. (Depending on the size of the tacos, this process must be repeated)
3. Peel onion and garlic and chop finely. Heat remaining oil in the air fryer and fry onions and garlic. Season with salt and pepper.
4. Wash and dice the tomatoes. Halve the avocado, remove the kernel, remove the pulp from the skin and cut into strips.
5. Cover the finished tacos with hack, tomato, avocado and cauliflower and garnish with a dollop of fresh cream.

427. Quinoa Salad with Tuna, Arugula & Pomegranate

INGREDIENTS

- 40 g of quinoa
- 1 can of tuna
- 8 cherry tomatoes
- 10 g salad
- 20 g arugula
- 20 g onions
- 1 lime freshly pressed
- 30 g pomegranate
- 5 g alfalfa sprouts
- 1 pinch of sea salt
- 1 pinch of black pepper

INSTRUCTIONS

1. Rinse quinoa in a fine strainer under running water. • Cook the quinoa until tender, then drain and drain. • Season with fresh lime juice, salt and pepper.
2. Rinse the tuna • Rinse the vegetables, salad and arugula, dry the salad and arugula in a salad spinner • Peel the onion, cut a quarter of it into fine rings • Rinse rice in a colander and dry in a kitchen crepe.
3. Pour the quinoa into a meal of prep glass, then add some lettuce and the tomatoes on top • Now add the tuna and onions • Add the arugula and sprouts and the pomegranate seeds as a topping.

428. Salmon in Cream Sauce with Peas & Lemon

INGREDIENTS

- 500 g salmon fillet, without skin
- 150 g peas green raw
- 200 ml whipped cream 30%
- 2 small shallots
- 1 toe garlic
- 20 g Parmesan
- 40 g butter
- 1 lemon medium

- 1 pinch of nutmeg
- 1 pinch of pepper white
- 1 pinch of sea salt

INSTRUCTIONS

1. Wash the salmon and pat dry, then cut into bite-sized pieces. • Peel the shallots and finely dice. • Peel the garlic and finely chop.
2. Heat butter in an air fryer, add shallots and garlic and fry the salmon pieces in it. • Add the cream and stir. • Add the peas and simmer briefly over medium heat.
3. Meanwhile, wash the lemon hot, dry and rub the bowl with the grater. • Halve the lemon and squeeze out the juice.
4. Add grated Parmesan, lemon peel and a little nutmeg to the air fryer and stir. • Season with lemon juice, salt and pepper.

429. Salmon Fillet with Almond Crust & Pea & Parsnip Puree

INGREDIENTS

For the salmon fillets

- 2 salmon fillets, 200 g each
- 50 g almond flakes
- 2 stalks dill
- 1 organic lemon
- 1 tbsp olive oil

For the puree

- 300 g parsnips
- 60 g peas, frozen, thawed
- 50 g potatoes
- 50 g milk
- 50 g whipped cream
- nutmeg
- sea salt
- pepper

INSTRUCTIONS

1. Wash the salmon fillets and pat dry • Heat the oil in air fryer and fry the fillets on both sides • Wash the dill and shake it dry, then chop • Place fillets in a dish and drizzle with lemon juice.
2. Add the almonds and dill to air fryer and mix with the rest of the oil • Pour the mixture over the salmon fillets and season with salt and pepper. • Cook fillets in a preheated air fryer at 140-160° C for about 20 minutes.
3. Peel the parsnips and potatoes and cut them into small cubes. • Cover the vegetables with salted water for 10-15 minutes, add the peas shortly before the end of the cooking time. • Drain and let vegetables evaporate in the air fryer.
4. Add the milk and whipped cream to the vegetables and make it into puree with a potato masher • Season the pea and parsnip puree with fresh grated nutmeg and salt and place on two plates.
5. Remove the salmon fillets with almond crust from the oven and add to the pea and parsnip puree

430. Asian Air Fryer with Shrimp & Vegetables

INGREDIENTS

- 250 g shrimp
- 400 ml vegetable broth
- 100 g mushrooms
- 40 g rice noodles

- 2 spring onions
- 1 tomato
- 1 lime
- 2 cloves of garlic
- ½ red chili pepper
- ½ green chili pepper
- 1 tbsp fish sauce
- 1 tbsp organic soy sauce
- 1 tbsp. Sesame oil
- 200 ml warm water
- sea salt
- pepper

INSTRUCTIONS

1. Wash shrimp and drain • Clean and slice the mushrooms • Clean the spring onions and cut into rings at an angle • Wash the tomatoes and cut into small cubes • Peel the garlic and cut into thin slices • Cut the chili peppers into thin rings.
2. Heat the vegetables in the air fryer. Turn off the air fryer and let the rice noodles cook in it. • Heat sesame oil in an air fryer and fry the shrimp with garlic. • Add mushrooms, chilis and tomato and sauté.
3. Halve the lime and squeeze out the juice. • Mix 200 ml warm water with fish sauce, soy sauce and a little lime juice and add to the air fryer. • Add the spring onions and season with salt and pepper. • Add rice noodles to the air fryer and mix well.

431. Grilled Salmon with Pumpkin & Steamed Beans

INGREDIENTS

- 2 salmon fillets, 200 g each
- 150 g pumpkin (Hokkaido or butternut squash)
- 200 g green beans
- 1 organic lemon
- 3 tbsp olive oil
- sea salt
- pepper

INSTRUCTIONS

1. Wash the salmon fillets and pat dry • Wash and dry the pumpkin, then cut in half and remove the seeds • Cut the pumpkin into 1-2 cm slices • Wash and clean the beans, then cover with water for 8-10 minutes.
2. Drizzle salmon and pumpkin with oil and cook on the hot grill. • Turn both after 3-4 minutes and grill on the other side. • Reduce heat and cook salmon fillets and pumpkin slices until they are over (the cooking time may vary depending on the condition).
3. Wash the lemon hot and dry • Rub the lemon peel with the grater, put in a bowl and set aside • Halve the lemon, squeeze the lemon over the salmon fillets with your hand and drizzle with lemon juice.
4. Spread the lemon peel on the fillets • Drain the beans into a sieve, drain and place on two plates • Add salmon fillets and pumpkin, season with salt and pepper and serve.

432. Air Fryer Chinese Shrimp Salad

INGREDIENTS

- 220 g shrimp, without head, with shell
- 100 g Chinese cabbage, raw
- 50 g red cabbage raw
- 10 cherry tomatoes
- 2 spring onions
- 1 carrot (carrot, carrot) raw
- 1 lime
- ½ paprika fresh yellow
- ½ paprika fresh red
- 6 stems of coriander, fresh
- 2 cloves of garlic
- 200 ml drinking water warm
- 5 tbsp soy sauce
- 4 tbsp olive oil

- 20 g honey
- 2 tsp sesame light
- 1 pinch of sea salt
- 1 pinch of black pepper

INSTRUCTIONS

1. Wash shrimp and drain, then cut lengthwise. • Peel the garlic and press it into a bowl with the garlic press. • Add the olive oil and shrimp to the garlic, stir and leave to stir.
2. Wash vegetables and herbs and drain • Remove the withered leaves and hard stalk from cabbage • Cut cabbage into thin strips • Halve tomatoes • Clean spring onions and cut them into strips.
3. Peel carrot and cut into thin sticks • Remove seeds from the pepper, then cut into rings or narrow strips • Pick coriander leaves from the stalk and chop • Place all prepared salad ingredients in a large bowl.
4. Halve the lime and squeeze out the juice. • Mix the soy sauce, lime juice, honey and water in a small bowl and add to the salad. • Season the salad with salt and pepper and mix everything together.
5. Put shrimp with garlic and oil in a hot air fryer and fry for a few minutes, then add to the salad and mix again. Sprinkle with sesame seeds and serve.

433. Butternut Squash with Tomatoes & Harissa

INGREDIENTS

- 400 g butternut pumpkin, organic
- 200 g tomato
- 2 shallots
- 2 cloves of garlic
- 6 stalks of parsley
- 500 ml vegetables Broth, homemade
- 150 ml red wine
- 3 tbsp olive oil
- 2 tbsp tomato paste
- 1 tsp Ras el hanout
- 1 tsp Harissa
- 1 pinch of black pepper
- 1 pinch of sea salt

INSTRUCTIONS

1. Peel the butternut pumpkin, remove seeds and cut into pieces of about 1 to 2 cm. • Wash tomatoes and cut them into pieces. • Peel and dice the shallots. • Peel and slice the garlic. • Wash the parsley and shake dry, peel the leaves and finely chop.
2. Heat olive oil in an air fryer and sauté the shallots and garlic. • Add the tomato purée and harissa and mix. • Add the butternut squash and sauté everything. • Deglaze everything with red wine and bring to the boil.
3. Add the tomatoes and add the stock • Season with Ras el hanout, salt and pepper and stir • Cover and simmer for 20-25 minutes.
4. Season with tomato, harissa, salt and pepper • Add the parsley and arrange on two plates.

434. Stuffed Pumpkin with Cauliflower Rice & Mushrooms

INGREDIENTS

- 2 medium Hokkaido pumpkins
- 300 g cauliflower
- 12 mushrooms brown
- 2 shallots
- 2 cloves of garlic
- 100 g leek raw
- 200 g Gouda grated
- 100 g Parmesan
- 1 lemon freshly squeezed
- 1 tbsp olive oil
- 1 tbsp butter
- 6 stalks of parsley
- 1 tsp Five spices powder
- 1 pinch sea salt

- 1 pinch of black pepper

INSTRUCTIONS

1. Brush the pumpkins, rinse, cut in half and remove core. • Clean and quarter the mushrooms. • Cut the peppers into small cubes. • Peel and cut the shallots and garlic.
2. Rinse the cauliflower, drain and then chop with the knife until it has a rice-like texture. • Cut the leek into rings. • Chop the parsley.
3. Melt oil and butter in an air fryer and sauté the shallots with garlic. • Add the leek and sauté. • Add the peppers, mushrooms and cauliflower and fry briefly.
4. Add the lemon juice and parsley and season with spices, salt and pepper • Divide the filling into the halves of the pumpkin, sprinkle with cheese and parmesan • Cook the pumpkins in a preheated oven at about 140° C for 20-30 minutes.

435. Pumpkin Au Gratin

INGREDIENTS

- 800 g nutmeg pumpkin
- 200 g Hokkaido pumpkin
- 200 g Gouda grated
- 200 ml whipped cream
- 2 cloves of garlic
- 6 stalks of parsley
- 1 pinch of sea salt
- 1 pinch of black pepper
- 1 pinch nutmeg dried
- 2 tbsp olive oil

INSTRUCTIONS

1. Wash the Hokkaido pumpkin and cut it into pieces. • Peel the nutmeg and cut it into pieces. • Peel the garlic. • Chop the parsley.
2. Heat olive oil in an air fryer and sauté the pumpkin. • Press the garlic press with the garlic press and add it • Add the cream and bring to a boil.
3. Add salt, pepper and freshly grated nutmeg and stir • Put everything in a large casserole dish and sprinkle with parsley and Gouda • Gratin pumpkin at about 175° C for 40-45 minutes in a preheated oven.

436. Roasted Pork Chop with Vegetables

INGREDIENTS

- 250 g pork chop, boneless
- 100 g zucchini, raw
- 40 g paprika fresh red
- 40 g paprika fresh yellow
- 40 g paprika fresh green
- 50 g mushrooms brown
- 5 stems of thyme, fresh
- 2 tbsp olive oil
- 1 tbsp butter
- 1 pinch of sea salt
- 1 pinch of black pepper

INSTRUCTIONS

1. Wash vegetables and drain • Slice zucchini at an angle • Cut peppers into strips • Clean and halve mushrooms • Wash thyme and shake dry.
2. Put pork chop in the hot air fryer, add the thyme and grill the meat on both sides. • Heat butter and oil in the second air fryer and fry the zucchini, peppers and mushrooms.

3. Season the vegetables with salt and pepper and place on a plate • Season the pork chop and add to the vegetables.

437. Quinoa with Roasted Pumpkin

INGREDIENTS

- 60 g quinoa
- 200 g Hokkaido pumpkin
- ½ onion / s red
- 50 g arugula
- 1 stalk of mint
- ½ lime freshly pressed
- 2 tbsp olive oil
- 1 pinch of Himalayan salt
- 1 pinch of black pepper
- 1 pinch of nutmeg dried

INSTRUCTIONS

1. Place the quinoa in a fine sieve and rinse under running water to rinse off the bitter substances. • Cover the quinoa in an air fryer with water. Simmer for 8-10 minutes until the granules are firm. • Drain the quinoa and allow it to evaporate.
2. Wash and dry the pumpkin, then cut in half and scrape out the seeds with a spoon • Cut the pumpkin into small pieces • Peel the onion, halve and cut into thin rings • Wash the arugula and drain well.
3. Heat oil in air fryer and sauté pumpkin • Add the quinoa and onion and season with salt and pepper • Wash the mint and shake dry, pick the leaves and chop them • Add the lime juice and mint and mix everything.

438. Roast Duck with Orange-Date Stuffing

INGREDIENTS

- 1 free-range duck, approx. 1.5 kg
- 2 oranges, organic quality
- 400 g Brussels sprouts
- 150 g celeriac
- 3 shallots
- 2 carrots
- 6 dates, pitted
- 1 bunch of thyme
- 4-5 sprigs of rosemary
- 4 branches of oregano
- 1 L of poultry or vegetable broth
- 200 ml red wine
- 50 g butter
- 2 tbsp olive oil
- 2 star anise
- 2 bay leaves
- 1 tsp Ras el hanout
- Pepper pink
- sea salt
- pepper

INSTRUCTIONS

1. Rinse the duck under running water and dab it dry • Wash the orange hot and grate dry, then cut into pieces • Wash and dry the herbs • Crush the dates roughly and add the orange and duck to the duck along with the herbs and pieces • The skin of the duck rubs in with salt and pepper.
2. Peel the shallots and finely dice • Peel and slice the carrots • Peel the celeriac and cut into small cubes • Heat oil in an air fryer. Roast the duck until brown • Add the shallots, carrots and celery and sauté.
3. Deglaze everything with wine and add the pieces of the second orange • Add half of the stock to the duck and let it boil down briefly • Add the star anise, bay leaves, Ras el hanout and paprika and stir.
4. Roast the duck in air fryer at 150° C for 2 hours, then pour in sauce from the roasting tin. • After 20 minutes, add the remaining stock and continue to cook the duck.

5. Whisk Brussels sprouts and remove the withered leaves • Halve Brussels sprouts and cover with steam over a little water. Cook for 5 minutes until firm. • Put Brussels sprouts in the air fryer.
6. Remove the duck from air fryer and place on a grill • Keep the duck warm in the oven • Remove the star anise, bay leaves and orange pieces from the sauce • Puree the vegetables with a blender • Bring the sauce to the boil again and season with salt and pepper.
7. Melt butter in an air fryer and fry the Brussels sprouts on all sides.

439. Vegetables with Beans, Peppers & Carrots

INGREDIENTS

- 100 g beans green
- 1 red fresh paprika
- 1 fresh green pepper
- 3 carrots
- 2 cloves of garlic
- 2 tbsp olive oil
- 1 tbsp butter
- 1 pinch of sea salt
- 1 pinch of black pepper

INSTRUCTIONS

1. Wash the beans, clean them and put them in a pot. • Cover the beans with water and bring to a boil. • Simmer the beans for about 5 minutes, then strain into a sieve.
2. Halve the peppers, remove the cores and partitions and rinse the halves under running water • Cut the peppers into strips • Wash the carrots thoroughly, halve the carrots lengthwise • Peel the garlic and cut into thin slices.
3. Heat butter and oil in an air fryer and add the carrots. • Add the peppers, beans and garlic and fry everything in the air fryer for 2-3 minutes, stirring the vegetables several times. • Season the vegetables with salt and pepper.

440. Roasted Avocado with Bacon

INGREDIENTS

- 2 medium avocadoes
- 1 lime freshly pressed
- 300 g bacon
- 1 tbsp olive oil
- 1 pinch of sea salt
- 1 pinch of black pepper

INSTRUCTIONS

1. Halve and core the avocados • Quarter the avocados, remove the pulp from the skin and sprinkle with lime juice to prevent the pieces from turning brown.
2. Spread the bacon slices on a board and roll in the avocado pieces one after the other. • Heat oil in an air fryer and fry the avocados wrapped in bacon on all sides.
3. Remove avocados from the air fryer, season with salt and pepper and serve hot.

441. Fried Cauliflower with Fresh Herbs

INGREDIENTS

- 600 g cauliflower
- 2 cloves of garlic
- 2 tbsp butter
- 2 stems of basil fresh
- 2 stems of parsley
- 1 tsp turmeric powder

- 1 pinch of sea salt
- 1 pinch of black pepper
- 2 tbsp olive oil

INSTRUCTIONS

1. Cut the cauliflower florets from the stalk, then wash and drain. • Peel the garlic and finely chop it. • Add the olive oil, garlic, turmeric, salt and pepper to a bowl and mix. • Add the cauliflower to the spice mixture and swirl through.
2. Heat butter in an air fryer and add cauliflower. • Fry the cauliflower florets from all sides. • Wash and dry the herbs, then chop and add to the cauliflower.

441. Fried Liver with Onion & Herbs

INGREDIENTS

- 500 g calf liver (alternatively beef liver)
- 1 large onion
- 4 stems of thyme
- 2 stems of sage
- 4 stalks of parsley
- 2 tbsp butter
- 1 tsp olive oil
- sea salt
- pepper

INSTRUCTIONS

1. Wash the liver and pat dry with kitchen paper • Clean the liver and cut into pieces • Peel the onion and cut into rings • Wash and dry the herbs • Finely chop the parsley.
2. Heat butter and oil in an air fryer and fry onions until golden brown. • Remove the onion and set aside. • Put liver, thyme and sage in a hot air fryer. • Fry the pieces of liver on all sides.
3. Remove from the air fryer and add salt and pepper to the meat. • Put onions back into the air fryer and heat briefly. • Put the fried liver with onions on two plates and sprinkle with parsley.

442. Green Asparagus with Salmon Fillet & Dill Butter

INGREDIENTS

- 2 salmon fillet, 250 g
- 400 g green asparagus
- 2 organic lemons
- 3 tbsp butter
- 2 tbsp olive oil
- 3-4 stalks Dill
- pepper
- Sea salt

INSTRUCTIONS

1. Wash the green asparagus and cut off the ends • Wash and drain the dill • Wash the salmon fillets and pat dry with a kitchen towel • Rinse the lemon hot, dry and cut into writing.
2. For the asparagus, heat 1 tbsp of oil and 1 tbsp of butter in air fryer and fry for several minutes. • Turn the bars several times so that they are fried from all sides.
3. In the second air fryer, melt 1 tbsp oil and 2 tbsp butter and fry the salmon on the side without skin for about two minutes • Turn the fillets and fry on the skin side. • Spoon the liquid oil-butter mixture over the fish with the spoon over and over,
4. Divide green asparagus into two plates and add one salmon fillet each. • Pour liquid butter over the fish and serve with dill and lemon slices.

443. Chicken Breast Strips with Asian Asparagus

INGREDIENTS

- 300 g chicken breast fillet, organic quality
- 500 g green asparagus
- 2 cloves of garlic
- 1 shallot
- 150 ml water
- 40 ml organic soy sauce
- 2 tbsp of sesame oil
- 2 tsp honey
- Lemon zest from an organic lemon
- Bamboo salt
- Colorful pepper

INSTRUCTIONS

1. Cut the meat into thin strips, making sure that the cuts are transverse to the longitudinal fibers. • Wash the asparagus spears thoroughly and peel the lower third if necessary. • Cut the green asparagus into pieces. • Peel and cut the shallot and garlic.
2. Heat oil in an air fryer and fry meat. • Remove the meat and set aside. • Put the shallot and garlic in the hot air fryer and sauté. • Add green asparagus and stir. • Mix the honey and soy sauce with 150 ml warm water and add to the asparagus.
3. Put the meat strips back into the air fryer with the green asparagus and toss. • Add the lemon zest to the meat and season with salt and pepper.

444. Salmon Fillet On Green Asparagus & Kohlrabi

INGREDIENTS

- 2 salmon fillets á 200 g
- 500 g green asparagus
- 50 g lamb's lettuce
- 1 large kohlrabi
- 2-3 branches dill
- 2 tbsp olive oil
- 1 tbsp butter
- 1 tsp pink berries
- sea salt

INSTRUCTIONS

1. Wash salmon and dry with kitchen towel • Pierce salmon skin with a sharp knife • Wash lettuce and dill and drain.
2. Cut off the asparagus leaves and peel the bottom as needed • Peel and dice the kohlrabi • Place the kohlrabi and asparagus in a large pot with steamer insert and cook until crispy in the hot steam.
3. Heat butter and olive oil in an air fryer and fry the salmon on the skin side. • Cover and cook the salmon over medium heat • Depending on how thick the fillet is, the salmon must roast for 10-20 minutes.
4. Arrange corn salad on both plates • Add the asparagus and kohlrabi and lay the salmon on the plates • Sprinkle salmon with chopped dill and sea salt and serve hot.

445. Roasted Trout with Butter & Lemon

INGREDIENTS

- 100 g butter
- 2 lemons
- 4 garlic cloves
- 4 stalks of dill fresh
- 4 stems thyme, fresh
- 1 pinch of sea salt
- 1 pinch of black pepper
- 2 rainbow trout except with head

INSTRUCTIONS

1. Rinse the trout under running water and drain on a kitchen towel. • Wash the lemons, dry them, then cut into slices. • Wash the herbs and shake dry.
2. Peel the garlic and chop it roughly. • Fill the trout with herbs, garlic and lemon slices. • Cut butter into pieces and melt about half of it in the air fryer. • Fry the trout on both sides for a short time.
3. Place the trout in a refractory dish and cook in a preheated oven at 175° C for 15-20 minutes. Remove trout from the oven and butter. Salt and pepper the fish and serve with the lemon boat.

446. Steak on Spring Onions with Cherry Sauce

INGREDIENTS

- 4 beef steaks à 180 g
- 1 bunch of spring onions
- 1 glass of cherries
- 1 shallot
- 6 stems of rosemary
- 2 tbsp balsamic vinegar
- 2 tbsp olive oil
- 2 tbsp butter
- 1 tbsp Xucker
- ½ tsp agar agar
- Sea salt
- pepper
- cinnamon sticks
- 100 ml water

INSTRUCTIONS

1. Clean spring onions and cut into strips at an angle • Finely chop the rosemary • Drain the cherries through a sieve, collecting the juice • Peel the shallot and finely chop.
2. For the sauce, heat 1 tbsp butter and sauté shallot. • Add Xucker and deglaze with cherry juice, vinegar and water and bring to a boil. • Simmer sauce for 5-10 minutes. • Stir agar agar in a little water, add to the sauce, stir and bring to a boil again • Season the sauce with salt, pepper and freshly grated cinnamon. • Remove the pot from the heat and add the cherries to the sauce.
3. Heat butter and oil in an air fryer and fry steaks for 2 minutes. • Turn the steaks and roast on the other side for about 2 minutes. • Put the steaks on a large plate and season. • Place a rosemary steak on each steak, with a second large plate Cover steaks and let them rest in the oven at about 50° C for 5 minutes.
4. Add spring onions to air fryer and sauté • Add the chopped rosemary, then season the onions with salt and pepper. • Remove the steaks from the oven and add to the spring onions. • Pour the cherry sauce and serve.

447. Peppers Au Gratin

INGREDIENTS

- 2 large red peppers
- 600 g ground beef
- ½ zucchini
- 1 shallot
- 1 tbsp olive oil
- 200 g Gouda, grated
- 12 stems of thyme
- sea salt
- pepper

INSTRUCTIONS

1. Wash vegetables and herbs and drain • Halve the peppers and remove the seeds • Cut the zucchini into small pieces • Peel the shallot and finely dice • Remove the leaves from 6 thyme stalks.

2. Heat oil in an air fryer and sauté the shallot with zucchini. • Take both out again and fry the minced meat. • Season the minced meat with salt and pepper and mix with the thyme leaves, zucchini and shallot.
3. Pour minced meat mixture into the halves of the pepper and sprinkle with Gouda • Put the peppers in a casserole dish and gratinate for 15-20 minutes in a preheated oven. • Cover the paprika buns with thyme and serve.

448. Shrimp on Salad

INGREDIENTS

- 250 g organic shrimp
- 125 g organic lettuce mix
- 6 cherry tomatoes
- ½ spring onion
- 1 tbsp olive oil
- 1 clove of garlic
- 1 organic lemon
- Sea salt
- pepper

INSTRUCTIONS

1. Brush shrimp with oil • Peel and chop the garlic • Rinse hot lemon, dry and grate the skin • Put the lemon, olive oil, garlic, a little salt and pepper in a bowl and mix • Add shrimp and leave for 10 minutes.
2. Wash the salad and dry in the salad spinner • Clean the spring onion and cut into thin rings • Wash and halve the tomatoes • Squeeze out the lemon • Put the salad and vegetables in a salad bowl, season with salt and pepper and drizzle with a little lemon juice.
3. Put shrimp and lemon-oil mixture in a hot air fryer and fry on both sides.

449. Entrecôte Steak

INGREDIENTS

- 500 g steak (1 piece)
- 50 g butter
- 1 garlic bulb
- 1 tbsp olive oil
- 2 stems of thyme
- sea salt
- pepper

INSTRUCTIONS

1. Rinse the meat and pat dry, salt and let rest briefly. • Heat oil and butter in an air fryer. • Cut the garlic bulb in half and place it in the air fryer with thyme.
2. Roast meat on each side for about 4-6 minutes. • Turn the steak several times.
3. Remove meat from air fryer and let it sit in the oven at 50° C for 6-8 minutes

450. Salmon Fillet with Dill

INGREDIENTS

- 2 salmon fillets á 250 g (by the fisherman)
- 1 organic lemon
- 1 tbsp butter
- ½ tsp olive oil
- ½ bunch dill
- sea salt
- Colorful pepper

INSTRUCTIONS

1.Wash lemon and cut into boat • Crush pepper and sea salt in a mortar • Heat butter and oil in air fryer and sear salmon first on the skin side • Turn and search the other side.

2. Season the salmon, put the dill with the salmon in the air fryer and cook for 10-15 minutes at 170° C. • Distribute salmon on two plates and serve with a lemon boat.

451. Chicken Breast with Julienne Vegetable Salad
INGREDIENTS

- 2 chicken breast fillets á 250 g
- 100 g carrots
- 100 g parsley root
- 50 g leek
- 50 g red pepper
- 2-3 sprigs of thyme
- 2 tbsp butter
- Himalayan salt
- pepper
- 1 tsp olive oil

INSTRUCTIONS

1. Peel, wash and clean carrots and parsley roots. • Cut the peppers in half, remove and wash the seeds. • Halve and wash the leeks. • Cut the whole vegetables into thin julienne strips.
2. Pluck the thyme leaves • Rinse off the chicken breast and dab dry • Massage the chicken breast with oil, salt, pepper and thyme • Fry in a coated air fryer until golden brown.
3. Blanch the vegetables and place them on plates together with the chicken breast fillet.

452. Beef Fillet with Tomatoes
INGREDIENTS

- 2 beef fillets, 150 g
- 6-8 cherry tomatoes
- 4-6 brown mushrooms
- 1 large potato
- 3-4 stems rosemary
- 3-4 stems thyme
- 2 tbsp butter
- 1 tbsp olive oil
- pepper
- Sea salt

INSTRUCTIONS

1. Tying beef fillets • Clean and halve the mushrooms • Rinse the tomatoes and herbs • Boil the potato whole with the shell in the pot, then cut into slices.
2. Heat olive oil and butter in an air fryer and sauté the fillets on both sides. • Place the herbs in the oven and cook the meat in a preheated oven for 10-12 minutes at 160° C.
3. Add the mushrooms, potato wedges and tomatoes to the fillets in the air fryer after about 5 minutes and cook.

453. Duck Breast with Wok Vegetables
INGREDIENTS

- 500 g duck breast fillets
- 200 g Chinese cabbage
- 200 g broccoli
- 200 g snow peas
- 12 brown mushrooms
- 2 spring onions
- 2 cloves of garlic
- 2 red chili peppers

- ½ red pepper
- about 4 cm of fresh ginger
- Juice of a lemon
- 100 ml vegetable broth
- 6 tbsp soy sauce
- 1 tbsp. Sesame oil
- 1 tsp honey
- Bamboo salt
- pepper

INSTRUCTIONS

1. Cut the duck breast fillets into strips • Cut the Chinese cabbage into small pieces • Cut the broccoli florets from the stalk • Clean the pomegranates • Brush the mushrooms and cut in half.
2. Clean the spring onions and cut into wide rings • Peel the garlic and ginger and cut into thin slices • Cut the chili peppers into rings • Cut the peppers into bite-sized pieces.
3. Heat the oil in the wok, fry the meat with onion and then set aside in a warm bowl. • Put the paprika, broccoli and snow peas in the hot wok and sauté.
4. Add mushrooms, garlic and ginger and sauté, then add Chinese cabbage and chili peppers. • Add the stock and add meat again.
5. Add soy sauce, honey and lemon juice and simmer briefly. • Season with salt and pepper and serve hot.

454. Roasted Chicken Breast with Tomato Salsa

INGREDIENTS

For the chicken breast

- 2 chicken breast fillets, 200 g
- ½ tsp of paprika
- ½ tsp turmeric
- Sea salt
- pepper
- 1 tbsp olive oil

For the salsa

- 2 tomatoes
- 50 g zucchini
- 1 red onion
- ½ bunch of coriander
- 1 red chili pepper
- 1 clove of garlic
- Juice of a lime
- Sea salt
- pepper

INSTRUCTIONS

1. Cut the tomatoes and zucchini into small cubes • Peel the onion and garlic and cut them to size. • Chop the chili and coriander.
2. Pour lime juice into a bowl and add minced ingredients • Season with salt and pepper and leave to soak.
3. For the chicken breast mix spices in a small bowl and rub fillets with them. • Heat olive oil in an air fryer and fry fillets on both sides.
4. Remove chicken breast fillets from the air fryer, cut up and spread tomato salsa on top.

455. Colorful Salad with Fried Mushrooms

INGREDIENTS

- 10 mushrooms
- 2 tomatoes
- 1 romaine lettuce
- 1 handful of corn salad

- 1 handful of arugula
- 1 handful of Lattughino red
- 1 tbsp olive oil
- sea salt
- pepper
- Balsamic vinegar

INSTRUCTIONS

1. Wash the lettuce leaves, dry in the salad spinner and place in the salad bowl. • Cut the tomatoes into small pieces and add to the salad. • Add the salt, pepper and some balsamic vinegar and stir.
2. Clean mushrooms and quarter them • Heat oil in an air fryer and sauté mushrooms. • Spread the salad on two plates and top with fried mushrooms.

456. Chicken with Chanterelles

INGREDIENTS

- 2 chicken legs, 200 g
- 100 g chanterelles
- 50 g mushrooms
- 1 shallot
- ½ bunch of thyme
- Sea salt & pepper
- 2 tbsp olive oil

INSTRUCTIONS

1. Rinse chicken thighs under warm water and dry • Peel and dice shallot • Remove thyme leaves from stalk.
2. In the air fryer, heat 1 tbsp of olive oil and sauté chicken legs. • Sprinkle chicken thighs with thyme and cook in preheated oven at 140° C for about 35 minutes.
3. Brush mushrooms with oil. • In a second air fryer, heat 1 tbsp of olive oil and fry the shallots. • Add the mushrooms and fry for a short time. • Season the mushrooms with salt and pepper and add to the chicken.

457. Shashlik

INGREDIENTS

- 500 g pork tenderloin
- 2 yellow peppers
- 12 cherry tomatoes
- 2 onions
- 1/2 bunch of parsley
- 2-3 sprigs of thyme
- 2 lemons
- Himalayan salt
- White pepper

INSTRUCTIONS

1. Dice the meat • Peel the onion and dice it small • Chop the parsley and thyme.
2. Put the onion, herbs, juice of the lemons and salt and pepper into a bowl and mix. • Add the meat cubes and marinate. • Cover with meat and keep covered for at least 4 hours.
3. Cut the peppers into pieces • Peel and sauté the second onion • Place the meat alternately with onions, peppers and tomatoes on the skewers and grill for 10-15 minutes.

458. Lamb Meatballs with Salsa

INGREDIENTS

- 400 g lamb minced raw
- 1 egg yolk, chicken egg
- 150 g soy yogurt
- 1 tsp mustard medium hot
- 1 pinch of pepper red cayenne
- 1 pinch of cumin dried
- 1 pinch of fennel seeds
- 1 pinch of sea salt
- 2 tbsp butter
- 1 tbsp olive oil
- 2 large tomatoes
- 1 medium onion red
- 2 cloves of garlic
- 1 chili peppers raw
- 1 pinch of sea salt
- 1 pinch of black pepper
- 1 lime small
- 10 stems of coriander, fresh
- 3 tbsp olive oil

INSTRUCTIONS

1. Carve tomatoes over Krenz, pour into boiling water for a short time and then skin. • Quarter the tomatoes and chop them into small pieces.
2. Peel onion and garlic and chop finely • Halve chili and core seeds • Place tomatoes, onion, garlic, a little chili and the remaining ingredients in a bowl and mince with the hand blender.
3. Put the minced lamb, yogurt, mustard and egg in a bowl and mix. • Pound all the spices in the mortar and add to the minced meat mixture, knead and make into small balls.
4. Heat butter and oil in an air fryer and fry the meatballs to a golden brown. • Serve the lamb meatballs with salsa.

459. Roasted Orange & Rosemary Chicken

INGREDIENTS

- 2 chicken thighs, with skin and bones
- 1 onion red
- 1 orange
- 5 stems of rosemary
- 8 stems of thyme fresh
- 10 garlic toes
- 2 peppers (chili) raw
- 1 pinch of sea salt
- 1 pinch of black pepper
- 1 pinch of paprika powder sweet
- 1 pinch turmeric powder
- 4 tbsp of coconut oil

INSTRUCTIONS

1. Preheat the oven to 180° C • Rinse the chicken legs, pat dry and divide at the joint
2. Mix salt, pepper, paprika and turmeric with 2 tbsp coconut oil and rub in the chicken meat.
3. Rinse chili peppers and dab them dry. • Rinse off rosemary and wedge dry. • Peel the onion and cut into small pieces. • Rinse the orange neatly with warm water and cut into slices.
4. Heat coconut oil in an air fryer.
5. Halve the garlic bulb diagonally and add to the oil.
6. Fry the chicken thighs on both sides until golden brown. • Add the chili peppers, orange slices, thyme and rosemary, place everything in the oven and bake for about 30 minutes until golden brown, turning it over several times.

460. Chicken Breast Fillet with Vegetables

INGREDIENTS

- 300 g chicken breast fillet
- 1 red pepper
- 100 g snow peas
- 2 sprigs of rosemary
- 2 sprigs of thyme
- 1 tsp butter
- sea salt
- Harissa
- 1 tsp olive oil

INSTRUCTIONS

1. Halve the paprika, core it and cut it into small pieces. • Clean the pomegranate. • Rinse the herbs, drain and then chop.
2. Cut chicken breast into pieces of approximately equal size. • Heat butter and olive oil in an air fryer and fry the fillet pieces. • Remove the meat and season with salt and pepper.
3. Add vegetables to the air fryer and fry. if you like it spicy, add some Harissa • Add herbs and toss.
4. Add the meat again and cook for several minutes on medium heat • Season with salt and pepper and serve.

Made in the USA
Monee, IL
07 August 2020